Lessing's Philosophy of Religion

and the German Enlightenment

Recent Titles in
AMERICAN ACADEMY OF RELIGION
Reflection and Theory in the Study of Religion Series

SERIES EDITOR
May McClintock Fulkerson, Duke University

A Publication Series of
The American Academy of Religion
and
Oxford University Press

AMERICAN ACADEMY OF RELIGION

Lessing's Philosophy of Religion and the German Enlightenment

Lessing on Christianity and Reason

Toshimasa Yasukata

OXFORD
UNIVERSITY PRESS

2002

OXFORD

UNIVERSITY PRESS

Oxford   New York

Athens   Auckland   Bangkok   Bogotá   Buenos Aires   Cape Town
Chennai   Dar es Salaam   Delhi   Florence   Hong Kong   Istanbul   Karachi
Kolkata   Kuala Lumpur   Madrid   Melbourne   Mexico City   Mumbai   Nairobi
Paris   São Paulo   Shanghai   Singapore   Taipei   Tokyo   Toronto   Warsaw

and associated companies in
Berlin   Ibadan

Published by Oxford University Press, Inc.
198 Madison Avenue, New York, New York 10016

Oxford is a registered trademark of Oxford University Press

Library of Congress Cataloging-in-Publication Data
Yasukata, Toshimasa, 1952–
Lessing's philosophy of religion and the German enlightenment / Toshimasa Yasukata.
p.   cm. — (American Academy of Religion reflection and theory in the study of religion series)
Includes bibliographical references and index.
ISBN 0-19-514494-5
1. Lessing, Gotthold Ephraim, 1729–1781—Religion.
2. Enlightenment—Germany.   3. Germany—Intellectual life—18th century.
I. Title.   II. Reflection and theory in the study of religion.
PT2418.R4 Y37   2001
832'.6—dc21   00-066901

2 4 6 8 9 7 5 3 1

Printed in the United States of America
on acid-free paper

For
Peter C. Hodgson

Preface

Presented in this book are the results of my endeavors over the past fifteen years to elucidate some important facets of the German Enlightenment, with particular attention to its eminent thinker Gotthold Ephraim Lessing (1729–81). My concern with him goes back to research on Ernst Troeltsch undertaken for my first doctorate, for which research was initiated at Kyoto University and completed at Vanderbilt University. My Ph.D. dissertation at Vanderbilt University was published in the American Academy of Religion Academy Series as *Ernst Troeltsch: Systematic Theologian of Radical Historicality* (1986). As is well known, Troeltsch considered the eighteenth-century Enlightenment the beginning of modern history. It marked, he maintained, a significant turning point from the religiously oriented culture of the Middle Ages to the eminently secular culture of modern times. After the Enlightenment "century of reason," everything changed. Religion was no exception. Christianity too underwent serious and drastic changes, hence Troeltsch's famous thesis as to the difference between early Protestantism (*Altprotestantismus*) and modern Protestantism (*Neuprotestantismus*).

It was this thesis that originally directed me to the study of Lessing. In order to reexamine Troeltsch's thesis, I intended to carry out a thorough study of Lessing's religious thought. The reason for taking up Lessing is that he seemed to be a key figure in bridging over the two Protestantisms. My initial study of Lessing thus began as a kind of case study. The more deeply I studied him, however, the more I became fascinated by his enigmatic thought in and of itself. As a result, quite apart from my original concern, clarification of his basic religious thought became an urgent task in its own right.

This study of Lessing has been far more difficult than my previous study of Troeltsch. The reason is not simply that Lessing's German is more difficult than Troeltsch's. The main cause of the difficulty is that Lessing was a "writer who revealed, while hiding, the reasons compelling wise men to hide the truth" (Leo Strauss). Accordingly, it took much perseverance and training before I could grasp his thought with any degree of accuracy. Because there was no specialist on Lessing the theologian or Lessing the philosopher of religion in Japan, and because there were for the most part no reliable books on him in Japanese, I had no choice but to read the bulk of his writings in the original

German, not to mention working my way through the immense secondary writings on Lessing one after another. For the first ten years, I groped vainly in the dark and felt as if I had missed my way and wandered deep into a forest. But one day, after years of assiduous effort at reading Lessing's original texts and after learning much from the untold secondary literature, a clear image of Lessing suddenly emerged from his writings. At that moment it seemed as if the dense fog veiling the deep forest had suddenly lifted, and a mysterious mountain had made its appearance high over the forest. The intuition that flashed over me at that moment guided my study thereafter.

Four years ago I finally completed my study of Lessing, put it into another doctoral dissertation, and submitted it to Kyoto University. The book *Lessing to Doitsu Keimō: Lessing Shūkyō Tetsugaku no Kenkyū* [Lessing and the German Enlightenment: A study of Lessing's philosophy of religion] (Tokyo: Sōbunsha, 1998), is a revised and enlarged version of my Litt.D. dissertation. The English version presented here is based on this Japanese work, but is not a literal translation from the Japanese. I have made every effort to make my work easy for the English reader to understand. For this purpose, I have often changed the wording and inserted new sentences as necessary. But there is no significant difference between the Japanese and English versions as regards the main points in my interpretation of Lessing's religious thought.

As was the case with my previous study of Troeltsch, I am deeply indebted to my former teacher, Dr. Wataru Mizugaki, now professor emeritus of Kyoto University. He constantly encouraged my study of Lessing and, at a crucial stage in the evolution of my Lessing work, kindly took the time to read and comment on parts of the original manuscript.

After my Litt.D. dissertation was completed in Japanese, it happened to come to the attention of Dr. Peter C. Hodgson, my American *Doktorvater* at Vanderbilt University. He stressed the need for an updated study on Lessing in English and warmheartedly urged me to translate my Lessing work and have it published in America. Without his stimulation and encouragement, this English version would never have come into being. I am very grateful to him for his encouragement and support.

I would also like to express my appreciation to Professor Mary McClintock Fulkerson of the Divinity School of Duke University for her assistance as Editor of the Reflection and Theory in the Study of Religion Series of the American Academy of Religion; Theodore Calderara, Editorial Assistant of Oxford University Press; and Nancy Hoagland, Editorial, Design, and Production Director for Academic Books of Oxford University Press.

Finally, Dr. David Reid, my former colleague and friend, deserves my special thanks. He read both the Japanese original and the English draft, corrected grammatical and bibliographical errors, made innumerable stylistic suggestions, and even retyped the entire manuscript in camera-ready form. If this book is at all readable as an English work, it is largely because of his refinements. No words are adequate to express my heartfelt gratitude for his extraordinary labor and friendship.

This book is dedicated to Peter C. Hodgson in commemoration of happy school days at Vanderbilt University (1980–85) when I absorbed his lectures and participated in his seminars with great enthusiasm and great benefit.

Toshimasa Yasukata
Iwate, Japan

Acknowledgments

Goethe, Johann Wolfgang von, *Goethe's Collected Works*, vol. 1: *Selected Poems*. Copyright 1983 by Princeton University Press. Reprinted by permission of Princeton University Press.

Goethe, Johann Wolfgang von, *Goethe's Collected Works*, vol. 4: *From My Life: Poetry and Truth*. Copyright 1987 by Suhrkamp Publishers New York, Inc. Reprinted by permission of Princeton University Press.

The Spinoza Conversations between Lessing and Jacobi: Text with Excerpts from the Ensuing Controversy, translated by G. Vallée, J. B. Lawson, and C. G. Chapple. Copyright 1988 by the University Press of America. Reprinted by permission.

Selections from "The Jews: A Comedy in One Act" and "Nathan the Wise," translated by Ingrid Walsøe-Engel and Bayard Quincy Morgan respectively, are taken from *Nathan the Wise, Minna von Barnhelm, and Other Plays and Writings*, edited by Peter Demetz. Copyright 1991 by The Continuum Publishing Company. Reprinted by permission.

Contents

Abbreviations

B *Werke und Briefe in zwölf Bänden.* Herausgegeben von Wilfried Barner zusammen mit Klaus Bohnen, Gunter E. Grimm, Helmuth Kiesel, Arno Schilson, Jürgen Stenzel und Conrad Wiedemann. Frankfurt am Main: Deutscher Klassiker Verlag, 1985– .

D *Lessing im Gespräch.* Herausgegeben von Richard Daunicht. Munich: Wilhelm Fink Verlag, 1971.

G *Werke.* In Zusammenarbeit mit Karl Eibl, Helmut Göbel, Karl S. Guthke, Gerd Hillen, Albert von Schirnding und Jörg Schönert. Herausgegeben von Herbert G. Göpfert. 8 Bde. Munich: Carl Hanser Verlag, 1970–79.

Hauptschriften *Die Hauptschriften zum Pantheismusstreit zwischen Jacobi und Mendelssohn.* Herausgegeben und mit einer historisch-kritischen Einleitung versehen von Heinrich Scholz. Berlin: Verlag von Reuther & Reichard, 1916.

JubA Mendelssohn, Moses. *Gesammelte Schriften.* Jubiläumausgabe. Herausgegeben von I. Elbogen, J. Guttmann, E. Mittwoch, A. Altmann et al. 20 Bde. Stuttgart-Bad Cannstatt: Friedrich Frommann Verlag, 1971ff.

LM *Sämtliche Schriften.* Herausgegeben von Karl Lachmann, dritte, aufs neue durchgesehene und vermehrte Aufl., besorgt durch Franz Muncker. 23 Bde. Stuttgart (Bd. 12ff.), Leipzig (Bd. 22f.), Berlin und Leipzig 1886–1924. Nachdruck, Berlin: Walter de Gruyter & Co., 1968.

LYB *Lessing Yearbook.* Bde. 1–11, Munich: Max Hueber Verlag, 1969–79; Bde. 12–21, Munich and Detroit: edition text + kritik GmbH and Wayne State University Press,

1980–89; Bd. 22ff., Detroit: Wayne State University Press, 1990ff.

R	*Gesammelte Werke.* Herausgegeben von Paul Rilla. 10 Bde. Berlin 1954–58. 2. Aufl., Berlin und Weimar: Aufbau-Verlag, 1968.

RGG	*Die Religion in Geschichte und Gegenwart.* Tübingen: J. C. B. Mohr, 1909–13; 2. Aufl., 1927–32; 3. Aufl., 1957–65.

W	*Lessings Werke.* Herausgegeben von Kurt Wölfel. 3 Bde. Frankfurt am Main: Insel Verlag, 1972.

WSA	*Wolfenbütteler Studien zur Aufklärung.* Heidelberg: Verlag Lambert Schneider, 1974ff.

WW	Jacobi, Friedrich Heinrich. *Werke.* 6 Bde. Herausgegeben von Friedrich Roth und Friedrich Köppen. Leipzig: Fleischer, 1812–25; Nachdruck, Darmstadt: Wissenschaftliche Buchgesellschaft, 1976.

Note on Texts and Translations

1. The study of Lessing presented in this book is based on five different editions of Lessing's works (see Abbreviations). The reason the use of any single edition is insufficient is briefly stated in note 8 of the introduction. Basically, I have used the 23-volume *Sämtliche Schriften* (LM) edited by Karl Lachmann and Franz Muncker, widely regarded as the best critical edition to date. An increasing number of researchers, however, have lately made use of the more compact 8-volume "Hanser," or "Göpfert," edition: *Werke* edited by Herbert G. Göpfert and published by the Carl Hanser Verlag (G). A new critical edition, which when completed will certainly be more comprehensive than any other, is now being published in the series *Bibliothek Deutscher Klassiker: Werke und Briefe in zwölf Bänden* edited by Wilfried Barner (B). This new standard edition will most likely replace all previous ones because of its scholarly precision, up-to-date information, and comprehensiveness. But because publication is still in process, the use of this edition as a main text is not yet possible. Consequently, I have used LM as my main text, while reference has also been made to G and B.

2. In citing Lessing's works, cross-references will be made and an abbreviated form of the text's name will be given in parentheses. For example, the form used in citing from the text of *Eine Duplik* is as follows: LM 13, 23–24; G8, 32–33 (*Eine Duplik*). In citing letters to or from Lessing, reference will be made to both LM and B, and necessary information is given in parentheses as follows: LM 18, 356 (Letter to Elise Reimarus of 28 November 1780); B 12, 361 (no. 1602), or LM 19, 31–33 (Letter from Moses Mendelssohn of 10 January 1756); B 11/1, 85–87 (no. 84).

3. The Lachmann-Muncker edition (LM) leaves old orthographic forms as they stood in Lessing's original writings. In compliance with G and B, however, this book in principle uses modern orthographic forms. But because some terms are still in old orthographic forms even in G and B, these terms are cited in the form in which they appear, as in *Gottesgelahrtheit*, *allmählig*, etc.

4.   The present study is based exclusively on Lessing's original German texts.
     It also makes extensive use of other German literature. For the benefit of
     American readers, however, all passages cited are given in English transla-
     tion, sources being indicated in the notes and bibliography as appropri-
     ate. An important title, on its first appearance, is given in English (with
     the German title in parentheses); thereafter only in English. Incidentally,
     when a title has two publication dates divided by a slash, as in *Die Reli-
     gion*, 1749/50, the slash mark signifies "or." For the passages cited, I have
     used existing standard translations wherever possible, though I usually
     identify the translation being used only on the first occasion, rather than
     each time. Where no translation exists, I have made my own English ren-
     dering. Because the German texts include a number of terms for which
     there are no exact equivalents in English, I have added the original Ger-
     man in parentheses whenever appropriate in the hope of conveying more
     vividly the flavor of Lessing's thinking.

Lessing's Philosophy of Religion

and the German Enlightenment

Introduction

Immanuel Kant once gave the following famous definition for the Enlightenment:

> *Enlightenment is man's release from his self-incurred tutelage. Tutelage* is man's inability to make use of his understanding without direction from another. This tutelage is *self-incurred* when its cause lies not in lack of reason but in lack of resolution and courage to use it without direction from another. *Sapere aude!* "Have courage to use your own reason!"—that is the motto of enlightenment.[1]

The Enlightenment, in this definition, is a movement that aimed at the universal achievement of a spiritually and intellectually mature state of being, the hallmark of which is independent and responsible use of one's own reason. According to Wilhelm Dilthey, however, Gotthold Ephraim Lessing (1729–1781) was the first to achieve this state in German intellectual history. Lessing was *der erste ganz mündige Mensch*,[2] the first modern German to really come of age. Among many contemporary intellectuals, he was the critical edge of the German Enlightenment and the very first thinker who, in complete freedom from bias toward all traditions, created a self-reliant and positive view of life. As confirmed by Hannah Arendt, *Selbstdenken*—independent thinking— continues to be a highly valuable legacy of the Lessingian Enlightenment.[3]

Lessing's Significance for German Intellectual History

Lessing is usually considered "an important nodal point" in the German intellectual history leading from Luther through Leibniz up to German idealism. According to the well-known literary historian Benno von Wiese, Lessing not only brought European rationalism to completion but also, being anchored in German religious and speculative traditions, transmuted it into a specifically German form. By so doing, he opened the way to the German classicism of Goethe and Schiller as well as to the German idealist philosophy of Fichte, Schelling, and Hegel.[4] In view of his position in this line of intellectual development, it is no exaggeration to say that Lessing demonstrated most clearly the closest of ties between the German Enlightenment and German idealism.

Lessing has enjoyed great popularity among the German people. Some of his admirers even assign him a status comparable to that of the Reformer Martin Luther. Heinrich Heine, for example, extols him as follows:

> No German can utter the name [of Lessing] without finding a greater or smaller echo resounding in his heart. Since Luther, Germany has produced no person greater or better than Gotthold Ephraim Lessing. These two men are our pride and our bliss.[5]
>
> I would say that Lessing succeeded Luther. After Luther emancipated us from the yoke of tradition and elevated the Bible to Christianity's sole authority, an obstinate bibliolatry arose . . . and the letter of the Bible became just as tyrannical a ruler as the earlier tradition. For emancipating us from this tyrannical reign of the letter, Lessing has rendered the greatest service. Just as Luther was not the only person who fought against tradition, so too it was certainly not Lessing alone who fought against the letter; but it was Lessing who fought the most formidable fight.[6]

There is no denying that Heine's extolment of Lessing contains a degree of hyperbole. Nevertheless, such words of praise may not necessarily be unjustified when we read them in the light of the following noteworthy remarks uttered by Johann Wolfgang von Goethe. This greatest of German writers, one of the noblest minds in German history, declares:

> Luther was a genius of a very significant kind. He has exercised great influence for a long time, and the number of days until the time when, in remote centuries, he will cease to be productive is unforeseeable. Lessing sought to refuse the noble title of genius, but his lasting influence testifies against what he thought of himself.[7]

Given Lessing's importance for German intellectual history, it is not surprising that hundreds of his complete or collected works have been edited, and that yet another new, critical edition is now being published.[8] The International Lessing Society now serves as a kind of common forum for all scholars engaging in the study of the literary and intellectual history of eighteenth-century Germany.[9] As one might expect from these facts, so many studies about Lessing already exist that it is almost impossible today for any single researcher to survey the whole spectrum of Lessing studies.[10] In addition to studies in the fields of literature, literary criticism, and dramaturgy, there are numerous studies in the fields of theology and philosophy of religion. Despite this body of research, no consensus has been attained to date regarding the real core of his theological and religious-philosophical thought. On the contrary, diametrically opposed interpretations prevail among researchers.

The reason for such interpretive contradictions must be assigned to Lessing himself. Dilthey, in his now classic monograph on Lessing, makes the following noteworthy observation:

> There are indeed convincing reasons to believe partly that he did not present the final and supreme results of his lifelong inquiry at all, and partly that he presented them to his contemporaries in half-concealed form. As over against those contemporaries who were theologically restricted and oppressed, he felt himself

a pedagogue. . . . He was the very first German thinker who, in complete freedom from every tradition and from every bias and aversion to it, faced real life and created a self-reliant and positive view of life. One cannot yet say this even about Leibniz, who is so incomparably original in his worldview. As Lessing proceeded toward this view of life in his last period, one feels that he became more and more lonely. For this voyage of discovery he did not have, and was unable to have, any companion just as he had once had none for his aesthetic exploration. He was in utter loneliness and yet took up the fight against all tendencies that took the theological tradition as their starting point, it being a matter of indifference to him whether they were friendly or hostile to this tradition. He had to conceal this isolated position, make temporary allies, and raise contemporaries to his own [view] gradually. This was his position. And this explains the possibility that what is in front of us is not fully his real opinion and that the final results of his lifelong inquiry are not set down in what lies before us.

Much immediate and enthusiastic interest on our side, and much of an enigmatic character on his, cling to Lessing studies. If there is anything at all in modern German literary history that requires rigorous methodical research, it is Lessing.[11]

It is true that a number of in-depth studies have been made to disclose what Dilthey called the "enigmatic character" (*Rätselhaftigkeit*) or "mystery" (*Geheimnis*) of Lessing. Nevertheless, as a theologian or philosopher of religion, Lessing is still a riddle to us.

Sixty years after Dilthey's monograph, however, Karl Guthke reported that "the irreconcilable contradictions of Lessing interpretation can be observed in the interpretations of his theological writings."[12] Fifteen years later, he again reported with regret that "Lessing the theologian is still a subject of dispute. The question at issue, ever since the eighteenth century, has to do with his Christianity."[13] The situation remains the same today. That is to say, no consensus has been attained to date as to the real core of his theological and religious-philosophical thought.

Lessing and Modern Protestant Theology

The first thing to bear in mind when considering Lessing's theology or philosophy of religion is that he was neither a theologian nor a philosopher by profession. He states his relationship to theology as follows: "I am a dilettante in the field of theology, not a theologian. I have never taken an oath to uphold any particular system."[14] In apparent endorsement of his statement, hardly ever does he receive serious treatment in textbooks on the history of Protestant theology.[15]

Lessing's relationship to philosophy is similar. Wilhelm Windelband gave Lessing high marks as "the only creative mind in German philosophy between Leibniz and Kant,"[16] but there are few books on the history of philosophy that contain more than passing remarks about Lessing.[17]

But as our study will shortly demonstrate, Lessing's contribution to both theology and philosophy was immense. Lessing as theologian or philosopher of religion was, in the profundity of his thought, far superior to ordinary Enlightenment thinkers. Indeed, he foreshadowed some of the significant theological and/or philosophical ideas that several great thinkers were later to advocate, thinkers such as Schleiermacher, Hegel, Kierkegaard, and Troeltsch.[18] According to Walter Nigg, Lessing was "the first thinker" who "took a look at the difficult situation of Christianity in modern times" and "examined the traditional theological foundations with respect to their durability in order to make them capable of being newly established, despite their evident cracks."[19] Lessing's famous dictum regarding double truths, namely, that "accidental truths of history can never become the proof for necessary truths of reason," was presented as a result of his thorough examination of the theological situation of his age. The metaphor of "the ugly broad ditch" (*der garstige breite Graben*), which he invented to describe the gap between the two kinds of truth, has functioned as "a kind of code, or shorthand, signaling 'the problem' of faith and history" in modern theology.[20]

As far as Lessing's significance for the history of philosophy is concerned, the problem of his "Spinoza confession" is of supreme importance. The "Spinoza controversy" (*Spinoza-Streit*) between Moses Mendelssohn and Friedrich Heinrich Jacobi, which initially began in the summer of 1783 as a private quarrel over the deceased Lessing's "Spinozism," eventually engaged almost all the best minds of late eighteenth-century Germany. Wizenmann, Herder, Goethe, Kant, Hamann, Reinhold, and other eminent thinkers took part in the dispute. It thus led to the "pantheism controversy" (*Pantheismus-streit*), a significant dispute that was to shape the main contours of nineteenth-century philosophy. This controversy is all the more important because it raised the problem of "the dilemma of a rational nihilism or an irrational fideism,"[21] a central concern of Fichte, Schelling, Hegel, Kierkegaard, and Nietzsche.

When we take the above points into consideration, there is considerable warrant for calling Lessing, as Gottfried Fittbogen once did, "the founder of modern Protestantism."[22] In fact Ernst Troeltsch, usually regarded as "the last great proponent of modern Protestantism," also regards Lessing as one of the thinkers who rendered substantial service in the formulation of "a new concept of Protestantism."[23] The following quotation epitomizes Troeltsch's view of Lessing: "Here again it was Lessing who, in his famous saying that the search for truth was preferable to the unsought possession of it, gave a typical characterization of modern religious feeling. In doing so he picked out precisely that thread in the web of Protestantism that the modern world is still eagerly weaving into its fabric."[24]

In yet another essay on theology and science of religion in the eighteenth century, Troeltsch counted among the "fathers of modern theology" such thinkers as Hamann, Jacobi, Fichte, Schelling, and Hegel. In Troeltsch's view these thinkers of idealist outlook are non-theologians who propelled theology forward" (*die Theologie treibende Nicht-Theologen*).[25] Borrowing this phraseology, I venture to assert that Lessing was the very first of the "non-theologians who propelled theology forward." Unquestionably, in eighteenth-century Germany, no lay thinker propelled theology forward more powerfully than Lessing. Accordingly, he may perhaps best be regarded as a typical example of what Troeltsch called "theology that does not belong to the guild" (*die unzünftige Theologie*).[26] The historical theologian Leopold Zscharnack, editor of one volume of Lessing's theological and religious-philosophical writings[27] and author of the monograph *Lessing and Semler*, seems to endorse my judgment when he states:

> Among lay thinkers during the time of the German Enlightenment, no one took greater part in the efforts of traditional ecclesiastical theology to come to terms with the modern spirit than Lessing, and no one was more engaged in ecclesiastical-theological questions than he. Unlike Herder, who was a professional theologian, Lessing was neither a minister nor a theologian by profession. Nevertheless, first as editor and literary critic, then as librarian of the ducal library at Wolfenbüttel, he rendered great service to theological inquiry and became, along with the general superintendent at Weimar, the theologian among German classicists. In this capacity, he emancipated intellectuals from the yoke of the traditional church with greater success than anyone else. On the other hand, he was also able to hand over to them, and to preserve for them, historical respect for its great intellectual and cultural heritage.[28]

It is certain, then, that any serious study of the history of modern theology cannot and ought not to disregard Lessing. Far from being a mere "dilettante in the field of theology," he was a "special admirer or lover of theology." In this character he engaged in theology with the utmost love and admiration for its subject matter. His seemingly humble self-appraisal, namely, that he was a *Liebhaber der Theologie und nicht Theolog*, should be taken, therefore, in the sense of his having a special appreciation and love for theology.

It may be possible to construe this self-appraisal as an ironic expression of his assurance and pride that he, though not a theologian by profession, engaged in theology with greater devotion and seriousness than any professional theologian. In fact, in his fragment *Bibliolatry* (1779), Lessing compared himself to Ion, the hero in Euripides' tragedy who worked as a servant at the temple of Apollo in Delphi. Said Lessing: "I, too, am at work, not in the temple but only near it. I, too, merely dust the steps beyond which the holy priest is content to sweep away the dust from the interior of the temple. I, too, am proud of this trifling work, for I know best in whose honor I do what I do."[29] In this quotation we can discern Lessing's serious commitment to theology, however humble his self-appraisal may seem to be. We agree unreservedly with Martin Haug when he says, "Lessing was not a theologian; but he belongs, in the essential part of his thinking and his literary activity, to the history of theology."[30]

Tasks of Lessing Studies

Taking Lessing as a "special admirer or lover of theology," we make it the precise aim of our inquiry to elucidate his theological and religious-philosophical thought. But as the history of previous Lessing studies demonstrates, this is a very difficult task that requires extraordinarily meticulous analysis.

The reason that Lessing, as theologian or philosopher of religion, has escaped the persistent pursuit of researchers for more than two centuries is that his thinking is essentially "inquiring" and "experimental" (*experimentell*),[31] with the result that it is always open to new possibilities. This accounts for the "fragmentary character"[32] of most of his theological and religious-philosophical writings. As pointed out by many researchers, fragmentariness, unsystematicness, ambiguity, and contradictoriness are prominent features of his theological and religious-philosophical thought. But these features should not be explained away as mere idiosyncratic traits. They must be understood, rather, within the wider context of the eighteenth-century German social and political situation, with which the country's religious and intellectual situation was inseparably connected.[33]

The territorial system based on the principle of *cuius regio, eius religio* outlived "the confessional age" far into the age of reason. To engage in open criticism of Lutheran orthodoxy, which was bound up with the territorial state, involved putting one's civil life in jeopardy.[34] To this extent, genuine freedom of religious belief did not yet exist in Lessing's Germany. On the other hand, however, as time went on, modern rationalistic ideas gained a foothold even among clergymen and theologians. As a result, *neology*[35]—an approach to theology based on advanced, enlightened ideas—was on the rise during the mid-eighteenth century in Germany. But Lessing was not content to reconcile the opposition between orthodoxy and the Enlightenment in the easy way the neologists did. He was thus led to search for "a third way,"[36] a way different from both Lutheran orthodoxy and neology. This option meant, however, that he had to engage in "theological battle on two fronts" (*der theologische Zweifrontenkampf*)[37] against both orthodoxy and neology, or again, in a "war on three fronts" (*Dreifrontenkrieg*):[38] against Reimarus's rationalism, Goeze's orthodoxy, and Semler's neology.[39]

But Lessing had neither ecclesiastical nor political patrons behind him. His only resources were his brain and his pen. The theological battle, therefore, was far from easy. At times he may have pretended to be a friend or ally to his enemies in order to deceive them. At other times he may have been forced to adumbrate his real opinions or knowledge of newly germinating truths instead of setting them forth in a straightforward way.[40] At still other times he may have had no choice but to conceal them from others entirely.[41] It is true that in his treatise *Berengar of Tours*, Lessing says (probably with neology in mind):

> I do not know whether it is a duty to sacrifice life and fortune for truth; at least the courage and resolution needed for this are not gifts that we can give to ourselves. But if one wishes to teach the truth, I know it is an obligation either to teach the whole truth or not to teach it at all. [It is a duty] to teach the truth clearly and plainly, without using enigmatic terms, without reservation, without distrust of its strength and usefulness. And the gifts needed for this lie within our power. Anyone who does not wish to acquire the gifts, or who does not wish to use them if he has acquired them, deserves only ill of human understanding.

[This is so] if one removes grave errors from us, but withholds the whole truth and wishes to please us with a garbled mixture of truth and falsehood. For the greater the error, the shorter and straighter is the road to truth. A subtle error, however, can keep us from the truth perpetually, since it is much more difficult for us to recognize it as an error.[42]

On the other hand, however, he defended a freemasonry attitude by saying that there are "truths which are better left unsaid" and that "the wise man *cannot* say what is better left unsaid."[43]

Be that as it may, Lessing was a first-rate tactician as well as a first-rate lover of truth. Given the ecclesiastical-political situation of mid-eighteenth-century Germany, it is understandable that he may have deemed it permissible, in the battle for truth, to skimp on human fidelity when circumstances compelled it.[44] In him realistic tactics coexisted with love for the truth, hence his frequently quoted phrases: "I must aim my weapons at my opponent; not all that I write γυμναστικῶς ["gymnastically," or as a mental exercise] would I also write δογματικῶς [dogmatically, or as an authoritative principle]."[45]

In addition, Lessing was born with a spirit of defiance and had a tendency to side with the underdog. As his friend Christoph Friedrich Nicolai testifies of his personality, "Lessing . . . could not tolerate anything that was overdecisive, and in polite or learned discussion often liked to take the side that was the weaker, or the one whose opposite someone was trying to assert."[46] Nicolai provides a telling illustration: "Many of Lessing's friends will still recall that during the Seven Years War he always supported Prussia at social gatherings while he stayed in Leipzig, whereas in Berlin [he supported] the cause of Saxony. He was thus an object of heartfelt hatred to true patriots in both places, patriots who . . . were a trifle fierce while the war lasted."[47] He also recalls that Lessing, in debate, often exercised "the skill either to take the weaker side or, if somebody presented the *pro*, to hunt immediately, and with rare acuteness, for the *contra*."[48]

This kind of antithetic spirit had a bearing on his attitude toward Christian apologetics. "The more insistently a person wanted to prove Christianity to me, the more doubtful I became. The more willfully and triumphantly another sought to trample it completely underfoot, the more inclined I felt to uphold it, at least in my heart."[49] The "polemical, antithetic character"[50] of Lessing's theological and religious-philosophical writings is, as many researchers have repeatedly pointed out, rooted in his inborn dialectical nature. He was by nature "a genuinely *dialectic thinker* of strict logic."[51] Hence it may be no exaggeration when Martin Haug says of this dialectical thinker's theological and religious-philosophical writings that "indeed almost all of Lessing's assertions (*Sätze*)" were "counterassertions" (*Gegensätze*).[52]

Given this state of affairs, it is clearly impermissible to take Lessing's theological or religious-philosophical statements at face value. What he wrote or said about theological or religious-philosophical topics must not be easily generalized into an abstract system. In interpreting his words, we must give special attention to the immediate, concrete context in which they were initially written or uttered. In particular, we must take into consideration the original assertions of his adversaries, assertions toward which his statements, intended as "counterassertions," were directed.

As a matter of fact, "most of Lessing's theological expressions grew out of dialogues. For this reason they have, to a large extent, a dialogical and ephemeral character."[53] Being a first-rate dramatist, Lessing often employed dramatic methods and techniques in his theological and religious-philosophical writings, with the result that his theological and religious-philosophical arguments contained theatrical elements. This is why his antagonist Goeze severely attacked his logic as "theater logic" (*Theaterlogik*).[54] Whether or not Goeze was right in this insistence, it is certain that Lessing's arguments were considerably more dramatic and dynamic than the ordinary theological argument. As Heinrich Scholz rightly observes, "the antithetical, the hypothetical, and the humorous" (*das Antithetische, das Hypothetische und das Humoristische*) are "three factors of infinite importance for Lessing."[55] We should not, therefore, take Lessing's theological and religious-philosophical statements literally, though we must take them seriously. We agree with Hermann Timm when he says:

> If we accept this proposal as a basis for interpretation, then his lifelong critique of theologians can only be understood as an overture of a negative sort. Also, and precisely in his theological writings, Lessing has given full play to his agonistic, sportsmanlike nature. He was a competitor and a virtuoso of irony, masterfully skilled in formulating points of opposition in the manner of a dramatic scene. Nearly as attractive as paradoxes, they were for the most part constructed in such a way as to convince [people] that the twisted words have the appearance of evident truths. In short, he was a master at rhetorically digging "ugly broad ditches."[56]

If this is the case, then Lessing's theological and religious-philosophical statements should not be taken as expressions of firm dogmatic convictions. He often engaged in "interpretive play for the sake of gymnastic training of the spirit."[57] As a result, most of his statements are experimental and heuristic. To borrow Whitehead's famous phrase, they are tentative results of his "adventures of ideas."

Thus arises the problem of the exoteric and the esoteric in his theology. This is said to be the most difficult problem in the interpretation of Lessing. Friedrich Loofs, the first to pose this question, drew a very negative conclusion. He ended his discussion of the matter by saying, "It would be nonsense, therefore, to attempt to identify a Lessingian 'theology'. For Lessing's exoterically expressed theological thoughts lie only in part on *one* level, and we know too little of his esoteric view."[58] His point is that the "exoteric teachings," the teachings Lessing set forth in public, do not reflect his real opinion or conviction, and they cannot be treated on a single level because they range over a variety of levels. At any rate, Lessing's "esoteric" view is concealed, Loofs concluded, behind the "exoteric" walls that we lack the ability to penetrate.

This problem, which has been blocking our understanding of Lessing, must be overcome in one way or another if we are to talk about Lessing's theology or his philosophy of religion. But how can we penetrate the exoteric walls that have blocked our access to his esoteric view? Or rather, does the way in which Loofs formulated the problem need to be called in question? In any case, we have to search for a new approach to Lessing's theology and philosophy of religion if we are to escape Loofs's dilemma.

The Question of Methodology for Lessing Studies

Whether we can even find such an approach is the question before us. Since the history of Lessing studies tells us that no cure-all method has been discovered, we should like to begin by reexamining old interpretive methods.

What interests us here is Lessing's own peculiar way of accepting or appropriating other people's thought into his system. Carl Schwarz simply called it "accommodation."[59] Martin Haug named it, more specifically, "pedagogic accommodation" (*die pädagogische Akkommodation*) or "the method of education" (*die Methode der Erziehung*).[60] Thielicke refined it into what he called the "method of assimilation" (*Angleichungsmethode*).[61] The point is that "Lessing's peculiar manner of thinking and writing"[62] should be clearly distinguished from the "substance of [his] thought" (*Gedankensubstanz*).[63] If we distinguish these two discrete things clearly, we will not have to reach a negative conclusion like the one Loofs drew from his premise.

In this connection, we give special attention to Lessing's utterances in his *Leibniz on Eternal Punishments*. What he stated here to vindicate Leibniz against the attacks of Johann August Eberhard can be applied to Lessing himself. For this reason his statements provide, as Henry E. Allison aptly observed, "important clues to his own philosophical position."[64] What, then, is the main point of Lessing's defense of Leibniz?

In refutation of Eberhard, who had accused Leibniz of accommodating his philosophical views to prevailing theological doctrines, Lessing made the following statement:

> One cannot truly say that he [Leibniz] sought to accommodate the prevailing doctrines of all parties into his system. . . . Leibniz, in his search for truth, never took commonly held opinions into consideration. But he firmly believed that no opinion could be generally accepted which was not in a certain aspect, in a certain sense, true. With this firm conviction, he often took pleasure in turning and twisting these commonly held opinions until he made their certain aspect visible, until he made their certain sense comprehensible. He struck fire from the flint, but he did not conceal his fire in the flint. . . . To be sure he believed in them [commonly held opinions], that is, in the supportable sense which he did not so much add to them as discover in them. The supportable sense was true, and how could he not believe in the truth? This should not be regarded as either duplicity or vanity. He did nothing more, or less, than the ancient philosophers were wont to do with their exoteric lectures. He observed a bit of prudence for which our most recent philosophers have become much too wise. He willingly set his own system aside and sought to lead each toward truth along the road on which he found him.[65]

According to Lessing, Eberhard's charge that Leibniz accommodated his views to prevailing theological views was utterly unjustifiable. Leibniz endeavored, rather, to accommodate the prevailing theological views to his philosophical system. He sought to find a "supportable sense" (*ein erträglicher Sinn*) in them. At any rate, Lessing continues, Leibniz accepted the orthodox doctrine of eternal punishment in its "supportable sense."

> I am convinced, rather, and believe myself able to prove, that Leibniz simply acquiesced in the ordinary doctrine of damnation, with all its exoteric grounds, [and that] he even wished to strengthen it with new grounds. [This is] because he recognized that it agreed better with a great esoteric truth of his own philosophy than the opposing doctrine. To be sure, he did not accept it in the crude and unseemly sense in which so many theologians accept it. But he found that even in this crude and unseemly sense, it still possessed more truth than the equally crude and unseemly concepts of the enthusiastic defenders of the restoration. And this alone induced him to have a bit too much to do with orthodoxy and its business rather than too little with the latter.[66]

On the basis of his meticulous analysis of these and other statements by Lessing, Thielicke summarizes the results in four points important for the question of method:

1. The mode of thinking specific to Lessing can be characterized as "assimilation to the opponent" (*Angleichung an den Gegner*). This mode of thinking always presupposes a "static substance of thought" (*eine ruhende Gedankensubstanz*), the existence of which alone makes such assimilation possible and easy. For this reason, "system" and "method" in Lessing must be separated in principle.
2. Assimilation consists, in the first place, not in adaptation or accommodation to the opponent, but rather in the accommodation of the prevailing doctrines of all parties to his system. Actual assimilation to the opponent, if any, exists only in the formal sense. That is to say, it consists in a calculation of the opponent's standpoint, presuppositions of thought, and language.
3. The exoteric mode of thinking must not be regarded merely as a matter of method exterior to Lessing's system. It belongs to the system itself. Consequently, it is not permissible to go behind the fundamental interweaving of exoteric and esoteric with a view to isolating Lessing's true or esoteric conviction. The exoteric and esoteric were, rather, systematically interwoven in his thought. The ultimate cause of such systematic interweaving is that Lessing, because he was still developing his ideas, could not advance from exoteric "believing" (*Glauben*) to esoteric "seeing" (*Schauen*).
4. The fact that Lessing was still in process of development forces him to ask questions and wait for answers. This "attitude of asking and waiting" accounts for the ambiguity in his thought with regard to transcendent revelation. It also throws light on the fact that his repeated tackling of the problem of revelation and reason, transcendence and immanence, was destined to remain fragmentary and failed to achieve clarity.[67]

These are the main points that Thielicke formulated as a result of methodical reflection on Lessing's theology or philosophy of religion. By and large, we can agree with his points insofar as questions of method are concerned.

The basic premises for our interpretation of Lessing bear some resemblance to the ones Thielicke employs. For the purpose of this inquiry we shall assume as working hypotheses, vindication for which will be presented in the course of our discussion, the following five points: (1) There was an enduring core of thought in Lessing's system, and it was this enduring core that made possible his elastic accommodation to all sorts of opinions. (2) Lessing as theologian or philosopher of religion was at once a first-rate inquirer and a first-rate pedagogue. This double role of tireless inquirer and skillful pedagogue inevitably demanded accommodation from him. (3) As a tireless and persevering inquirer, Lessing constantly sought the truth and sensed, ahead of his time, a germ of advanced knowledge as yet unavailable to his contemporaries. As a skillful and patient pedagogue, however, he considered it more appropriate to keep the higher knowledge of which he had had a foretaste secret until his contemporaries became ripe for it. (4) Possession of the germ of higher truth and the necessity for its concealment caused the peculiar interweaving of exoteric and esoteric in his system. The exoteric and esoteric, however, were so closely related that one could not be isolated from the other. (5) Lessing was still in the ever-changing stream of historical process. Despite possessing the germ of advanced knowledge, he had not yet obtained the whole truth, but was waiting for its fuller manifestation in future.

Our approach to Lessing thus owes a great deal to Thielicke's methodical refinement. Nevertheless, the actual mode of procedure we propose to follow is completely different from his. Unlike Thielicke, we will not place a one-sided emphasis on Lessing's last work, *The Education of the Human Race* (*Die Erziehung des Menschengeschlechts*). Nor will we attempt to interpret Lessing's theology or philosophy of religion solely or primarily in subjective-existentialist terms. We propose, rather, to interpret Lessing's theological and religious-philosophical thought from a great variety of his writings, which are in most cases fragmentary and often contradict each other. We also propose to pay greater attention to the historical context within which each text came into being, and to interpret his thought in correlation with this historical context. What is attempted here is not a systematic reconstruction of Lessing's philosophy of religion. Ours is, rather, a trial interpretation of Lessing's theological and religious-philosophical thought in several of its important aspects. It is, as it were, an assay into the hidden and presumably rich vein of Lessing's thought. This "intellectual assay" is intended, however, for systematic reconstruction in future. Such reconstruction can only be attempted after this and other assays of a similar kind bear fruit. The main purpose of this book, then, is to elucidate Lessing's "basic ideas" (*Grundgedanken*), with special concentration on his theological and religious-philosophical writings, for the sake of such a future task.

1

Lessing and Christianity

It is often said that "Lessing became a philosopher in debating with Christianity."[1] As this statement implies, Lessing's relationship with Christianity has a long and deep-rooted history. His engagement with theology did not suddenly blossom with his publication of *Fragments from an Unnamed Author* (*Fragmenten des Ungenannten*) or the ensuing "fragments controversy" (*Fragmentenstreit*). It goes back, rather, to the Leipzig period (1746–48) when he was a seminary student, or even further back to his boyhood in the parsonage at Kamenz. This chapter, accordingly, surveys Lessing's general relationship with Christianity and Christian theology. The aim of this survey is to lay the groundwork for more detailed studies in the chapters that follow.

Lessing's Formative Period (*Bildungsjahre*)

Born 22 January 1729 in the parsonage at Kamenz in Saxony, Lessing was destined to come to grips with Christianity throughout his life. He was the first great thinker among the many men of letters and philosophers in Germany who came from a Lutheran parsonage. As "the first free writer of the German language" (*der erste freie Schriftsteller deutscher Sprache*), he emancipated himself from the yoke of Christian tradition, yet respected its intellectual and cultural heritage more than his successors. The way he preserved "the religious traditions of his ancestry," moreover, was unique. He did this not so much by "appropriating them respectfully" as by having "serious doubt" (*klüglicher Zweifel*)[2] about them.

Lessing's father, Johann Gottfried Lessing (1693–1770), was a learned pastor of Lutheran orthodoxy who had mastered theology and philosophy at the University of Wittenberg. His mother, Justina Salome Lessing (née Feller, 1703–1777), had herself been raised in a parsonage as a Lutheran pastor's daughter. Gotthold Lessing, born and reared within Lutheran Christianity, formed his own personality in serious dialogue and inner battle with this earliest of Protestant traditions.

In 1741 Lessing entered the famous ducal school of St. Afra in Meissen. There he stood out for his "intellectual acumen and excellent memory."[3] The schoolmaster is said to have compared him to "a horse that must have double

14

fodder" (*ein Pferd, das doppeltes Futter haben muß*)[4] because Lessing mastered all subjects with extraordinary eagerness and understanding. In particular, the young boy showed keen interest in classical philology and mathematics. At the same time, however, he felt within himself an irresistible bent for story writing and even at that young age wrote his first play, *The Young Scholar.*

On graduating from St. Afra at the age of seventeen, a year earlier than his classmates due to his academic excellence, he entered the University of Leipzig to study theology. It was then customary for sons of the parsonage to study theology, for the time in which Lessing spent his youth was, to borrow Dilthey's expression, "a time in which the whole of German culture was theological."[5] At that time, the famous theologian and philologist Johann August Ernesti was a member of the theological faculty at the University of Leipzig. But the young Lessing's eyes had already been opened to the wider world of the humanities, and he experienced a budding love for literary creation. As a result, he found most of the lectures offered at the school of theology rather tedious and boring. The teachers who attracted him most were the philologist Johann Friedrich Christ and the philosopher of mathematics Abraham Gotthelf Kästner. But his initial desire to study theology did not last long. He soon put aside theological study to study the world of real life.

Leipzig, known in those days as "a small Paris," was full of charms and temptations for a lad fresh from the country.[6] What attracted young Lessing was the theater, to which he was introduced by Christlob Mylius, a cousin seven years older than himself, who was working as a journalist in Leipzig. In one of the few extant letters to his mother, Lessing reflects on his development during the time he spent in Leipzig.

> I graduated from school young, in the conviction that my entire happiness was to consist in books. I came to Leipzig, a place where one could see the whole world in small size. For the first few months I lived an even more sequestered life than I had lived in Meissen. Always among my books, occupied only with myself, I rarely thought of other people or, perhaps, of God. . . . This state, however, did not last long. My eyes were opened—should I say fortunately, or unfortunately, for me? The future will decide which is the case. I came to see that books would make me a scholar, but never a man. I ventured forth among my fellows. Good God! What a difference I perceived between myself and them! A boorish shyness, a neglected and awkward body, utter ignorance of the manners of society, a gloomy, unfriendly bearing in which every one believed he could read my contempt for him—these were the good qualities that my self-criticism disclosed. I felt such shame as I had never felt before. The effect was a fixed determination to better myself in this, cost what it may. You know what I started. I learned to dance, to fence, to vault. . . . I advanced so far in these things that those who, in anticipation, had denied me all talent in these respects came to admire me in some degree. My body had become a bit more suitable, and I sought society in order that now I might also learn to live. I laid aside serious books for a time in order to make myself acquainted with others, which are far more pleasant, and perhaps quite as useful. I took up comedies first. It may seem unbelievable, but they rendered great service to

me. From them I learned to distinguish between good and forced behavior and between rude and natural behavior. From them I learned to know true and false virtues, and learned that vices would disappear because of their ridiculousness and shamefulness. (Letter to his mother of 20 January 1749.)[7]

Frequenting local theaters and spending excessive amounts of time in the company of playwrights, actors, and actresses eventually caused Lessing to drop out of the university. To the great disappointment of his parents, he fled to Berlin to lead a hand-to-mouth life as a cub writer and editor. He hoped to become someday "a German Molière" (*ein deutscher Molière*).[8] But in the eyes of his devout parents, his wish to become a writer of comedies was painfully like the biblical parable of the prodigal son. Worrying about his son's spiritual condition and salvation, the father-pastor wrote stern letters remonstrating against his seemingly immoral life. In reply to one of these letters, the twenty-year-old freelance journalist defended himself with the following memorable words:

> Time will tell whether I have respect for my parents, conviction in my religion, and morality in my path through life. Time will tell whether the better Christian is one who has the principles of Christian teaching memorized and on his tongue, often without understanding them, who goes to church, and follows all the customs because he is used to them; or whether the better Christian is one who has held serious doubts and, after examining them, has attained conviction, or at least is still striving to attain it. The Christian religion is not something to be swallowed blindly and taken in good faith from parents. Most of us simply inherit it from them, as we do their possessions, but our parents too show by their behavior the kind of honest Christians they are. As long as I see that one of the most important commandments of Christianity, "*Love thine enemy*," is observed no better than it is now, I shall continue to doubt whether those people who say they are Christians, really are Christians. (Letter to his father of 30 May 1749.)[9]

Ernst Cassirer perceives in this defiant statement "genuine Lessingian devoutness."[10] Be that as it may, this letter is vivid testimony to the fact that "serious doubt" about the religious traditions of his forebears formed the starting point of the young Lessing's engagement with Christianity.

In serious dialogue and inner battle with the Christian tradition as he knew it from strict, yet benevolent, parents, Lessing gradually came to form his own philosophy of religion. He had to go through many trials and errors, many twists and turns, before eventually attaining to "a high eminence from which he believes it possible to see beyond the limits of the allotted path of his present day's journey."[11] Only in the works brought to fruition when he served as librarian at the ducal library in Wolfenbüttel, especially in *Nathan the Wise* (*Nathan der Weise*, 1779) and *The Education of the Human Race* (*Die Erziehung des Menschengeschlechts*, 1780) did there come into being what can be called an authentic "Lessingian philosophy of religion."

Lessing's formative period (*Bildungsjahre*) covers the years from 1748 to 1760. Having fled Leipzig, he began his career as a freelance journalist, changing his residence every few years: Berlin (1748–51), Wittenberg (1751–52),

Berlin again (1752–55), Leipzig (1755–58), and once more back to Berlin (1758–60). During this formative period, he may seem to have led an impious, godless life that had little to do with the religion in which he was raised. But this was not the case. He never lost his serious interest in Christianity. The fragments written during this period bear witness to his deep concern with religion in general, and with Christianity in particular. For example, in the preface to the fragment *Religion* (*Die Religion*, 1749/50), it is stated that "religion has for many years been the theme that invokes my more serious poetic inspirations."[12] Other fragments ascribed to the same early years, such as *Some Thoughts about the Moravians* (*Gedanken über die Herrnhuter*, 1750) and *The Christianity of Reason* (*Das Christentum der Vernunft*, 1751/52), testify to the young Lessing's deep and continuing concern with religion. They also illustrate the salient characteristics of his developing religious thought.

Toward the end of 1751, Lessing, temporarily interrupting his activity as a journalist and editor, went to Wittenberg, where his younger brother Johannes Theophilus was staying, in order to enter a Magister, or M.A., program.[13] At the University of Wittenberg, he made an intensive study of religious thought in the period of the Reformation. The results of his historical studies are collected in his *Vindications* (*Rettungen*, 1754). These vindications focused attention on a number of thinkers whose ideas had been unjustly ignored or distorted due to public prejudice or malice. His aim was to do justice to them and to rehabilitate their reputations from a disinterested and objective point of view. The fact that Lessing, running against the stream of general opinion, chose to shed new light on these heretical or apostate thinkers and thoughts may be useful in clarifying his motivation for publishing, during his Wolfenbüttel period, the *Fragments from an Unnamed Author*.

The Breslau period (1760–65) is of great importance for the development of Lessing's thought. When Berlin, the capital of Prussia, was besieged and occupied by Austrian troops in October 1760, Lessing was about to embark on a new kind of employment, one that signified a major change in his life. From Friedrich Bogislaw von Tauentzien, a general officer newly assigned to Breslau, he received an invitation to serve as the officer's secretary. Having become acquainted with Tauentzien through his friend Edwald von Kleist[14] during his second stay in Leipzig (1755–58), Lessing went to Breslau to take up this post and stayed there four and a half years. He did not return to Berlin until May 1765.

During his stay in Breslau, Lessing enjoyed a pleasant life and had more free time and greater economic stability than ever before. He took advantage of this opportunity to conduct intensive philosophical studies of Leibniz and Spinoza, on the one hand, and to carry out in-depth studies of the church fathers, on the other. Samuel Benjamin Klose provides us with a contemporary report on this period:

> In the last years of his stay in Breslau, he began to concern himself with theological studies. He drafted an outline for a major treatise on the persecution of

Christian martyrs, and proposed to one of his friends that they read the church fathers together. According to his affirmation, he found in Justin Martyr religious theses utterly different from those prevalent in modern times. At the same time, Spinoza's philosophy became an object of study. He read those who wanted to refute Spinoza. Among them, Bayle, in his judgment, was the one person who understood Spinoza least. For him, the person who entered most deeply into Spinoza's true meaning was Dippel. Nevertheless, Lessing never expressed his ideas on this topic at all, either to Jacobi or to his most trusted friends.[15]

In any event, the philosophical and theological studies Lessing carried out during his Breslau period caused a significant turn in the direction of his thought. These studies emancipated him from the spell of Enlightenment theology. With his eyes opened to a higher worldview, he was now able to adopt his own religious-philosophical stance in controversies between orthodoxy and Enlightenment. Subsequent chapters will develop this point in more detail. But it is important to observe here that Lessing's involvement with theology did not begin suddenly during his Wolfenbüttel period but had a long history, traceable to the religious education that began at home with his father.

Lessing and the Fragments Controversy (*Fragmentenstreit*)

The fragments controversy, a dispute ignited by his publication of parts of Hermann Samuel Reimarus's unpublished manuscripts under the title *Fragments from an Unnamed Author*, made Lessing's name immortal in the history of Protestant theology. Reimarus, a deceased professor of Oriental languages at a Gymnasium in Hamburg, was highly respected during his lifetime for his warm personality and academic excellence. His contemporaries regarded him as a good Christian. He was regarded as standing up for the Christian religion, even if he was not in complete agreement with Lutheran orthodoxy. In his heart of hearts, however, he had become a radical deist. In secret he entertained highly critical and radical ideas about Christianity, expressing his critiques in voluminous, unpublished manuscripts drawn together under the title *Apology for Rational Worshippers of God* (*Apologie oder Schutzschrift für die vernünftigen Verehrer Gottes*). For fear of civil persecution, he did not want to take the risk of publishing the manuscripts. He showed them to only a few of his most trusted friends and to his two children—but not to his wife!

Lessing had the good fortune of becoming close friends with Reimarus's children, Johann Albert and Elise, during his stay in Hamburg (1765–70). He borrowed their father's unpublished manuscripts under the pledge of never disclosing the author's real name. Beginning in May 1770 he assumed the office of librarian at the famous Herzog-August-Bibliothek at Wolfenbüttel. On 13 February 1772 he was granted, from the hand of the Duke of Brunswick, the privilege of immunity from censorship, on condition that he would never attack the Christian religion. From 1774 onward, he began to publish a series of precious manuscripts and other acquisitions that he had discovered in the library. He smuggled the Reimarus manuscripts into the library and, pretending he had found them in its holdings, published them under the title *Fragments from an Unnamed Author.* He camouflaged the author's identity by providing the false supposition that the author might be Johann Lorenz Schmidt, the deist who had translated the banned Wertheimer Bible of 1735. In 1774 Lessing first published a small and comparatively moderate part of the Reimarus manuscripts under the title *On Tolerating the Deists.* It evoked, as he had expected, no significant response. Three years later, he published five other fragments that stood at the heart of Reimarus's attacks on the Christian doctrine of revelation. To these fragments he appended his own "Editor's Counterpropositions" (*Gegensätze des Herausgebers*). This publication of more fragments, allegedly anonymous, aroused sharp refutations and reproaches from all sides, especially from the camp of Lutheran orthodoxy. This led to the exceptionally bitter dispute called the fragments controversy.

The controversy began innocuously enough. Johann Daniel Schumann, director of a lyceum in Hanover, attempted to refute the unnamed author by writing the treatise *On the Evidence of the Proofs for the Truth of the Christian Religion.* Lessing countered Schumann with his famous booklets *On the Proof of the Spirit and of Power (Über den Beweis des Geistes und der Kraft)* and *The Testament of John (Das Testament Johannis)*, to which Schumann responded with *J. D. Schumann's Answer to the Letter Sent Him from Brunswick on the Proof of the Spirit and of Power.* Johann Heinrich Ress, the Archdeacon and Superintendent of Wolfenbüttel, then attacked the unnamed author by writing a treatise called *Defense of the History of the Resurrection.* When Lessing responded with *A Rejoinder (Eine Duplik)*, Ress made a further attempt to defend the gospel account of the resurrection by writing yet another treatise, *The History of the Resurrection of Jesus Christ without Contradictions: In Opposition to A Rejoinder.* Later, other people such as Friedrich Wilhelm Mascho and Georg Christoph Silberschlag took part in the controversy. But Lessing did not attempt to refute them publicly, presumably because he judged these opponents too insignificant to fight against.[16]

But with the participation of Johann Melchior Goeze (1717–1786), pastor of the Church of St. Catherine in Hamburg and Hauptpastor, or Pastor Primarius, of the Hamburg pastors, a drastic change in the nature and pace of the controversy took place. Unlike his predecessors, who had been preoccupied with refuting the statements of the unnamed author, Goeze took aim not so much at the unnamed author as at the editor of the fragments. The fragments were a "hostile blasphemy"[17] against the Christian religion, to be sure, but Lessing was a blasphemous person who "derided the entire Christian world to its face." The fragments were a "disgraceful abortion," but the "Editor's Counterpropositions" were "more poisonous than the poison in the fragments themselves."[18]

Representing Lutheran orthodoxy, Goeze launched a fierce attack against Lessing with his publication of *Something Preliminary against Court Councillor Lessing's Direct and Indirect Malevolent Attacks on Our Most Holy Religion, and on Its Single Foundation, the Bible* together with another pamphlet called *Lessing's Weaknesses.* Lessing, to defend both the unnamed author and himself, published a series of polemical writings: *A Parable*; *Axioms, If There Be Any in Such Things*; *Anti-Goeze* in eleven installments; and *The Necessary Answer to the Very Unnecessary Question of Hauptpastor Goeze in Hamburg*. Moreover, he even went so far as to put into print the most radically critical fragment of Reimarus's manuscripts, *On the Purpose of Jesus and His Disciples*.

This head-on confrontation between Lessing and Goeze became hopelessly mired in personal invective. But when it began to look as if he might lose the battle, Goeze appealed to the civil authority. In July 1778 all of Lessing's publications became subject to strict censorship, and in August of the same year, Lessing was required to receive permission from the government of Brunswick before he could publish anything.

Having been prohibited from continuing his anti-Goeze controversy within the territory of the Duke of Brunswick, Lessing decided to return to "his old pulpit, the theater,"[19] to resume the theological battle. He then wrote "a play, the content of which has some analogy with his present disputes."[20] Lessing characterized this play, his famous *Nathan the Wise*, as "a son of his approaching old age, [a son] whom the polemic helped to bring to birth."[21]

But if Lessing is right in saying that "Nathan's attitude toward *all* positive religions has always been *my own*,"[22] then we have to take the dramatic work *Nathan the Wise* into consideration in order to understand the full spectrum of his theological or religious-philosophical thought. Thus the task of elucidating Lessing's theology or philosophy of religion will inevitably require a much broader scope of research than that of ordinary theological studies.

Lessing's Theological Position

Since detailed analyses of the main aspects of Lessing's theological or religious-philosophical thought will be attempted in chapters 2 through 7, our task here is to make clear the basic characteristics of his thought. We approach this limited task by asking why Lessing ventured to publish Reimarus's manuscripts as *Fragments from an Unnamed Author*.

Reimarus himself had chosen not to publish his manuscripts, with their radical criticisms of Christianity, for fear of possible persecution against himself and his family. Why, then, did Lessing risk putting them into print?

To our question, Lessing himself provides two significant answers. In his *A Confutation against Friedrich Mascho*, he states: "I have pulled him into the world because I no longer wanted to live under the same roof with him alone. He incessantly pestered me; and I confess that I was not always able to resist his whispers as much as I could have wished. So I thought, somebody else must either bring us closer together, or separate us further; and this somebody else can be nobody other than the public."[23] Again, in the first installment of his *Anti-Goeze*, Lessing says: "God knows that I have no objection to the fact that you and all schoolmasters in Lower Saxony are campaigning against my unnamed author. On the contrary, I am pleased with this. For I brought him to light for the very purpose that a goodly number of people could examine and refute him."[24]

If we take these statements at face value, Lessing was not completely in accord with Reimarus, but wished, rather, to resist him if he could. On the other hand, he could not deny that there was a grain of truth in Reimarus's radical historical criticism of the biblical accounts. This thrust him, unavoidably, into an extremely ambivalent state, which was naturally intolerable to him. But because he was unable to extricate himself from this state by his own power, he appealed to the general public for rescue. He thus took it on himself to publish Reimarus's manuscripts anonymously so that the general public might be able to examine and judge them.

Nevertheless, we cannot take Lessing's statements at face value. For his was an exceptionally ironical mind, and he had a genius for tactics. Furthermore, a glance at his "Editor's Counterpropositions" shows that he had already taken a definite stance toward Reimarus, or, rather, had already taken a stance at a certain distance from him. This implies that Lessing was not actually in need of adjudication by the public, for he himself had already attained, by the time he decided to publish the *Fragments from an Unnamed Author*, his own theological position, a position transcending both orthodoxy and deistic rationalism.

Why, then, did he make these fragments available to the public? In my view, the answer can be found in the "Editor's Counterpropositions." Here Lessing proclaims: "Truly, he is yet to appear. On both sides he is yet to appear: the man who disputes religion in such a manner, and defends religion in such a manner, as the importance and dignity of the subject requires. With all knowledge, with all love for the truth, with all seriousness!"[25] Lessing, who had regarded Reimarus as a person who came close to "the ideal of a genuine disputer of religion," now expected that the *Fragments from an Unnamed Author* would awaken "a man who would come just as close to the ideal of a genuine defender of religion."[26] Thus we can perceive, in his publishing of Reimarus's fragments, an audacious attempt to mobilize and revitalize the theological situation of that time. Unlike the neologians, he did not want to mediate between orthodoxy and Enlightenment in an easygoing manner, but intended to attain a deeper understanding of Christian truth through a dialectical process of disputation and defense.

How did Lessing locate himself in the theological situation of that day? It is true that he looked down on Lutheran orthodoxy, but he despised enlightened rational theology, or neology, even more. As he put it with characteristic verve, "our new-fashioned clergymen" are "far too inconsequential [as] theologians, and not nearly consequential enough [as] philosophers" (*die Theologen viel zu wenig, und Philosophen lange nicht genug sind*).[27] In a letter of 2 February 1774 to his brother Karl, he explains his paradoxical relationship to Lutheran orthodoxy.

> Now without investigating how much or how little I have reason to be satisfied with my fellow men, I must tell you, however, that you truly form a completely

false idea of me on this point, that you understand my entire attitude toward orthodoxy very incorrectly. Am I supposed to begrudge the world's seeking to be more enlightened? Am I supposed not to wish from the heart that everyone could think about religion rationally? I should despise myself if my scribblings were devoted to any end but that of helping to further these great intentions. But let me [decide] in my own way how, in my view, I can do this. And what is simpler than this way? I should not wish the impure water, long unusable, to be preserved; it is only that I should not wish it to be poured away before we know where we can get purer; I simply do not want it poured away unthinkingly, leaving the child to be bathed in liquid manure. And what else is the new-fashioned theology, as compared with orthodoxy, but liquid manure as compared with impure water?

With orthodoxy, thank God, there was a tolerably clear understanding. A curtain had been drawn between it and philosophy, behind which each could go its own way without interfering with the other. But what is happening now? This curtain is being torn down, and under the pretext of making us reasonable Christians, we are turned into extremely unreasonable philosophers. I beseech you, dear brother, look rather less at what our modern theologians discard than at what they want to put in its place. We are one in our conviction that our old religious system is false. But I cannot say with you that it is a patch-work created by bunglers and quasi-philosophers. I know of nothing in the world on the study of which human intelligence has been more acutely displayed and exercised. What is really a patchwork created by bunglers and quasi-philosophers is the religious system that they now want to put in place of the old—and with far more influence on reason and philosophy than the old arrogated to itself. And yet you take it amiss that I defend the old system? My neighbor's house is on the point of collapsing. If he wants to pull it down, I will willingly help him. But he wants to prop it up and support it in a way that entails the complete ruin of my house. He must stop this, or I shall take care of his collapsing house as if it were my own.[28]

This citation shows that Lessing had now attained a position that transcended the three main trends of the time (orthodoxy, neology, and deistic rationalism) and that he wanted to contribute to the development of theology in his peculiarly realistic manner by relating himself dialectically to each of these trends.

Lessing and the Pursuit of Truth

Lessing was himself a child of the Enlightenment and deemed it the supreme end of his literary activity to make everyone think about religion rationally. For him, orthodoxy was something like "impure water, long unusable," to be thrown away sooner or later. But he did not side with "the new-fashioned theology," or neology. According to him, this newfangled theology, "under the pretext of making us reasonable Christians," merely "turned us into extremely unreasonable philosophers." For this reason, neology was a greater obstacle than orthodoxy to the ultimate goal to which Lessing devoted himself, the goal of human enlightenment. Neology was to orthodoxy as liquid manure was to dirty water. Both were impure—that is to say, untruth—but dirty water (orthodoxy) was more tolerable than liquid manure (neology). That is why Lessing, in leveling caustic criticisms at neology, often took the side of orthodoxy.

Yet Lessing sought "to take care of his [neighbor's] collapsing house [orthodoxy] as if it were [his] own," because he did not want his neighbor to "prop it up and support it in a way that entails the complete ruin of [his own] house." His attempt to "defend the old system" was not, therefore, from the bottom of his heart. In his heart of hearts, he was willing to help his neighbor pull down the collapsing house if the latter wished it.[29] Nevertheless, his taking the side of orthodoxy should not be taken as a mere pose. It is attributable, rather, to the fact that Lessing himself did not "know where we can get purer [water]." In other words, he did not possess this purer water (truth) but was in search of it.

Seen from this viewpoint, Lessing's act of publishing Reimarus's fragments can be construed as an act intended to serve the search for truth. In our interpretation, Lessing, by publishing these sensational fragments, sought to create a stir in the stagnant theology of his time. Making the fragments public would, he hoped, provoke a heated discussion or controversy between the "genuine disputer of religion" and the "genuine defender of religion" for the purpose of attaining a deeper understanding of the truth. He was convinced, in fact, that controversy could contribute to the search for truth. As he put it, "controversy has fostered the spirit of investigation (*Geist der Prüfung*); it has kept prejudice and reputation off balance; in short, it has prevented rouged untruth from establishing itself in place of truth."[30]

Such an attitude, incidentally, is characteristic of Lessing. We have already seen the young Lessing's letter of 30 May 1749 to his father, the letter in which he defended himself against his father's remonstrations. In this letter we found him saying that although "most of us simply inherit it from them [our parents], as we do their possessions," nonetheless "the Christian religion is not something to be swallowed blindly and taken in good faith from parents." "Time will tell," he went on, that "one who has held serious doubts and, after looking into the matter, has attained conviction, or at least is still striving to attain it," is a better Christian than "one who has the principles of Christian teaching memorized and on his tongue, often without understanding them, who goes to church, and follows all the customs because he is used to them."[31] We may be able to sense something of the noble spirit of this son of the parsonage, the spirit that did not deviate from the search for truth, no matter how far he deviated from the academic or clerical course that his parents had wanted their son to take. In any event, it is evident that having "serious doubts" about Christianity formed the starting point of Lessing's lifelong religious quest.

Lessing declares it his duty "to test with his own eyes *quid liquidum sit in causa Christianorum*" (what it is in the Christian cause that may be taken as certain). Hence he hunts out all sorts of theological books and reads whatever he can lay his hands on: first apologetic, pro-Christian books, then polemical, anti-Christian ones.[32] According to his reminiscences, however, "the more conclusively the one wished to prove [the truth of] Christianity, the more doubtful I became, while the more wantonly and triumphantly the other wished to stamp it into the ground, the more I felt inclined, at least in my heart, to support it."[33]

But it was probably in his Breslau period, no later than the beginning of 1771, that Lessing, having passed through the storms of doubt and skepticism, began to take a more positive attitude toward Christianity. In his letter to Moses Mendelssohn of 9 January 1771, he makes a significant statement about the retrieval of lost truths:

> I am now going to study Ferguson properly. I can see already from the table of contents that this is the kind of book I have missed here, where for the most part I have only books that sooner or later dull my understanding and waste my time. When one does not think for a long time, he ends up not being able to think at all. Is it really good, though, to contemplate and concern oneself seriously with truths with which one has lived and, for the sake of peace, must continue to live in constant contradiction? I can already see from afar many such truths in the Englishman.
>
> Among them are some which I have long ceased to regard as truths. Still, it is not merely since yesterday that I have been concerned lest, while discarding certain prejudices, I may have thrown away a little too much, which I shall have to retrieve. It is only the fear of dragging all the rubbish back into my house that has so far hindered me from doing this. It is infinitely difficult to know when and where one should stop, and for the vast majority of men, the object of their reflection lies at the point where they become tired of reflecting.[34]

Many scholars see in this statement Lessing's retrieval or reevaluation of the Christian revelation.[35] Whether the truths that Lessing "can already see from afar" and wishes "to retrieve" signify the revealed truths of Christianity or something else, one thing is certain: it is about this time that there occurs a decisive turn in his pursuit of truth. There now begins a truly theological or religious-philosophical investigation not motivated by doubt but nourished by the Christian revelation. Against the background of his erstwhile meandering pursuit of truth, the following famous words should be read:

> The worth of a man does not consist in the truth he possesses, or thinks he possesses, but in the pains he has taken to attain that truth. For his powers are extended not through possession but through the search for truth. In this alone does his ever-growing perfection consist. Possession makes him lazy, indolent, and proud.
>
> If God held all truth in his right hand and everlasting striving for truth in his left, so that I should always and everlastingly be mistaken, and said to me, "Choose," I would humbly pick the left hand and say, "Father, grant me that. Absolute truth is for thee alone."[36]

We must bear in mind that such words can be spoken only by the mature Lessing as one who recognizes that he "has set himself upon a high eminence from which he believes it possible to see beyond the limits of the allotted path of his present day's journey."[37]

Salient Features of Lessing's Theological Thought

We have sought to explain the characteristics of Lessing's theological thought mainly in formal terms. Now let us try to elucidate its salient features in material terms. Since more detailed analysis will be attempted in the chapters that follow, our concern here is to characterize the general aspects of Lessing's theological thought. For this task, we give special attention to the "Editor's Counterpropositions" that Lessing appended to Reimarus's fragments when he published them as the work of an unnamed author.

In order to cushion the general reader, who was likely to be shocked by the unnamed author's rationalistic criticism of the biblical accounts, Lessing says:

And now enough of these fragments. A reader who would have preferred me to spare him altogether is surely more timid than well instructed. He may be a very devout Christian, but he is certainly not a very enlightened one. He may be wholehearted in upholding his religion; but he should also have greater confidence in it.

For how much could be said in reply to all these objections and difficulties! And even if absolutely no answer were forthcoming, what then? The learned theologian might in the last resort be embarrassed, but certainly not the Christian. To the former it might at most cause confusion to see the supports with which he would uphold religion shattered in this way, to find cast down the buttresses by which, God willing, he would have made it safe and sound. But how do this man's hypotheses, explanations, and proofs affect the Christian? For him it is simply a fact, this Christianity which he feels to be true and in which he feels blessed. When the paralytic experiences the beneficial shocks of the electric spark, does it worry him whether Nollet or Franklin or neither is right?

In short, the letter is not the spirit, and the Bible is not religion. Consequently, objections to the letter and to the Bible are not by the same token objections to the spirit and to religion. For the Bible obviously contains more than is essential to religion, and it is a mere hypothesis to assert of this superfluity that it must be infallible throughout. Moreover, religion was there before a Bible existed. Christianity was there before the evangelists and apostles wrote. A long period elapsed before the first of them wrote, and a considerable time before the entire canon was complete. Therefore, while much may depend on these writings, it is impossible to suppose that the entire truth of the religion depends on them. If there had been a period in which it had already spread abroad and in which it had gained many souls, and if, nevertheless, not a single letter of what has come down to us had yet been written down, then it must also be possible that everything which the evangelists and apostles wrote could have been lost—and yet that the religion which they taught would have continued. The religion is not true because the evangelists and apostles taught it. They taught it, rather, because it is true. The written traditions must be interpreted by their inner truth, and no written traditions can give a religion inner truth if it has none.

This, therefore, would be, in the worst case as I have said, the general answer to a large part of these fragments.[38]

The words cited above constitute the material at which Goeze leveled his most caustic criticism. In fact, they contain the gist of Lessing's own theological thought, which is distinct not only from Reimarus's deistic-rationalistic biblical criticism but also from the Lutheran biblicism represented by Goeze. Here we focus attention on four points: (1) the relationship between "piety" and "enlightenment" in Lessing; (2) his emphasis on experience; (3) his sharp distinction between the letter and the spirit, between the Bible and religion; and (4) his concept of the inner truth of religion.

First of all, Lessing says that any reader who would be frightened by the unnamed author's radical criticism of the biblical accounts "may be a very devout Christian, but he is certainly not a very enlightened one." He admonishes the reader not only to "be wholehearted in upholding his religion" but also "to have greater confidence in it." Needless to say, the Christian commended by Lessing is both "very devout" and "very enlightened." Such a Christian, however, need not be disturbed, says Lessing, by the unnamed author's "hypotheses, explanations, and proofs," but can trust wholeheartedly in the gospel. For such "hypotheses, explanations, and proofs" have to do only with the letter, not with the spirit of the Christian religion.

What is implied here is that a Lessingian understanding of the Enlightenment does not annul piety as such. It is true that Lessing is critical of "simple" or "inferior" piety that is utterly incompatible with rational thinking. But he affirms a "higher" piety that is compatible with such thought. True piety, according to him, unifies *pietas* and *scientia* in a higher synthesis.

Secondly, and closely related to true piety in this sense, is Lessing's assertion that evidence for the Christian faith is based on inner experience. According to him, what is important is "simply a fact, this Christianity which he *feels* to be true and in which he *feels* blessed." The fact that one feels the Christian religion to be true and feels blessed in it suffices. No further proof or explanation is necessary. To demonstrate this assertion, he introduces the example of a patient suffering from paralysis. "When the paralytic *experiences* the beneficial shocks of the electric spark, does it worry him whether Nollet or Franklin or neither is right?" That is to say, once the paralytic experiences the benefits of the electric spark, it makes no difference to him who first discovered the law of electricity, or which theory best explains electrical phenomena. It is worth noticing that Lessing italicizes the words "feel" (*fühlen*) and "experience" (*erfahren*). For him religion is a matter of the "heart" (*Herz*), not of the "brain" (*Kopf*). What is important, therefore, is not a theory about religion, but to actually "feel" or "experience" it.[39]

It may be this emphasis that leads Lessing, in his *Some Thoughts about the Moravians*, to stress "practical Christianity" (*das ausübende Christentum*) in contrast to "contemplative Christianity" (*das beschauende Christentum*).[40] In this significant early fragment, he defends the simple and devout faith of the Moravians against the criticism leveled at it by orthodox theologians who cling to a sophisticated dogmatic system. He declares, "Man was created for action and not for speculation";[41] "what is the use of believing correctly, if one does not live correctly?"; "in knowledge we are angels and in living [we are] devils" (*der Erkenntnis nach sind wir Engel, und dem Leben nach Teufel*).[42] In any event, it is one of the basic characteristics of Lessing's thought that greater value attaches to praxis than to theory, to experience than to teaching, and to ethics than to dogmatics. In each pair, the former predominates, though his ideal is their synthesis.

Thirdly, by his sharp distinction between the letter and the spirit, between the Bible and religion, Lessing not only defends the Christian religion against Reimarus's radically deistic criticism of the biblical accounts but also devastates Lutheran orthodoxy's adherence to the letter of the Bible. "In short, the letter is not the spirit, and the Bible is not religion. Consequently, objections to the letter and to the Bible are not by the same token objections to the spirit and to religion." For the same reason, Lutheran orthodoxy's position that each and every letter of the Bible is infallible can no longer be supported. "For the Bible obviously contains more than is essential to religion, and it is a mere hypothesis to assert of this superfluity that it must be infallible throughout." What is of great importance, though, is that Lessing supports his assertion by appealing to the Reformer Luther on this point, where it is precisely the Protestant "scriptural principle" that is at stake.

> Oh, that he could do it, he whom I should most like to have as my judge!—
> Thou, Luther!—Great, misunderstood man! And by none less understood than
> by the shortsighted, obstinate people who, with your slippers in their hand and
> an affected noisy zeal, saunter along the road which thou hast prepared!—
> Thou hast released us from the yoke of tradition. Who will release us from the
> more intolerable yoke of the letter? Who will finally bring us a Christianity
> such as thou wouldst now teach, as Christ himself wouldst teach?[43]

Heinrich Heine has great appreciation for Lessing's struggle with Lutheran orthodoxy and for his efforts to emancipate the German people from the tyranny of "the letter of the Bible." He regards Lessing as "the heir to Luther."

This interpretation of Lessing as the legitimate successor to the Lutheran Reformation may well be questionable, but the adequacy of such an interpretation is not our concern here. What interests us here, rather, is that Lessing, while interpreting the spirit of the Reformation in an utterly new, modern direction in his theological controversy with Lutheran orthodoxy, has recourse to Luther's *spirit*, not to Luther's *writings*.

> The true Lutheran does not wish to be defended by Luther's writings but by
> Luther's spirit; and Luther's spirit absolutely requires that no man may be pre-
> vented from advancing in knowledge of the truth according to his own judg-
> ment.[44]

Lessing's interpretation of "Luther's spirit" may well be open to censure as a one-sided subjectification of the Reformation principle. But it must not be taken as an arbitrary subjectivization of Protestant Christianity or an unqualified elevation of private religion. For Lessing advocates autonomy in pursuing not only knowledge of the truth but also the "inner truth" of the Christian religion.

It follows, fourthly, that Lessing's concept of the "inner truth" (*die innere Wahrheit*) of the Christian religion deserves special attention. One may well suspect that this concept too agrees with "subjective religion." For one may easily associate it with a mystically or spiritualistically grounded theology.

Lessing's adversary, Goeze, who regards Lessing's sharp distinction between the inner truth of Christianity and the written traditions of the Bible as an "empty word," criticizes him on precisely this point.

> Where does he wish to obtain the knowledge of the inner truth of the Christian religion if not from the scriptural traditions, or from the writings of the evangelists and apostles, in proper connection with the writings of the Old Testament?[45]

Goeze evidently fears that Lessing's advocacy of the inner truth of Christianity, when separated from the historically given, objective foundation of the scriptural traditions, can easily lead to the enthronement of arbitrary subjectivity. Lessing's answer to his Lutheran reviler is worth special consideration.

> This inner truth is not a kind of wax nose that every knave can mold as he likes to fit his own face. Where [do I] get the inner truth? From the Christian religion itself. That is why it is called inner truth, the truth that requires no authentication from outside.[46]

An account of this concept of inner truth will be given in chapters 3 and 4. Suffice it here to say that the inner truth of the Christian religion as Lessing affirms it is neither proved nor disproved by historical facts attested in the Bible. It is meant, rather, to be a truth intrinsic to the Christian religion as such. Though human participation may play an important role, this truth is by no means a sheerly subjective truth grasped in the inwardness of the believer. It is a truth for which evidence becomes manifest when the believer participates in "the reality of revelation" (*die Wirklichkeit der Offenbarung*).[47] To illustrate it by means of the foregoing example of the paralytic, the inner truth of the Christian religion is something like the truth that the paralytic personally experiences when he feels "the beneficial shocks of the electric spark," or when he encounters the "beneficial effectiveness" (*wohltätige Wirksamkeit*) of electricity.

Thus far we have observed, prior to a detailed analysis of particulars, the general characteristics of Lessing's theological and/or religious-philosophical thought from a macroscopic point of view. Changing the lens for a microscopic one, we shall consider various aspects of his thought in greater detail in the chapters that follow. Inevitably, there will be some overlapping with what has just been outlined in this chapter. Such will be the case especially in chapters 2 and 3, where the description is mainly historical. Accordingly, I wish to beg the reader's indulgence in advance for these overlappings.

2

The Religious Thought of the
Young Lessing

In German intellectual history, philosophers and men of letters who began life in a Lutheran parsonage are by no means rare. Hölderlin, Nietzsche, Dilthey, and Hesse are among those who might be named. (Herder, incidentally, was the son of the cantor, or precentor, of a Lutheran church.) But Lessing stands out as the first great German thinker to be born in a parsonage.

His grandfather, Theophilus Lessing (1647–1735), was a local dignitary who had published a book on religious toleration[1] in his youth and rendered long and notable service to his community as mayor of the city of Kamenz. His father, Johann Gottfried Lessing, as we have seen, was a Lutheran orthodox pastor, while his mother, Justina Salome, was the daughter of another Lutheran pastor who sprang from a venerable line of pastors. Our Lessing, therefore, was born into the Christian tradition and grew up within it. In this chapter we wish to trace the young Lessing's development, focusing on his religious thought.

The Young Lessing and His Religious Skepticism

In Berlin, Lessing began his freelance career as a reporter for the *Berlinische Privilegierte Zeitung*, or *Berlin Licensed Newspaper*. Changing residence every few years, he engaged in numerous activities as a columnist, literary critic, dramatist, and editor. On the face of it, his life and activities during this period seem to have had nothing whatever to do with the Christian religion. But the truth is that he did not lose his initial interest in religion at all. We have already seen that in his preface to the fragment *Religion (Die Religion,* 1749/50), Lessing clearly stated that "religion has for many years been the theme that invokes my more serious poetic inspirations."[2] Furthermore, as we will shortly observe, other fragments ascribed to the same early years, fragments such as *Some Thoughts about the Moravians (Gedanken über die Herrnhuter,* 1750), *The Christianity of Reason (Das Christentum der Vernunft,* 1751/52), and a number of literary criticisms in the *Berlinische Privilegierte Zeitung* or *Das Neueste aus dem Reiche des Witzes,* testify to the deep and continuing involvement with religion on the part of the young Lessing.

As 1751 drew to a close, Lessing broke off his freelance activity in Berlin in order to study for a Magister degree at the University of Wittenberg, where his younger brother, Johannes Theophilus, was then studying. This decision may reflect, in part, his acceptance of the strong wishes of his parents for him to complete university study. At any rate, Lessing took advantage of this opportunity to carry out intensive historical studies on the religious thought of the Reformation period by making use of old documents and sources in the university library.

These studies, contained in his *Vindications* (*Rettungen*, 1754), are composed of four investigations: the *Vindication of Hieronymus Cardanus*; the *Vindication of Inepti Religiosi and of its Anonymous Author*; the *Vindication of Cochläus*; and the *Vindication of Horace*. All four of these vindications are intended to exonerate and reappraise, from a more impartial, scientific standpoint, thinkers whose ideas had been unjustly neglected or misrepresented because of bias or ill will. It is important that Lessing, contrary to accepted opinion, chose to study, and if possible to exonerate, these heretical or apostate thinkers. This fact will help us to clarify his motive for publishing, during his Wolfenbüttel period, the *Fragments from an Unnamed Author*. But this matter we leave in abeyance for the time being.

More than once we have noted that entertaining "serious doubt" about Christianity formed the starting point of Lessing's lifelong religious quest. The fragment *Religion*, written in iambic hexameter, is a testimony to this point of view. In its preface the young poet briefly alludes to the background and main theme of the poem. He says that it deals with his religious skepticism, which is also the skepticism of his age, in the form of "a soliloquy . . . conducted in silence on a lonely day of annoyance." "Self-knowledge has always been the shortest way to religion, to which I add that it is also the surest."[3] He asks what we discover when we look back to the moment of birth, and replies that we see it is as something we share with the beasts, as a birth even more miserable than theirs. We first realize we are human, he goes on, when, after long years of spiritlessness and emotionlessness, we find vices in ourselves and learn that our vices are more powerful than our virtues. "Who is excluded from this miserable lot? Even the wisest man is not excluded. It is only that in him vices reign under beautiful masks and are less harmful due to the nature of their objects. But in him vices are just as strong as they are in the most depraved souls among the rabble." In the face of this reign of vices, the poet deeply laments. "What a sight! To find nothing but vices in the whole range of the human heart! And are they from God? Tormenting doubt!" But a religious intuition occurs to him. "Yet perhaps our spirit is more divine on this account. Perhaps we were created for the truth, for we are not [created] for virtue." Nevertheless, another doubt soon occupies his heart. "For the truth? How multiform is it? Each one believes that he possesses the truth, but each has it in a different way. No, only fallacy is our portion, and delusion our science." Thus assaulted by a storm of doubts, the poet, in search of a solution, asks himself, "What is man? Where does he come from? [He is] too bad for a God, too good for chance."[4]

Whether or not this poem is "a document of priceless value for insight into the development of Lessing's worldview,"[5] it is certain that "Lessing is here far removed from Enlightenment theology of any sort."[6] He is highly critical of both neology and Leibniz-Wolffian optimism, and the tone of his speech is very much like that of Lutheran orthodoxy. For example, he denounces the rationalistic position of the Enlightenment with sententious words like these: "Damned school-wisdom! You whims of wise fools!" (l. 35); "I too was misled by school-wisdom, puffed up with my own arrogance, / And took even a philosophical blade of grass for the truth." (ll. 61–62) He does, however, make a frank confession of human sinfulness and of the impotence of the will:

> Pride, lust for revenge, obstinacy have often betrayed in children's deeds / The sharp glance of the teacher in a quite masculine way. / Ah! Why does your poison rage in marrow and blood / With self-spoiling yet welcome fury, / Before the malleable spirit learns to know virtue? / From it nature, not the spirit itself, removed the spirit. / No! It did not remove itself, for it was asleep in the soul, / Still a wavering concept of good and evil, / And when the spirit awoke, and when I wanted to choose, / Ah! I was already determined to do wrong in my choice. (ll. 129–38). . . . In vain do you raise up in me free strength of will! / I will, I will!—And yet I am not virtuous. (ll. 167–68). . . . Oh heart, black as the Moor, and spotted as the panther! (l. 342)

On the face of it, the poet's standpoint, making human misery "the guide to religion" (*der Wegweiser zur Religion*),[7] seems Lutheran. It is doubtful, however, whether Lessing at this point in time represents the standpoint of Lutheran orthodoxy. For what concerns the poet with regard to religion is not so much its saving message as its epistemological content.[8] Hans Leisegang ought to have been more circumspect, therefore, than to pass the following judgment:

> In any event one thing is certain. Lessing has already abandoned the standpoint of [Lutheran] orthodoxy. For his religion, or the religion he seeks, lacks the key concept around which all things organize themselves in Lutheran orthodoxy, the concept of faith that holds the whole orthodox system together from within.[9]

In contrast, Johannes Schneider asserts that "the fragment must be judged as it stands before us. To supplement it and read anything into it is impermissible."[10] So far as this fragment is concerned, we are of the same opinion as Schneider. We too think that "we must be content with the statement that in the first canto there is nothing that contradicts the teaching of [Lutheran] orthodoxy."[11] We do not know why Lessing abandoned the poem midway, when he had originally intended to write large-scale, hexametric poems. But we must reckon with the fact that the poem remains fragmentary.[12]

The Young Lessing and His Theological Critique

Next to be considered is Lessing's *Some Thoughts about the Moravians* (1750). In this fragment, the young Lessing lays the Christianity of his day on the dissecting table, considering it analytically with extraordinary theological insight. Presenting a broad outline of the history of both philosophy and Christianity, he makes a number of sharp criticisms not only about the dogmatism of Lutheran orthodoxy but also about the speculative theology of the Enlightenment. The fundamental proposition of this fragment, a proposition of exceptional importance, is this:

> Man was created for action and not for speculation. Yet precisely because he was not created for speculation, he inclines more toward the latter than the former. His maliciousness always leads him to do what he should not, and his presumptuousness to do what he cannot. He should have limits set for himself.[13]

To verify this proposition, he surveys the general development of Western philosophy and the history of Christianity.

The great hero of ancient philosophy, according to Lessing, was Socrates, "a preacher of truth" (*ein Prediger der Wahrheit*). Admonishing the presumption of the sophists, Socrates taught people to abjure heavenly things and "reverse their gaze" so as to look within themselves. That is, he persuaded us to fathom "the uninvestigated depths" and "the most secret corners." But those who followed him perverted his teachings. Few followed the way of practical knowledge that Socrates had shown. "Plato began to dream, and Aristotle to syllogize."[14] Later philosophy, both in antiquity and in medieval times, was under the spell of one or the other of these two philosophers. In time, Descartes appeared and opened the door to the sanctuary. The truth seemed to take new form at his hands. But modern philosophy, subjected to mathematics by two outstanding minds of the following generation, namely, Newton and Leibniz, became less practical. Thus present-day philosophers "fill the head while the heart remains empty. They lead the mind to the highest heaven, while the soul, through its passions, is set lower than the beast."[15]

The history of Christianity traces a similar path. The religion of Adam was "simple, easy, and vital" (*einfach, leicht und lebendig*). But this state did not last long. Adam's descendants treated this simple religion as they pleased, so that "the essentials were submerged beneath a deluge of arbitrary propositions."[16] Thus "the correct concept of God" was replaced by the false concept of a "Being who cannot live without morning and evening offerings."[17] In order to rescue the world from this ignorance and help truth prevail over superstition, Christ came as "a teacher enlightened by God" (*ein von Gott erleuchteter Lehrer*).[18] Therefore Christ's true purpose, in a nutshell, was precisely "to reestablish religion in all its purity."[19]

> As long as the Church was at war, it was concerned to give its religion, through an irreproachable and marvelous life, that rigor which few enemies were capable of withstanding. As soon as it was at peace, however, it lost its rigor and began to adorn its religion, to bring its doctrines into a certain order, and to reinforce divine truth with human proofs.[20]

As a result, "practical Christianity" (*das ausübende Christentum*) was superseded by "contemplative Christianity" (*das beschauende Christentum*).[21]

The Reformation intended to restore Christianity to its original purity. But squabbles over trivial matters between two leaders (namely, Luther and Zwingli) thwarted the original intention. As Lessing puts it:

> What an adverse fate it was that let two men differ over words, a mere trifle, when they could so much more skillfully have set about reinstating religion in its former splendor, had they but joined forces. Blessed men . . . who steadied the trembling crowns on the heads of kings. . . . But how was it that virtue and holiness gained so little from your improvements? Of what good is right belief in a wrong light?[22]

Finally, having thus described the Reformation as a movement that brought about intellectual advancement but failed to bring about a corresponding moral improvement, Lessing turns to the Christianity of his own day and finds that it has reached its lowest ebb.

> And now for the present. Should I deem it fortunate or unfortunate that such an excellent combination of theology and philosophy has been achieved, one in which it is only with pain and distress that the one is separable from the other, in which one weakens the other; the former attempting to compel belief through proofs, and the latter supporting proofs with belief? I say now that because of this perverse manner of teaching Christianity, a true Christian has become far more rare than in the dark ages. In knowledge we are angels, and in living [we are] devils.[23]

The preceding paragraphs outline the argument Lessing develops in *Some Thoughts about the Moravians*. To restate a few important points, in this fragment the young Lessing conceives of the "simple, easy, and vital" religion of Adam as the ideal religion. He regards the history of biblical religion as a process of degradation from natural religion to positive religion. Furthermore, he treats Christ as "a teacher enlightened by God." Thus there can be no question about the deistic tendency of his thought.

Nevertheless, we can also discern here some features of Lessing's thought that differ from deism. His words in the *Berlin Licensed Newspaper* of 30 March 1751 bring out some of these features:

> It is fortunate that there is still a theologian now and then who remembers what is practical about Christianity in an age when most theologians get lost in sterile disputes. Sometimes they condemn a simple Moravian; sometimes they give a much simpler mocker of religion new material for mockery through their so-called refutations; sometimes they quarrel over impossible reconciliations before they have laid the foundations for such reconciliation through cleansing the heart of bitterness, squabbling, slander, and oppression, and through spreading that love which alone constitutes the essential mark of the Christian. To patch up a single religion before considering [how to] bring people to harmonious exercise of their obligations is an empty fancy. Does one make two bad dogs good if one confines them in a shed? It is not concord in matters of opinion but concord in virtuous conduct that makes the world peaceful and happy.[24]

A clear-cut distinction between faith and knowledge, respect for devout faith, a preference for practical moral conduct over metaphysical speculation, and understanding of Christianity as a religion of love—all these characteristics are typical of Lessing's religious thought.

The Ideal of Universal Humanity as Expressed in the Comedy *The Jews*

The one-act comedy *The Jews* (*Die Juden*, 1749), written when he was twenty years of age as the fifth of Lessing's dramatic pieces,[25] is an important document from which to judge the religious thought of the young Lessing. The outline of the play is very simple.

A baron and his daughter are attacked on the highway by rascally, bearded "Jews." The victims come within an inch of being killed, but in the nick of time an anonymous traveler, accompanied by his servant, rescues them. The people nearby, including the baron, firmly believe that the criminals are Jews. But the traveler who rescues the baron and his daughter discloses the truth of the matter. It turns out that the real criminals, the warden Stich and the steward Krumm, are disguised Christian subjects of the baron, whereas the gracious traveler proves to be a Jew. The baron, heartily ashamed of his prejudice against Jews, sincerely apologizes to the traveler.

Lessing explains how this comedy came into being:

> It was the outcome of a very serious consideration of the disgraceful oppression under which one people had to groan. I mean the [Jewish] nation, which a Christian can hardly regard without some kind of respect. From this nation, I thought, many heroes and prophets have arisen. . . . Yet does one doubt today whether an honest man is to be found among this people? My enthusiasm for theater was so great that everything which came into my head at that time metamorphosed into comedy. I soon got the notion, therefore, of trying to see what effect it would have on the stage if one demonstrated virtue in this people where it was not expected at all. I am eager to hear the verdict.[26]

In view of this remark, it might be possible to regard this comedy as "a splendid vindication of a despised people" (*eine vortreffliche Ehrenrettung eines verachteten Volkes*).[27] But the point Lessing really wanted to make seems to be not so much a vindication of the Jewish people as such but an impeachment of the prejudice, hypocrisy, and intolerance against Jews prevalent in Europe on the part of allegedly Christian society. The deep-seatedness of the prejudice against Jews in his age is well expressed in words uttered by the characters. Both the steward Martin Krumm, who wants to have his own crime imputed to Jews, and the baron, who was rescued by the anonymous Jew, speak with one voice in their prejudice against Jews.

> *Traveler:* Your master absolutely insists that they were Jews. It's true they had beards, but their speech was the normal speech of a peasant from these parts. If they were disguised, as I most certainly believe, then the twilight really did come in handy for them. For I simply can't understand how Jews would be able to make the streets unsafe when so few of them are tolerated in this country.
>
> *Martin Krumm:* Yes, yes, I'm positive that they were Jews too. Perhaps you aren't really well enough acquainted with that godless trash yet. As many as

there are of them, without exception, are swindlers, thieves, and highwaymen. And that's why it's a people which the Good Lord has cursed. It's a good thing I'm not the king. I wouldn't leave one of them, not a single one of them, alive. Oh! may God protect all upstanding Christians from these people. If the Good Lord didn't hate them himself, then why, in that terrible catastrophe a while back in Breslau, why did twice as many of them die as Christians? . . . [28]

Baron: You know, it really was Jews who attacked me. Just now my steward told me that he came upon three of them on the highway a few days ago. The way he described them to me, they looked more like criminals than honest people. And why should I even have any doubts about it? A people that is so bent on profit asks little whether it makes it justly or unjustly, by cunning or by force. They seem to be made for trade, or, to call a spade a spade, for swindling. Polite, free, enterprising, discreet, these are characteristics that would make them laudable, if they didn't use them all too often for our misfortune.—*(He stops a moment.)*—Jews have already caused me no end of harm and aggravation. . . . Oh! they are the most evil, the most despicable people— What do you say? You seem quite depressed.

Traveler: What should I say? I must say, that I have heard this complaint very often—

Baron: And isn't it true that their facial features have something about them that sets us against them right away? It's almost as if you can see the spitefulness, unscrupulousness, selfishness, deceit, and perjury clearly in their eyes— But why are you turning away from me?

Traveler: As I hear, sir, you are such a great expert in physiognomy, and I'm worried lest mine—

Baron: Oh! You insult me! How could you even suspect such a thing? Without being an expert in physiognomy I must tell you that I have never seen such an upright, magnanimous, and pleasant expression as yours.

Traveler: To tell you the truth: I am not partial to general judgments about whole peoples— You won't take this liberty of mine the wrong way.—I would like to believe that among all nations there were good and evil souls. . . . And among the Jews [as well]—[29]

The contrast between a prejudice against the Jews, deep-seated in Christian society, and a universal humanism transcending all sectarianism and partisanship, is sharply delineated here. Does the following conversation between the baron and the traveler suggest Lessing's idea of humanity, which found its ultimate expression in *Nathan the Wise*, the masterpiece of his later years?

Baron: All I see of you delights me. Come, let's see that the culprits are put into safe custody. Oh, how worthy of respect would all Jews be if they were all like you!

Traveler: And how delightful the Christians, if they all had your character![30]

Be that as it may, an explanation is hardly needed for the fact that *The Jews*, written by the twenty-year-old freelance journalist, has resonances with the cardinal idea of *Nathan the Wise*. This one-act play is, to be sure, an immature piece with many theatrical difficulties. Yet it is, as Hans Mayer asserts, "anything but an insignificant piece of juvenilia to be relegated to graduate seminars and read there only because of the author's general importance."[31] It may be no exaggeration to say that this one-act play demonstrates Lessing's real ability as an Enlightenment thinker more straightforwardly and acutely than *Nathan the Wise*. For in this play the young author sets forth his opinion frankly. According to Lessing, the espousal of freedom, equality, and tolerance in general terms is insufficient for realizing what the Enlightenment aims at. The touchstone for testing the real value of the Enlightenment is, rather, a matter of seeing whether and how, with an eye to those living in the real ghetto, one can overcome *in practice* the general prejudice against Jews.[32]

In response to the practical problem posed by the young Lessing, Johann David Michaelis, a professor of Oriental languages and theology at the University of Göttingen, published in the *Göttingen'sche Anzeigen von gelehrten Sachen* a comment which, though generally favorable, was in part highly critical:

> The unknown traveler is . . . so thoroughly good, so nobly minded, so careful to do his neighbor no wrong, . . . educated, so that while it is not impossible, it is exceedingly unlikely that such a noble temperament could have come to be found among a people whose fundamental beliefs, way of life, and education color their dealings with Christians all too noticeably with animosity, or at least with a decidedly cold reckoning against Christians. This impossibility is a hindrance to our pleasure, the more so that we wish this noble and lovely image had truth and reality to it. But even run-of-the-mill virtue and honesty are so rarely to be found among this people that the few examples that are in truth to be found cannot diminish as much as one would like the hatred felt against them.[33]

Michaelis's criticism was pertinent to some extent. The traveler in Lessing's one-act play was, to be sure, too good, too noble a man. It no doubt struck at least some people as exceedingly unlikely that such an ideal person could have turned up in real history.

But about the time he read Michaelis's review, Lessing happened, by good fortune, to make friends with a young Jewish man of noble mind, a man very much like the hero in the play. This was Moses Mendelssohn from the ghetto in Dessau.[34] The personal encounter between the young ex-parsonage freelance journalist, who throughout his life felt himself "a beloved bastard of a noble gracious lord,"[35] and the future great Jewish philosopher, in praise of whom the phrase "*Von Moses bis Moses war keiner dem Moses gleich*" was later coined,[36] was certainly good fortune not only for both young men but also for the German Enlightenment. Their friendship was to yield an exceptionally beautiful and moving page in German intellectual history.

Lessing's Speculative Reflections in *The Christianity of Reason*

Despite his assertion that "man was created for action and not for speculation," Lessing did not refrain from metaphysical speculation altogether. The early fragment *The Christianity of Reason* (1751/52) gives ample testimony of his metaphysical speculation. It also provides important suggestions for a proper understanding of his last significant work, *The Education of the Human Race*.[37]

This fragment, twenty-seven paragraphs in all, can be regarded as an attempt to demonstrate the "reasonableness of Christianity" (*Vernunftgemäßheit des Christentums*) and thus to bridge, from the perspective of reason, the gap between faith and knowledge. Its basic standpoint accords with Leibniz-Wolffian philosophy; it opposes a Pierre Bayle-like critique of Christianity.

In the first twelve paragraphs, Lessing attempts a rational demonstration of the Trinity, the nucleus of all Christian doctrines. According to Lessing, God as the most perfect Being has from eternity been able to concern himself only with the consideration of the most perfect thing (§1). Consequently, from eternity God has been able to contemplate only himself (§2). "To conceive, to will, and to create are one with God." Therefore, "anything that God conceives, he also creates" (§3). "God can think in only two ways: either he thinks of all his perfections at once, and of himself as including them all, or he thinks of his perfections individually, one by one, each one in its own grade" (§4). By contemplating himself from eternity in all his perfection God created "a being lacking no perfection that he himself possessed" (§5). This being is nothing other than what scripture calls "the Son of God" or "the Son-God" (§6). This being is identical with God himself (§7) and can therefore be called "an image of God, indeed an identical image" (§8). Between God and this being there must exist the greatest harmony (§9). Scripture calls this harmony between God and the Son-God "*the Spirit which proceeds from the Father and the Son*" (§10). "In this harmony is everything that is in the Father and also, therefore, everything that is in the Son; this harmony is therefore God" (§11). As a result, God the Father, the Son-God, and the harmony between them form a unity, "*all three are one*" (§12).

The next nine paragraphs belong to the sphere of "physics" or "cosmology." In Lessing's view, "God contemplated his perfections individually, that is, he created beings each of which has something of his perfections" (§13). The entirety of all these beings is called "the world" (§14). God contemplated the most perfect world in the most perfect way, and thus created the real world (§15). "The most perfect way of thinking of his perfections individually is to think of them separately in infinite grades of greater and less, which follow one on another in such a way that there is never a jump or gap between them" (§16). Accordingly, the beings in this world must form a great series of being that corresponds to grades of perfection (§17). "Such a series must be an infinite series, and in this sense the infinity of the world is incontestable" (§18). "God creates only simple things, the complex being a secondary consequence of his creation" (§19). "Since each of these simple beings has something which the others have, and none can have anything which the others have not, there must be harmony among these simple things" (§20). After long centuries, the day will sometime come when all phenomena in nature can be explained by the natural sciences (§21).

The last six paragraphs belong to the sphere of "ethics." Lessing has it that the simple beings in the world are, "as it were, limited gods" whose perfections must be similar to the perfections of God (§22). The "consciousness of his perfection and the power to act in accordance with his perfections" belong to God's perfection (§23). Accordingly, "the various grades of his perfections" must be connected with "various grades of the consciousness of these perfections" and "the power to act in accordance with them" (§24). "Beings which have perfections, which are conscious of their perfections, and which have the power to act in accordance with them, are called moral beings" (§25). The law that moral beings can follow is derived from their own nature. It can be none other than the imperative: *"Act in accordance with your individual perfections"* (*handle deinen individualistischen Vollkommenheiten gemäß*) (§26).[38] "Since, in the series of beings, there cannot possibly be a gap, there must also exist beings which are not sufficiently and clearly conscious of their perfections . . . " (§27).

The fragment breaks off here. But it is clear that the metaphysical speculation which Lessing evolved in this fragment is far removed from the standpoint of Lutheran orthodoxy. The historian of philosophy Heinz Heimsoeth sees in this fragment "the path leading from Nicholas of Cusa through Leibniz directly to Lessing."[39] Building on Heimsoeth's suggestion, Wolfgang Gericke assumes a history-of-thought stream running from Nicholas of Cusa through the Italian Renaissance philosophers, German natural philosophy, and Leibniz to Lessing. He calls this stream "the spiritualistic tradition" (*die spiritualistische Tradition*).[40] This point will call for closer examination in chapter 7. But in view of both this history-of-thought tradition and Lessing's reliance on Leibniz-Wolffian philosophy, we must take account of Hans Leisegang's brilliant identification of Lessing's worldview as "a monistic personalism" (*ein monistischer Personalismus*).[41] For even if it is evident that Lessing's metaphysical speculation is in accord with Leibniz's and Wolff's philosophy, the proposition that "to conceive, to will, and to create are one with God" clearly distinguishes his worldview not only from Leibniz-Wolffian dualism but also from Spinozistic monism. This proposition suggests, rather, a direction that brings Leibniz-Wolffian dualism and Spinozistic monism into a synthesis.[42]

Yet to call Lessing's worldview "a monistic personalism" is one thing, and to lay the philosophical foundation for it is quite another. It is not too much to say that the really difficult question about the concept of God culminates in this "monistic personalism." So far as we can tell, Ernst Troeltsch's argument in his *Glaubenslehre* best illustrates the difficulty.

Troeltsch, wishing to defend the prophetic-Christian personalistic idea of God, sought to conceive of God in terms of the duality between "essence" (*Wesen*) and "will" (*Wille*), a duality that involves an inner tension within the concept of God. But when he attempted a philosophical explanation of the concept of God, he frequently came close to tripping himself up over monistic pantheism. Though he sought to reconcile "what is true about theism and pantheism" (*die Wahrheitsmomente des Theismus und des Pantheismus*) by means of the idea of "God's self-replication and self-enrichment" (*die Selbst-*

vervielfältigung und Selbstbereicherung Gottes),[43] when it came to philosophical elaboration for this idea, his argument fell short.[44] Nonetheless, the idea underlying his argument is, as he himself acknowledges, "the idea of panentheism" (*der Gedanke des Panentheismus*).[45]

It is precisely at this point that Troeltsch's concept of God seems to come into contact with Lessing's metaphysical speculation. For the God Lessing speaks of in his *The Christianity of Reason* is not the impersonal One that Spinoza taught, but the thinking, willing, and creating God in whom these three actions are one. But the one-and-the-sameness of thinking, willing, and creating in God signifies that what God conceives of exists in reality. This implies that real things exist within God. Thus there is no question but that the worldview expressed in this fragment suggests that Lessing has a tendency toward "panentheism," the doctrine that God includes the world as a part, though not the whole, of his being, and thus that everything which exists exists within God.[46]

It is evident, moreover, that even though Lessing seems to have given up this speculation for a time due to Mendelssohn's objections,[47] he did not reject what he had proposed in *The Christianity of Reason*, but reintroduced it in modified form in §73 of *The Education of the Human Race*.[48] This shows that Lessing's concept of God has a significant resemblance to the God-concept that Troeltsch presented in his *Glaubenslehre*. For the present it will suffice to say that Lessing's alleged "Spinozism," which became a burning question among his friends and fellow scholars after his death, is attributable not only to his adherence to "monistic personalism" but also to the difficulty of seeing it through philosophically.[49]

The next thing to note, especially for a proper understanding of Lessing's later thought, is that he conceives of beings in the world as "limited gods" (*eingeschränkte Götter*). Such beings share in God's perfections, and Lessing includes among God's perfections "the consciousness of his perfection and the power to act in accordance with his perfections." If, following Leisegang, we apply this insight to anthropology, we arrive at the following categories for human beings: (1) human beings who have perfections but are not conscious of them, (2) human beings who have perfections, and are conscious of them, yet have no power to act in accordance with them, and (3) human beings who have perfections, are conscious of them, and have the power to act in accordance with them. If, in place of the word "perfections," we substitute the term "reason," we then arrive at the following developmental stages of reason: (1) latent reason (*latente Vernunft*), (2) conscious reason (*bewußte Vernunft*), and (3) willing and acting reason (*wollende und handelnde Vernunft*). To regard the development of reason in these ways, moreover, offers an important key for explicating the profound thought that Lessing presents to his readers in his last work, *The Education of the Human Race*.[50] But this sort of metaphysical conjecture takes us beyond the limits of our present task.

The last issue taken up in *The Christianity of Reason* is the weighty question of whether sins and evils in the actual world can be explained in the framework of Lessing's moral and rational worldview, and if so, how. If what

God contemplated in his perfections individually, and thus created, were the beings of this world, how, then, do the evils and sins that exist in the world relate to God's perfections? We can only conjecture that one of the reasons the young Lessing had to break off the metaphysical speculation attempted in this fragment is that he found himself incapable of dealing with this theodicean problem within his moralistic and rationalistic frame of reference. Admittedly, however, this is speculation on our part, and for the time being, at least, we will do well to stop speculating at the point where Lessing stopped.

Thus far we have analyzed Lessing's religious thought with special attention to his early writings, particularly *Religion, Some Thoughts about the Moravians, The Jews,* and *The Christianity of Reason.* These poetic, theological, dramatic, and philosophical writings show that the young Lessing has not yet worked out his own theological position but vacillates among four ways of thinking: Lutheran orthodoxy, pietism, deism, and Leibniz-Wolffian metaphysics. Nevertheless, these writings, however fragmentary, contain many of the germs of the religious-philosophical thought of his mature years. True, many twists and turns and much more time will be needed before he reaches the "high eminence" from which he can see beyond the limits of the prevailing forms of knowledge. Yet this analysis of Lessing's early writings endorses the validity of the saying that "genius displays itself even in childhood." For even in his early years, Lessing displayed brilliantly something of his later genius both as a theological critic and as a philosopher of religion.

3

The Controversy between
Lessing and Goeze

In May 1770, Lessing put an end to his long career as a freelance journalist to take up public service as a librarian at the famous Herzog-August-Bibliothek in Wolfenbüttel.[1] Beginning 13 February 1772, the Duke of Brunswick permitted him immunity from censorship on condition that he never take advantage of this immunity to attack Christianity. Two years later Lessing began to publish valuable manuscripts and other library acquisitions in a series entitled *Contributions to Literature and History from the Treasures of the Ducal Library at Wolfenbüttel* (*Zur Geschichte und Literatur: Aus den Schätzen der Herzoglichen Bibliothek zu Wolfenbüttel*). Into this series, he quietly inserted certain portions of the unpublished manuscripts of the late Hermann Samuel Reimarus,[2] publishing them as *Fragments from an Unnamed Author*. These documents, as we have seen, Lessing had borrowed from the author's son and daughter, Johann Albert and Elise Reimarus. In publishing them, he must have made a shrewd calculation. For he first published a small and inoffensive portion as if it were nothing important. He seems to have thought that publication of this innocuous portion would facilitate the later publication of more radical portions. In any event, he first brought out this harmless portion under the title *On Tolerating the Deists*. He even went so far as to camouflage the author's identity by offering the false surmise that the author might be Johann Lorenz Schmidt, the deist who had translated the banned Wertheimer Bible of 1735.

As he had expected, this initial publication elicited no significant reaction. Three years later, Lessing published five more manuscripts, attaching to them his own "Editor's Counterpropositions." The titles of the five manuscripts, translated into English, are: "On the Decrying of Reason in the Pulpit," "The Impossibility of a Revelation that All Men Can Believe on Rational Grounds," "The Passage of the Israelites through the Red Sea," "That the Books of the Old Testament Were Not Written to Reveal a Religion," and "On the Resurrection Narrative." In these extremely radical and by no means innocuous manuscripts, Reimarus presented his sharpest attacks on the Christian doctrine of revelation. Their publication evoked sharp reactions of refutation and reproach, especially from representatives of Lutheran orthodoxy. This marks the beginning of the "fragments controversy" (*Fragmentenstreit*).

41

Beginning and Development of the Controversy

In the first phase of the fragments controversy, the target of people's reproach and criticism was, as observed earlier, the unnamed author. In addition, all the critics were men of minor importance. Thus Lessing was able to continue in his chosen role as a mere editor of the fragments. He was able to behave as if he were no more than a disinterested spectator.

The intervention of Johann Melchior Goeze,[3] however, brought about a complete change in the character and pace of the controversy. Goeze, already notorious as "the Inquisitor" and representing himself as the defender of Lutheran orthodoxy, took aim at Lessing and attacked him fiercely. To this end, he published two acrimonious booklets: first, *Something Preliminary against Court Councillor Lessing's Direct and Indirect Malevolent Attacks on Our Most Holy Religion, and on Its Single Foundation, the Bible (Etwas Vorläufiges gegen des Herrn Hofrat Lessings mittelbare und unmittelbare feindselige Angriffe auf unsre allerheiligste Religion, und auf den einigen Lehrgrund derselben, die heilige Schrift)*; and second, *Lessing's Weaknesses (Lessings Schwächen)*.

Lessing took up the gauntlet and counterattacked in print, publishing his own polemical writings: *A Parable (Eine Parabel)*; *Axioms, If There Be Any in Such Things (Axiomata, wenn es deren in dergleichen Dingen gibt)*; the eleven-installment *Anti-Goeze*; and *The Necessary Answer to a very Unnecessary Question by Hauptpastor Goeze in Hamburg (Der nötigen Antwort auf eine sehr unnötige Frage des Herrn Hauptpastor Goeze in Hamburg)*. Going further, Lessing even put into print the most offensive portion of Reimarus's fragments under the title *On the Purpose of Jesus and His Disciples (Von dem Zwecke Jesu und seiner Jünger)*.

As a result of a misunderstanding (to be described below) and the mutual hatred to which it gave rise, the initially theological dispute between Lessing and Goeze eventually deteriorated into personal abuse and vituperation. More important, when the tide of controversy turned in Lessing's favor, Goeze appealed to the Duke of Brunswick. As a result, Lessing was deprived of his earlier privilege of freedom from censorship. In July 1778 every product of his pen was strictly censored, and from August 1778 he was forbidden to publish anything without advance permission from the government of Brunswick.

No authority in the world, however, could prevent this "lover of truth" from writing. When it became impossible to carry on his controversy with Goeze within the territory of the Duke of Brunswick, Lessing determined to return to "his old pulpit, the theater,"[4] and to continue his theological battle with Goeze from that vantage point. This was when he decided to write the play *Nathan the Wise*.

The foregoing paragraphs constitute a rough description of the course of the Lessing-Goeze controversy, "the second stage of the fragments controversy."[5] Before undertaking a theological analysis of this controversy, however, we must consider a few important things. First is the matter of the personal relationship between Lessing and Goeze. In point of fact, Lessing and

Goeze had already become acquainted with each other long before their confrontation over the Reimarus fragments. Their personal relationship began in Hamburg some eight years before the beginning of this controversy. In his documents, Lessing left behind the following remark: "On 24 October 1769 I met personally with the Hauptpastor, Goeze, for the first time. At his repeated invitation, I visited him and found him to be a man who was very natural in his demeanor and by no means unsuitable with regard to his knowledge. We first spoke of the public library in this city."[6] At their first meeting they seem to have exchanged views on the city library in Hamburg, which was in a deplorable state, on Goeze's magnificent collection of Bibles, and so on.[7] The talks with Goeze seem to have held a certain charm for Lessing because he visited Goeze several times. His brother Karl wrote about Lessing's visits with Goeze:

> Goeze, then the Hauptpastor, or, to use Bahrdtian terms for religious reason, the head stallion of the orthodox herd in Hamburg, received a few social calls from Lessing. During these visits, they admittedly did not establish which books of the Old and New Testaments were canonical, or the value of the old and new theaters in Hamburg, but spoke of other recondite matters. The Lutheran zealot, who felt himself powerless to impose ecclesiastical penance on Lessing, knew how to entertain a secular scholar just as Christ had known how to eat with tax collectors and sinners.
>
> Lessing, who took to every intelligent man regardless of what cap he wore, found pleasure in Goeze's erudition—and, enlightened slanderers might add, in his Rhine wine. He visited him often, without placing His Reverence under the embarrassment of a return visit. Lessing's friends and acquaintances soon got wind of this news, and began to tease him about it in tones at once abusive and earnest. They were utterly astonished, however, when he candidly confessed, making no secret of it, that he esteemed Goeze's erudition and even his theology. The sophisticated took this as expressing a spirit of contradiction, the super-sophisticated as mockery.[8]

The good relationship between the two seems to have continued for a while even after Lessing moved to Wolfenbüttel. On his way to other places, Goeze once stopped off in Wolfenbüttel to see Lessing. Unfortunately, however, they did not meet on that occasion because Lessing happened to be gone on business for Brunswick.

But something occurred that led to a rift in their relationship. The origin of the rift was that Goeze, in connection with his biblical research, asked Lessing to provide him with some information from the holdings in the ducal library. For some unknown reason, Lessing neither provided this information nor gave any reply whatever.[9] Growing resentful at Lessing's ignoring of his request, Goeze publicly blamed "a [certain] famous librarian in a big out-of-town library"[10] for neglecting his duty. When he became aware of Goeze's resentment, Lessing immediately thought that he ought to apologize for his neglect in a personal letter to Goeze. But he carelessly forgot to write the letter. Lessing did not think the matter very important, but Goeze thought it very important and was quite incensed.[11]

Another thing that had a bearing on their controversy was the matter of their respective circumstances. Goeze, a family man, had four children, but two died in infancy and a third while attending university. In 1774 he lost his beloved wife, with whom he had shared married life for twenty-eight years. With regard to his position, he adhered to the extremely strict doctrines of Lutheran orthodoxy so bigotedly that he caused discord among his fellow pastors. As a result, in 1770 he had to resign his post as Hauptpastor of the Hamburg pastors, a position he had held since 1760. Thus both as a family man and as a public man, Goeze lived in growing isolation and loneliness.[12]

In Lessing's case, on the other hand, the position of director of the Herzog-August-Bibliothek at Wolfenbüttel took the place of his erstwhile easygoing life as a freelance journalist. But he was still far from well-off. For this and other reasons, the period of his engagement to the beautiful widow Eva König lasted over five years. They married in October 1776.[13] Eva became pregnant the following year and gave birth to a boy on Christmas Day of 1777. But the newborn baby, Traugott, died within twenty-four hours. What was worse, his mother, because of the difficult labor, fell into a comatose state and died on 10 January 1778. So Lessing's happy married life ended suddenly in bitter grief and woe. It was precisely at this time, when Lessing was in the depths of despair, that Goeze opened his assault.[14] For this very reason, Goeze's inquisitorial accusations must have been extremely difficult for him to bear. But he somehow summoned up the energy to set his grief aside and counterattack the Inquisitor of Hamburg.

The controversy between Lessing and Goeze thus involves complicated non-theological factors. It is important to keep these personal factors in mind as we discuss the Lessing-Goeze controversy. We turn now to the substance of the controversy, with particular attention to its early phase when the two combatants were still comparatively dispassionate.

Goeze's Attack

The cause of the controversy, as noted above, was that Lessing, in the capacity of editor, published part of the deceased Reimarus's manuscripts under the title *Fragments from an Unnamed Author*. Goeze grew angry at the publication of such "blasphemous" documents and took an active part in the ongoing theological controversy that their publication had provoked. The target of Goeze's attack was what Lessing had appended to the fragments under the title "Editor's Counterpropositions" (*Gegensätze des Herausgebers*). Goeze focused his polemic on what Lessing had set forth as "the foundation for the Counterpropositions."[15] What Lessing asserted there bears repeating:

> In short, the letter is not the spirit, and the Bible is not religion. Consequently, objections to the letter and to the Bible are not by the same token objections to the spirit and to religion.
>
> For the Bible obviously contains more than is essential to religion, and it is a mere hypothesis to assert of this superfluity that it must be infallible throughout.

Moreover, religion was there before a Bible existed. Christianity was there before the evangelists and apostles wrote. A long period elapsed before the first of them wrote, and a considerable time before the entire canon was complete. Therefore, while much may depend on these writings, it is impossible to suppose that the entire truth of the religion depends on them. If there had been a period in which it had already spread abroad and in which it had gained many souls, and if, nevertheless, not a single letter of what has come down to us had yet been written down, then it must also be possible that everything which the evangelists and apostles wrote could have been lost—and yet that the religion which they taught would have continued. The religion is not true because the evangelists and apostles taught it. They taught it, rather, because it is true. The written traditions must be interpreted by their inner truth, and no written traditions can give a religion inner truth if it has none.[16]

Goeze took an utterly negative stance toward Lessing's assertions. He declared:

> In the entire passage I do not find a single proposition that, in the context in which it stands, I can regard as correct. The editor regards everything therein as genuine axioms, to be sure, but some of them still require very strong proof, while the remainder, and these constitute the majority, are demonstrably false.[17]

What Lessing sets forth with regard to letter and spirit, Bible and religion, is, Goeze contends, nothing but a tissue of "ambiguous, vague, shaky, and erroneous propositions."[18]

After passing this judgment on Lessing's assertions in general, Goeze undertakes to refute his propositions one by one. The main points of his refutation are the following:

1. Lessing's usage with regard to letter and spirit does not accord with the New Testament. Lessing understands the Bible under the category of letter, and religion under the category of spirit. Against Lessing's assertion that "the letter is not the spirit, and the Bible is not religion," we must therefore assert the converse: *"the letter is the spirit, and the Bible is religion."*[19]

2. Since the basic proposition that "the letter is not the spirit, and the Bible is not religion" is erroneous, the proposition that immediately follows, namely, that "objections to the letter and to the Bible are not by the same token objections to the spirit and to religion," cannot be true. Letter and spirit, the Bible and religion are one. Consequently, "objections to the letter are also objections to the spirit, and objections to the Bible are also objections to religion."[20]

3. With regard to the proposition that "the Bible obviously contains more than is essential to religion," this actually contains two propositions. The first is that "the Bible obviously contains what is essential to religion." The second is that "it contains more than is essential to religion." But this means that in the first of these two propositions, Lessing "admits what he has denied in the preceding proposition." Consequently, this proposition is contradictory.[21]

4. The proposition that "it is a mere hypothesis to assert of this superfluity that it must be infallible throughout" is false. The refutation is brief: "No, this is not a hypothesis, but incontrovertible truth."[22]

5. The proposition that "moreover, religion was there before a Bible existed" is also false because it contradicts the true proposition: "religion was not there before revelation existed." The distinction between revelation and the Bible "consists only in accidental, insignificant things." In any event, Lessing's proposition, which is nearly synonymous with "religion was there before revelation existed," is erroneous.[23]

6. The proposition that "Christianity was there before the evangelists and apostles wrote. A long period elapsed before the first of them wrote, and a considerable time before the entire canon was complete" might be conceded to some extent. Nevertheless, it must be asked anew, "*Was Christianity already there before Christ and the apostles preached?*"[24]

7. "Therefore, while much may depend on these writings, it is impossible to suppose that the entire truth of the religion depends on them." This proposition is to be refuted as follows. The truth of the Christian religion certainly depends on itself and is in accordance with God's characteristics and will. Nonetheless, "*our convictions of the truth of the Christian religion*" depend on the Bible alone. If the Bible had not been written and handed down to us, would there have remained any trace of what Christ did and preached?[25]

8. "If there had been a period in which it had already spread abroad and in which it had gained many souls, and if, nevertheless, not a single letter of what has come down to us had yet been written down, then it must also be possible that everything which the evangelists and apostles wrote could have been lost—and yet that the religion which they taught would have continued." This proposition is "a tangible sophism." The error becomes evident when, for the phrase "not a letter . . . had yet been written down," we substitute the phrase "not a word . . . had yet been preached." The Christian religion has its origin not in the writings of the evangelists and apostles, but in the sermons of Christ and the apostles. The correct proposition is, consequently, "the whole of the Christian religion rests on the teachings and deeds of Christ, as on its immediate ground. But where can we now learn about these teachings and deeds except from the writings of the evangelists and apostles? Therefore, if the latter were lost, the former must certainly be lost, too."[26]

9. The proposition that "the religion is not true because the evangelists and apostles taught it. They taught it, rather, because it is true" is also nonsense. The evangelists and apostles are men who taught and wrote, inspired by the Holy Spirit. One should say, then, that "the Christian religion is true because the evangelists and apostles taught it, or more properly, because God himself taught it."[27]

10. Therefore, the proposition that "the written traditions must be interpreted by their inner truth, and no written traditions can give a religion inner truth if it has none" must be refuted. Lessing's statements as to a

sharp distinction between the inner truth of the Christian religion and the scriptural tradition are merely empty words. "Where does he wish to obtain the knowledge of the inner truth of the Christian religion if not from the scriptural traditions?"[28]

Goeze concludes his first attack, *Something Preliminary*, with the words:

> I would be terrified of the hour of my death if I had to worry about the fact that on that day an account might be demanded of me as to the diffusion of these malicious essays, which are extremely dangerous to many souls and so detrimental to the honor of our great Redeemer. I wish that in future the editor would supply, out of the treasures of the library he serves, something better than poison and scandal.[29]

These threatening words are tantamount to an ultimatum, the final demand of a pastor to an unbeliever. With such menacing tones, Goeze may have succeeded in suppressing other people whom he regarded as enemies of Lutheran orthodoxy. But this sort of threat had the opposite effect on Lessing. Goeze's first polemic, therefore, only added fuel to the fire.

Lessing's Defense

In order to defend himself from Goeze's vehement attack, Lessing published, in due course, his *Axioms*. In this treatise he examined and refuted Goeze's arguments one by one and defended what he had set forth in his "Editor's Counterpropositions." He did not, however, resort to all-out confrontation from the start. Instead, he began with a strategy intended to evade attack. The first piece he issued in his fight against Goeze was *A Parable* in three parts: "a parable," "a request," and "a challenge." This small piece is full of metaphors and allegories, but it well reflects the characteristic features of Lessing's theological thought.

> There was once "a wise and active king" who ruled "a large, large kingdom." In its capital, he had "a palace of immeasurable scale and peculiar architecture." The scale was immeasurable because in the palace he gathered around himself all the assistant and tools that he needed for his government. The architecture was so peculiar that it conflicted with all known rules of building. Nevertheless, it aroused everyone's admiration for its simplicity and majesty, its durability and comfort. The whole palace stood, after long, long years, in the same purity and perfection it had had when the original builder completed it. From outside, it seemed a bit incomprehensible; from inside, however, there was light and good sense everywhere. Connoisseurs of architecture were especially annoyed by its external appearance, for it had only a few windows here and there, some larger, some smaller, some round, some square, while on the contrary it had an exceptional number of doors and gates of many shapes and sizes.
>
> People could not understand how there came to be enough light in so many rooms when the windows were so few. Only a few people perceived that the highest windows received their light from above. Many people were confused by the fact that the palace had a great number and variety of corridors, for they

thought that a big entrance on each side would have been more majestic and convenient. They failed to see that these corridors allowed anyone summoned to the palace to come swiftly and unerringly to the place where he or she was needed.

Disputes thus arose among the connoisseurs of architecture. The fewer opportunities they had to see the inside of the palace, the more vehemently they disputed. On the face of it, there were things that would seem to have solved the disputes very easily, but in reality they complicated the disputes and supplied the fuel for their continuation. Many connoisseurs of architecture possessed plans, which they claimed to be the plans of the original builder. These plans had been written in words and signs that were almost as good as lost today. Consequently, each connoisseur interpreted these words and signs as he liked. Each imagined an ideal new building based on his old plans. All were so preoccupied with the imagined ideal building that often they were not content with believing in the authenticity of their plans and interpretations in their own right but sought to persuade and even compel other to believe in them too.

Only a few people took another view, saying, "What do your plans matter to us? Whether it is this plan or that is all the same to us. It is enough that we learn at every moment that the most benevolent wisdom fills the whole palace and that from it nothing but beauty, order, and well-being spread over the whole land." These people were often badly treated. For when, in a lighthearted mood, they examined one of these plans in detail, they were rebuked by the possessor of the plan, as if they had been murderous arsonists intent on destroying the palace itself. They made little of the reproach, however, and thereby proved themselves qualified to join the people who worked within the palace. They had neither time nor desire to meddle in the disputes.

But one night, at midnight, when disputes about the original architect's plans were not so much resolved as dormant, the night watchmen began, all at once, to shout, "Fire! Fire in the palace!" What happened then? Everyone jumped out of bed and rushed to the place where he kept his most valued possession, namely, his own plan of the palace—as if the fire had occurred not in the palace but in his own house. "Let us save the plan at least!" each one thought. "The palace cannot be utterly destroyed by the fire there so long as the plan is preserved here!"

So everyone ran out in the street, each carrying his own plan in his hands. Instead of running swiftly to the palace to help extinguish the fire, each one pulled out his plan and tried to locate where the fire might be. One would cry, "Look, neighbor! Here's where it's burning! Here's where we can best get at the fire!" Then another would cry, "Not there, but here, neighbor, here!" Whereupon a third would interject, "What are you two talking about? It's burning here!" Then each tried to uphold his own claim. "What would it matter if it was burning there? The fire is certainly here!" "You can put it out there!" "I am not going to put it out there!" And while they were busy arguing, the palace, if there had been a real fire, would have burned to the ground. But the startled watchmen had mistaken the northern lights for a conflagration.[30]

From this outline of Lessing's parable, the basic ideas, expressed metaphorically, are clear. God is compared to "a wise and active king of a large, large kingdom" and religion to "a palace of immeasurable scale and peculiar architecture." The palace (religion) is incomprehensible to those trying to understand it from without; but the inside of the palace is full of "light from above"

(*Licht von oben*). The architecture of the palace reflects "the most benevolent wisdom" (*die gütigste Weisheit*), and good taste can be perceived everywhere. But the connoisseurs of architecture (orthodox theologians) are not content to experience the palace itself and the "beauty, order, and well-being" (grace and peace of the Spirit) that spread from the palace over the whole land. Instead, they take undue interest in the palace's "architecture" (theological doctrines) or "plans" (the Bible) and argue over the interpretation of "words and signs that are almost as good as lost today" (the letter). They quarrel over unimportant details all the more because they have little experience of "the inside of the palace" (the inner truth of religion).

Lessing's own position is succinctly implied in the words, "What do your plans matter to us? Whether it is this plan or that is all the same to us. It is enough that we learn at every moment that the most benevolent wisdom fills the whole palace and that from it nothing but beauty, order, and well-being spread over the whole land." This assertion is in complete agreement with what he asserted in his "Editor's Counterpropositions":

> But how do this man's hypotheses, explanations, and proofs affect the Christian? For him it is simply a fact, this Christianity which he feels to be true and in which he feels blessed. When the paralytic experiences the beneficial shocks of the electric spark, does it worry him whether Nollet or Franklin or neither is right?[31]

But why, then, instead of remaining content with "the beneficial shocks of the electric spark," did Lessing venture to publish Reimarus's sensational fragments, knowing full well that they might provoke bitter controversies like the "disputes over the plans"? Why did he toss into the Christian world live coals that a "night watchman" like Goeze, mistaking them for a conflagration, would use to create an uproar?[32]

The answer that Lessing gives in *A Request*, which immediately follows *A Parable*, is that he did so precisely because he was a librarian. Lessing compares the difference between Goeze as pastor and himself as librarian to that between a shepherd (*Schäfer*) and a botanist (*Kräuterkenner*).[33] As he puts it, the primary concern of the shepherd is for the safety of the sheep in his care, and he takes interest in herbs only insofar as they have to do with his sheep. The botanist, on the other hand, wanders the mountains and valleys to study herbs. And what pleasure he feels when he finds a new herb, one for which there is no recorded name in authoritative botanical books, "How indifferent he is as to whether this new herb is poisonous or not!"[34]

Lessing goes on to give the following account of the professional difference between the librarian and the pastor:

> We are much the same, dear Hauptpastor. . . . I am a supervisor of book treasures. . . . When I find among the treasures entrusted to me something that I believe is unknown, I publish it. I do so first of all in our catalogs, and little by little, as I learn that it fills this or that gap and helps to correct one thing or another, I also do so publicly. And I am utterly indifferent as to whether this person declares it important or that person unimportant, whether it benefits one

person or injures another. Useful and destructive are relative concepts, just as relative as large and small.

On the other hand, you, Reverend Sir, appreciate literary treasures only as regards the influence that they can exert on your flock, and prefer being too solicitous to being too negligent. What matters to you, whether something is known or unknown, is the possibility that it could offend even one of the least [of these] who are entrusted to your spiritual supervision.[35]

Having thus clarified their professional differences, Lessing goes on to make an earnest request, namely, that Goeze not interfere with what he does as a librarian, since he for his part has no wish to find fault with what Goeze does as a pastor. In response to Goeze's judgment day threat, Lessing declares that even if what he has published proves detrimental to Christianity, and even if he might be terrified *at the moment* of death, he will not be terrified *at the prospect* of death. On the contrary, he justifies his action in publishing what Goeze regards as "the worst that one can think"[36] with the words, "I have done what sensible Christians today wish that the ancient librarians in Alexandria, Caesarea, and Constantinople had done, had they been able, with the writings of Celsus, Fronto, and Porphyry."[37]

In any event, Lessing asserts that one does not have to overreact, as Goeze did, to the appearance of anti-Christian books. One can, in his opinion, trust with perfect serenity in the advance of the Christian religion. In his words,

> Christianity proceeds at its unchanging, gradual pace, and eclipses do not pull the planets from their orbits. But the sects of Christianity are its phases, which can endure only through the immobilization of all nature, when sun, planet, and observer all stand fast at one point. God protect us from this frightful immobility![38]

Goeze's judgment day threat thus poses no menace whatever to Lessing. He can even ask of Goeze the pastor that he "at least censure [him] less severely for having been honest enough to rescue from oblivion not only some very unchristian fragments but also a very Christian writing by Berengar."[39] He requests his onetime acquaintance to remain unruffled by the publication of *Fragments from an Unnamed Author*, repeating what he has already asserted in his "Editor's Counterpropositions." That is, even if one cannot answer all the objections and difficulties that the unnamed author raises from a rationalistic or deistic point of view, what does that matter to us? For despite such scholarly attacks, *religion* remains intact. It remains "steady and unstunted" in the hearts of "those Christians . . . who have inwardly felt its essential truths."[40]

Lessing initially intended to complete his reply to the first half of Goeze's *Something Preliminary* with the two tracts *A Parable* and *A Request*. But before he finished, Goeze published the second half of *Something Preliminary*. On reading it, Lessing quickly wrote a third tract, *A Challenge*, and published all three at once. He found it intolerable that Goeze would brand him an enemy of the Lutheran church. As the son of an upright Lutheran orthodox pastor, Lessing adamantly declares:

I simply will not be decried by you as a man who means less well by the Lutheran Church than you do. For I am conscious of being a far better friend to it than a man who wishes to persuade us that all tender feeling for his remunerative pastorate . . . is holy zeal for the cause of God.[41]

Asking which of the two has more "sparks of the Lutheran spirit,"[42] Lessing hauls Luther into court as a judge. He says:

Oh, that he could do it, he whom I should most like to have as my judge!—Thou, Luther! . . . Thou hast released us from the yoke of tradition. Who will release us from the more intolerable yoke of the letter?[43]

In the end, Lessing declares war against "the Inquisitor of Hamburg" in the following defiant and challenging words:

But there is only one thing I will not tolerate: your pride, that denies reason and learning to any person who uses reason and learning differently from the way you use them. Most of all, you infuriate me by continuing to treat my unnamed author, whom you know only from disparate fragments, in such an inept and immature way. For man weighed against man—not cause against cause—this unnamed author was *of such* weight that in all manner of learning, seven *Goezes* could not outweigh one of him. Believe me in this, Mr. Hauptpastor, take my word for it.

And now, very briefly, to my knightly challenge: *Write, Mr. Hauptpastor, and let your supporters write, as much as you will; I too shall write. If, in the least thing that concerns me or my unnamed author, I admit that you are right where you are not right, I shall never again be able to hold my pen.*[44]

The die was cast! A noble man like Lessing could not withdraw now. He had to fight out his battle to the best of his ability, no matter what it cost him.

Lessing's *Anti-Goeze*

According to Henry Chadwick, the eleven-part *Anti-Goeze* that Lessing churned out in record time is "mere theological Billingsgate."[45] It contains a few brilliant theological discussions, to be sure, but in most cases is nothing more than a vindication of his publication of the *Fragments from an Unnamed Author* as well as a castigation of his adversary by all possible means. This being the case, it will be unnecessary to discuss each essay in detail. We intend, rather, to focus on the most important points in Lessing's arguments.

In the first essay, Lessing boldly declares his determination to fight against Goeze. He says to his opponent: "You can *outshout* (*überschreien*) me every week; you know *where*. But you shall certainly not *outwrite* (*überschreiben*) me."[46] He continues:

God knows that I have no objection to the fact that you and all schoolmasters in Lower Saxony are campaigning against my unnamed author. On the contrary, I am pleased with this. For I brought him to light for the very purpose that a goodly number of people could examine and refute him. I also hope that he will in the near future come into the right hands, where he does not yet seem to be.

Thus I believe that I have really rendered greater service to the Christian religion
through making him known than you, with all your magazines and news-
papers.[47]

Accordingly, he maintains that Goeze's censure is misconceived. Goeze casts
Lessing in the role of an enemy of Christianity, but is really barking up the
wrong tree. Lessing asks:

How is it, since I have more confidence than you in the Christian religion, that
I should be an enemy of the Christian religion? Since I notify the public health
department of a poison that lurks in the dark, am I supposed to have brought the
pestilence into the land? Briefly, Reverend Sir, you are making a mistake if you
believe that the unnamed author would have remained completely outside the
world had I not helped him in.[48]

By the same token, the publishing of the unnamed author's fragments is
warranted, Lessing asserts, in light of "Luther's spirit" (*Luthers Geist*). For
when Luther sought to translate the Bible into German in defiance of the
ecclesiastical practice of the day, he did so on his own authority and on his
own responsibility. Hence Lessing boldly declares:

The true Lutheran does not wish to be defended by Luther's writings but by
Luther's spirit; and Luther's spirit absolutely requires that *no* man may be prevented from advancing in knowledge of the truth according to his own judgment. But *all* are prevented if only *one* is forbidden to communicate his advance
in knowledge to others. For without this communication at the individual level,
no progress whatever is possible.[49]

Whatever objections Luther specialists may raise against Lessing's interpretation of Luther, or however one-sided it may be, the fact remains that Lessing
himself is firmly convinced that he has the authority of Luther, thus interpreted, on his side. Because of this conviction, he can say with a clear conscience: "I have had the fragments printed; and I would still have them printed
even if people like Goeze were to condemn me and the whole world to the
deepest abyss of hell."[50] But polemics aside, Lessing, as a dialectical thinker,
held the lifelong conviction "that new objections will lead to new debates,
more penetrating doubts to more penetrating solutions."[51] Goeze's censorious
attacks are therefore powerless against Lessing.

Against Goeze, who reproves him for his allegedly unchristian conduct,
Lessing maintains that what is unchristian (*unchristlich*) is "that which argues
against the spirit of Christianity, or against the ultimate purpose of Christianity."[52] What, then, is the ultimate purpose of Christianity? As he puts it, "the
ultimate purpose of Christianity is not our salvation, which may come how it
will, but our *salvation by means of our enlightenment*." Consequently, "to
contribute nothing to the enlightenment of *many people*," he says, is far more
contrary to the spirit of Christianity than making "*a few people, perhaps,*
angry."[53] In his opinion, "the true Christian plays neither the coward nor the
braggart." The hallmark of the true Christian, rather, is to be "mistrustful of
one's reason" and "proud of one's feelings."[54]

It is very interesting that in his sixth essay Lessing, in order to justify his having published the *Fragments from an Unnamed Author*, refers to the fact that Jerome translated Origen's Περὶ Ἀρχῶν into Latin under the title *De Principiis*. Bringing his erudition into full play, he defends himself brilliantly.

> When Jerome *translated* from Greek a work that in his judgment was most pernicious to the Christian religion, namely, Origen's book Περὶ Ἀρχῶν—take good note of the word "translated," [for] *to translate* is much more than merely *to edit*—when he translated this dangerous work so as to rescue it from the bunglings and mutilations of another translator, Rufinus, that is, so as to present it to the Latin world in its full strength; and when the schola tyrannica [school of Tyrannius] reproached him on this account, as if he had a punishable offense on his soul, what was his answer? O impudentiam singularem! Accusant medicum, quod venena prodiderit [Oh, what singular impudence! They accuse a doctor of making poisons known to the public].[55]

In other words, if editing and publishing the *Fragments from an Unnamed Author* deserves the condemnation of the Christian church, how can it be that Jerome escaped condemnation when he translated Origen's anathematized book? Ought the great benefactor of orthodox faith to be regarded as an enemy of the church on this account? But if Jerome's act of translating Origen's book is permissible (and even Goeze must allow as much), then Lessing's less reproachable act of editing and publishing the *Fragments from an Unnamed Author* must, by the same token, naturally be permitted.

For Goeze, however, the issue is not merely the fact that Lessing edited and published the *Fragments*. What is more important, and more reprehensible, to him is that while acting as editor, Lessing took on himself the "advocacy of the author" (*die Advokatur des Verfassers*).[56] Though he had already touched on this issue in his third essay, Lessing takes it up again in his seventh, where he offers the following explanation:

> Advocacy? The advocacy of the author?—What kind of advocacy did my unnamed author have, which I took upon myself in his place? An advocate [is one who] has the right to plead a certain case before certain tribunals. I was not aware that my unnamed author possessed such a right.[57]

According to Lessing, Goeze intentionally misunderstands and distorts the relationship between the unnamed author and himself. Consequently, he makes the following objection:

> I never said that. Rather, I have said precisely the opposite. I have said, and proved, that even if the unnamed author is right and wins the argument at however many individual points, nonetheless, on the whole, what he apparently wishes to conclude therefrom does not follow.[58]

Yet even so, Lessing argues, "I am not, and cannot be a true, authentic advocate for my unnamed author, an advocate who would be of one mind and one spirit with his client as to the dispute in question."[59]

As the foregoing citations show, Lessing tries to keep a clear distance between himself and the unnamed author. In fact, as indicated in chapter 1, his theological position is substantially different from that of Reimarus. Goeze, however, because "gall has mastered his sight and made him violate boundaries,"[60] pays no attention to such differences. For him, "it does not matter what intelligent persons believe in secret, if only the rabble, the dear rabble, remain neatly in the groove in which clergymen alone know how to lead them."[61] From Goeze's perspective, any disturbing elements must be suppressed or eliminated wholesale, regardless of "trivial" differences between them. Lessing bitterly impeaches the Goezes of this world for their fanatical intolerance:

> Oh, you silly fools! You would like to banish the tempest from nature because it buries a ship in a sandbank here and shatters another against the rocky coast there.—Oh, you hypocrites! For we know what you really are. You are not concerned about this unfortunate ship. For you may depend on it: the only thing that concerns you is your own little garden, your own petty comfort, [your own] petty entertainment.[62]

Compared to such "silly fools," Lessing argues, "my unnamed author was a decent man."[63] In his ninth essay, Lessing portrays him as follows:

> Though my unnamed author admittedly puts every revealed religion in a tight spot, he is by no means a man devoid of all religion. I know no one but him in whom I have found, with regard to purely *rational* religion, such a true, complete, and warmhearted concept.[64]

At any rate, Lessing's relationship to the unnamed author is not that of a counsel to a defendant. To use Lessing's own words, he is not acting for the benefit of the unnamed author as an "advocate who wishes to win his case." He "merely speaks as an honest man who does not wish to see him damned so tumultuously."[65] He defends the unnamed author only because accusers, including Goeze, "have to this day never refuted him at all; they have only inveighed against him."[66]

With this, we have considered the main points of the Lessing-Goeze controversy. Our consideration shows that from the very start this controversy involved many factors that were too personal for it to be fought as a genuinely theological dispute. As a result, it eventually and inevitably turned into something completely different from what Lessing had first expected. Lessing was partly responsible for this undesirable result, to be sure. But far greater responsibility falls on Goeze. For when Lessing published Reimarus's fragments as if their author were anonymous, his intention was to break the ice of the frozen theological situation of his time and thus to render service in the manifestation of the truth. In his view, therefore, provoking theological controversy by publishing Reimarus's *Fragments* can be regarded as "a means for the pursuit of truth."[67] Having found in Reimarus a person who came close to "the ideal of a genuine disputer of religion," Lessing wished for "a man who would come just as close to the ideal of a genuine defender of religion."[68] He expected, moreover, that such a man would pass ruthless countercriticism on the deist. He seems to speak straightforwardly when he says: "For I brought him to light for the very purpose that a goodly number of people could examine and refute him."[69]

But the "truth question" (*Wahrheitsfrage*)[70] that Lessing raised when he published the *Fragments* was distorted into an issue of an entirely different kind, namely, a social and political one. For the adversary who appeared on the stage was, to use Boehart's term, a man of "fortress mentality" (*Festungsmentalität*).[71] Goeze was incapable of playing "a hermeneutical game for gymnastic fitness of spirit."[72] Lessing wanted to discuss the question of the truth claim of Christian revelation in an open forum, hoping thereby to advance understanding of revelation beyond the level of comprehension that had hitherto prevailed. Goeze, on the other hand, shunned the open forum, and once the discussion became public, soon had recourse to the civil authorities (*Obrigkeit*) to bring it to a halt as quickly as possible.[73] Hence the unhappy situation that Lessing deplored as "a dialogue but no dialogue" (*ein Dialog und kein Dialog*).[74] Contrary to his intention, the controversy between Lessing and Goeze turned into a personal quarrel characterized by faultfinding and mudslinging.

But the controversy was not entirely barren. For one thing, the breaking off of the controversy because of political intervention provided the immediate occasion for the birth of the immortal classic *Nathan the Wise*. For another, out of Lessing's lonely and heroic fight against a Lutheran orthodoxy bound up with state power, a truly modern Protestantism shortly came into being.

4

Lessing's "Ugly Broad Ditch"

An impromptu statement sometimes takes on immortality. An image or meta-phor, though produced almost offhandedly, sometimes attains universal valid-ity. Lessing's famous metaphor or image of the "ugly broad ditch" (*der garstige breite Graben*) is a case in point. This image has played the role of "a kind of code or shorthand"[1] signifying the hiatus between revelation and rea-son in general, and the divorce between faith and history in particular—a problem that is "a really serious and difficult problem of modern life."[2]

What, then, is Lessing's "ugly broad ditch"? To quote the words within which this metaphorical image is found: "That, then, is the ugly, broad ditch which I cannot get across, however often and however earnestly I have tried to make the leap. If anyone can help me over it, let him do it, I beg him, I adjure him. He will deserve a divine reward from me."[3] This quotation alone, how-ever, does not tell us what the ditch is like. It is when we broaden our view that it becomes clear to us that the ditch has to do with "Lessing's proposi-tion."

Lessing's proposition, as is well known, is the statement that "accidental truths of history can never become the proof for necessary truths of reason" (*zufällige Geschichtswahrheiten können der Beweis von notwendigen Ver-nunftswahrheiten nie werden*).[4] It is evident, therefore, that Lessing's "ugly broad ditch" is a metaphor for the divorce between "accidental truths of his-tory" and "necessary truths of reason." As to how we should interpret this metaphorical image in practice, however, there have been such a great variety of interpretations—sometimes diametrically opposed to each other—that even today the question of how to interpret it constitutes one of the most difficult tasks in Lessing studies.

This variety of interpretations is attributable not necessarily to differences in the theological or religious-philosophical standpoints of the interpreters but to Lessing himself. Henry Chadwick, one of the most brilliant patristic schol-ars in England and the editor and translator of *Lessing's Theological Writ-ings*,[5] says, "The tract [namely, *On the Proof of the Spirit and of Power*] is of importance for understanding Lessing; yet it may be doubted whether any writing equally influential in the history of modern religious thought has been marked by a comparable quantity of logical ambiguity."[6] According to him, "the latent obscurity and confusion" involved in this tract had already been perceived by Samuel Taylor Coleridge. The great English romantic poet, who loved Lessing's style of writing and argument and took it for a model, left the following memo: "Year after year I have made a point of reperusing the *Kleine Schriften*, as masterpieces of style and argument. But in the Reasoning [employed in this tract] I feel at each reperusal more and more puzzled how so palpable a *miss* could have been made by so acute a mind."[7] More recently, Gordon E. Michalson, Jr. has pointed out what he calls "serious confusion"[8] in Lessing's argument.

In view of this state of affairs, we wish to discuss the theological problems of Lessing's "ugly broad ditch" by closely analyzing the tract *On the Proof of the Spirit and of Power* in the hope of explicating the significance of Lessing's proposition for the present.

The Proof of the Spirit and of Power

On the Proof of the Spirit and of Power (*Über den Beweis des Geistes und der Kraft*, 1777) was published during an early stage of the fragments controversy. It was a flat rebuttal of *On the Evidence of the Proof for the Truth of the Christian Religion*,[9] a treatise by Johann Daniel Schumann, director of a lyceum in Hanover, intended to refute the *Fragments from an Unnamed Author*. Purporting to represent Lutheran orthodoxy, Schumann denied the unnamed author's bold assertion as to "the impossibility of a revelation which all men can believe on rational grounds." Instead, he attempted to give a conventional "historical proof of Christian truth," asserting that the truth of Christianity could be demonstrated by the fulfillment of prophecies and by miracles. In this regard he appealed to Origen's *Contra Celsum*, book 1, chapter 2, which mentions the proof of the spirit and of power.[10] But in Lessing's eyes, the use that Schumann made of Origen's text was erroneous. So Lessing published his confutation, incisively indicating the difficulties in the apologetics of this representative of Lutheran orthodoxy. The title of the tract arises directly out of these circumstances, but can be traced as far back as Paul's dictum in 1 Cor. 2:4: "καὶ ὁ λόγος μου καὶ τὸ κήρυγμά μου οὐκ ἐν πειθοῖς σοφίας λόγοις, ἀλλ᾽ ἐν ἀποδείξει πνεύματος καὶ δυνάμεως" (RSV: "my speech and my message were not in plausible words of wisdom, but in demonstration of the Spirit and power").

What argument, then, does Lessing present in this tract? First of all, he distinguishes sharply between direct experience of prophecies and miracles and their indirect mediation. He says:

> Fulfilled prophecies, which I myself experience, are one thing; fulfilled prophecies, of which I know only from history that others say they have experienced them, are another.
>
> Miracles, which I see with my own eyes, and which I have the opportunity to verify for myself, are one thing; miracles, of which I know only from history that others say they have seen and verified them, are another.[11]

Having made this sharp distinction, he continues:

> If I had lived at the time of Christ, then of course the prophecies fulfilled in his
> person would have made me pay great attention to him. If I had actually seen
> him perform miracles, if I had had no cause to doubt that true miracles existed,
> then in a worker of miracles who had been marked out so long before, I would
> have gained so much confidence that I would willingly have submitted my
> intellect to his, and I would have believed him in all things in which equally
> indisputable experience did not tell against him.
>
> Or: if even now I experienced that prophecies referring to Christ or the Chris-
> tian religion . . . were fulfilled in a manner admitting of no dispute, if even now
> believing Christians performed miracles that I had to recognize as true miracles,
> what could prevent me from accepting this proof of the spirit and of power, as
> the apostle calls it?[12]

But Lessing insists that he cannot unconditionally accept the "proof of the
spirit and of power" to which Origen, and through him Schumann, appealed.
The reason is that Lessing is no longer in the same position as Origen who, living in an age when miracles still occurred, experienced them so assuredly that
he could appeal to what the apostle called the proof of the spirit and of power.
In contrast, Lessing lives "in the eighteenth century, when miracles no longer
happen."[13] Between the early days of Christianity, when believers felt vividly
the power of the spirit to do miraculous things, and the century of the Enlightenment in which Lessing lives, there is a temporal distance of over a thousand
years. This vast temporal distance causes a serious problem for modern believers, since miracles, once frequent, have ceased to occur. As Lessing puts it:

> The problem is that reports of fulfilled prophecies are not fulfilled prophecies,
> that reports of miracles are not miracles. *These*, the prophecies fulfilled before
> my eyes, the miracles that occur before my eyes, are *immediate* in their effect.
> But *those*—the reports of fulfilled prophecies and miracles—have to work
> through a *medium* that takes away all their force.[14]

So far, Lessing's argument is thoroughly consistent and coherent. The point
he makes is that historical knowledge, because it is transmitted through some
medium to those of us living at the present time, is incapable of conveying the
absolute certainty that immediate experience can claim. Hence he asserts that
historical knowledge, because of its indirectness, is unable to provide grounds
for faith. To be sure, he does not deny that the evangelists' reports of prophecies and miracles are as reliable as historical truths can ever be. But if they are
only as reliable as other historical documents, is there any justification for giving them special treatment "as if they were infinitely more reliable"?[15] How is
it possible to regard the narrative of the evangelists as something "of great,
permanent worth, the loss of which would be irreparable"?[16] This stance, says
Lessing, is utterly impossible. Nothing can justify such treatment. It is impermissible, therefore, to promote historical truths, which are by nature only
probable and relatively credible, to the status of eternal truths. In short, to use
an impressive phrase from his *Rejoinder*, what Lessing denies is "the wish to
hang nothing less than the whole of eternity on a spider's thread" (*an den*

Faden einer Spinne nichts weniger als die ganze Ewigkeit hängen zu wollen).[17] According to him, historical truths cannot be *demonstrated* in the same way that mathematical truths are demonstrated. But "if no historical truth can be demonstrated, then nothing can be demonstrated by means of historical truths. That is to say, *accidental truths of history can never become the proof for necessary truths of reason.*"

To discuss this issue is the primary task of this chapter. We begin by noting that there is a subtle, but very significant displacement or shift in Lessing's argument. In order to make this clear, we propose to continue listening to his statements for a time.

Even if it is historically true that Christ raised the dead, or that he himself rose from the dead, how is it possible to draw the conclusion, Lessing asks, that God has a Son of the same essence as himself, or that the resurrected Christ is the Son of God? If a person cannot object to the statement about the resurrection of Christ on historical grounds, must one therefore accept the doctrine of the Trinity as true? What is the connection between "my inability" (*mein Unvermögen*) to raise any significant objection to the former and "my obligation" (*meine Verbindlichkeit*) to believe something against which my reason rebels?[18] Hence he boldly asserts:

> But to jump, with that historical truth, to a quite different class of truths, and to demand of me that I should form all my metaphysical and moral ideas accordingly; to expect me to alter all my fundamental ideas of the nature of the Godhead because I cannot see any credible testimony against the resurrection of Christ: if that is not a μετάβασις εἰς ἄλλο γένος, then I do not know what Aristotle meant by this phrase.[19]

This statement is followed in short order by another that we have already encountered: "That, then, is the ugly, broad ditch which I cannot get across, however often and however earnestly I have tried to make the leap. If anyone can help me over it, let him do it, I beg him, I adjure him. He will deserve a divine reward from me."[20]

The foregoing paragraphs indicate the main thrust of Lessing's argument in *On the Proof of the Spirit and of Power.* Analysis suggests that in the early part of the tract his argument points to the temporal distance between historical events attested in the biblical narrative and present-day believers, to the probable character of historical knowledge, and to the absolute certainty of immediate experience. At issue here is what Michalson calls the "temporal ditch." What is at stake in the latter part of the tract, however, is the issue of what Michalson calls the "metaphysical ditch" between time and eternity, between the accidental and the necessary.[21] The subjects under discussion are thus changed in a deft and clever manner.

In this secret shift from the "temporal ditch" to the "metaphysical ditch" certain problems are hidden—as well as Lessing's real strength. To be sure, his strength as a master of tactics with a special genius for rhetoric exhibits itself perfectly in his argument of the ditch. But the ultimate cause for what critics have called "so palpable a *miss,*" "logical ambiguity," or "serious confusion" also lie in this surreptitious and, as it were, "deceptive" change of subjects. For at first Lessing concedes that he would willingly have submitted his intellect to Christ's and would have believed in all his miraculous deeds if he had actually seen them with his own eyes, if he had had the opportunity to verify them for himself. That is to say, he declares that he is willing to accept historical truths as eternal ones so long as they are rooted in his own immediate experience. Afterward however, he insists that historical "events," because historical knowledge is merely probable and is incapable of attaining absolute certainty, cannot serve as a basis for eternal truths. Thus his argument in the early part seems to contradict that in the latter part.

Truths of History and Truths of Reason

The sharp distinction between "truths of history" and "truths of reason," incidentally, is not Lessing's invention. Leibniz, as is well known, had already clearly distinguished the two kinds of truth. In his theory of knowledge we find that he differentiated between "truths of reason" (*les vérités de raisonnement*; *Vernunftwahrheiten*) and "factual truths" (*les vérités de fait*; *Tatsachenwahrheiten*). "Truths of reason are necessary and their opposite is impossible; factual truths are contingent and their opposite is possible."[22] Necessary truths of reason come from the understanding alone and are governed by "the principle of contradiction" (*principe de la contradiction*), while contingent, factual truths come from experience or sense-observations and are governed by "the principle of sufficient reason" (*principe de la raison suffisante*).[23]

Leibniz's sharp distinction between these two kinds of truth, and his closely related exclusion of historical truths from the realm of absolute, or eternal, truths, can be traced back further to Spinoza. In his *Tractatus Theologico-Politicus*, Spinoza says:

> Natural divine law . . . does not depend on the truth of any historical narrative whatever, for inasmuch as this natural divine law is comprehended solely by consideration of human nature, it is plain that we can conceive it as existing as well in Adam as in any other man. . . . The truth of a historical narrative (*fides historiarum*), however assured, cannot give us the knowledge or, consequently, the love of God, for love of God springs from knowledge of him, and knowledge of him should be derived from general ideas, in themselves certain and known, so that the truth of a historical narrative is far from being a necessary requisite for our attaining our highest good.[24]

Lessing's proposition as to the two kinds of truth undoubtedly presupposes and follows in the wake of these lines of thought from Spinoza and Leibniz. But the proposition is not merely a refashioning of their thought. For Lessing also discusses, though indirectly, a contemporary problem concerning the existential "appropriation" (*Aneignung*) of truth by asking about the historical reliability of the Christ-event. What is important is that it is this issue, rather than the differentiation between two kinds of truth, that is at stake for him. That is to say, what really matters to him is how a modern person of sound understanding can appropriate the Christian message, including what is offensive to human reason, and still attain Christian conviction without surrendering his intellect (*sacrificium intellectus*).

The reason "appropriation" can become a theological problem of great importance for the modern person is that heteronomous elements involved in the truth claim of traditional Christianity offend the autonomy of human reason. Between the Christian message and the present-day believer there is, to borrow yet another term of Michalson's, an "existential ditch."[25] Consequently, in order to believe in the Christian message, the modern person has to surrender his intellect, or to put it more positively, has to make a "leap" (*Sprung*) or a "decision" (*Entscheidung*) in the Kierkegaardian sense.[26] Needless to say, the first to raise this problem most acutely was Kierkegaard himself. He considered the essence of the knowledge of truth to be its "appropriation," and sought throughout his life to carry out this task.[27] Yet as he himself declares in "a word of thanks to Lessing" in the *Concluding Unscientific Postscript to the Philosophical Fragments*, it was Lessing who first showed him the importance of appropriation. Kierkegaard says:

> His merit consists precisely in his having prevented it. I refer to the fact that he religiously shut himself up within the isolation of his own subjectivity; that he did not permit himself to be deceived into becoming world-historic and systematic with respect to the religious, but understood and knew how to hold fast to the understanding that the religious concerned Lessing, and Lessing alone, just as it concerns every other human being in the same manner; understood that he had infinitely to do with God, and nothing, nothing to do with any man directly. This is my theme, the object of my gratitude—now if I could only be sure that Lessing really does exemplify this principle![28]

The topic of "Lessing and Kierkegaard" comes into view, then, as one that would be well worth pursuing. Since space is limited, however, we cannot discuss this issue here. We must remain content to refer the reader to others' studies.[29]

Yet one can perceive the self-assertion of modern, autonomous selfhood in Lessing's own words:

> I do not for one moment deny that in Christ prophecies were fulfilled. I do not for one moment deny that Christ performed miracles. But since the truth of these miracles has completely ceased to be demonstrable by miracles still occurring now, since they are no more than reports of miracles . . . , I deny that they can and should bind me in the least to faith in the other teachings of Christ.
>
> What does bind me then? Nothing but these teachings themselves. Eighteen hundred years ago they were so new, so alien, so foreign to the entire mass of truths recognized in that age, that nothing less than miracles and fulfilled prophecies were required if the multitude were to attend to them at all.[30]

In this passage, one can see Lessing's true character as a thinker of the Enlightenment. The sentence that contains the verb "bind" (*verbinden*) implies a resolute attitude to refuse anything heteronomous so as to preserve the autonomy of human reason.[31] That is to say, Lessing wants to reject anything, whatever its authority, that would seek to "bind" him from outside. It is important to note, in this connection, that Lessing justifies the claim for autonomy in religious knowledge by referring to the spirit of Martin Luther.

> The true Lutheran does not wish to be defended by Luther's writings but by Luther's spirit; and Luther's spirit absolutely requires that *no* man may be prevented from advancing in knowledge of the truth according to his own judgment.[32]

It is questionable, to be sure, whether interpreting "Luther's spirit" as a claim for free inquiry in the matter of religion is correct. But the idea that the "teachings themselves" bind human reason without violating the autonomy of human reason is worthy of notice. This idea, it would seem, has a profound connection with that of the "inner truth" of religion.

The "Inner Truth" of Religion

As we have already seen, in his "Editor's Counterpropositions," Lessing boldly insisted on the "inner truth" of religion. He emphatically declared, "The [Christian] religion is not true because the evangelists and apostles taught it. They taught it, rather, because it is true. The written traditions must be interpreted by their inner truth, and no written traditions can give a religion inner truth if it has none."[33]

What, then, is the "inner truth" of religion? On the face of it, this concept gives the impression that it blends easily with the notion of "subjective religion."[34] For people easily associate it with a theological concept that has a mystic or spiritualistic background.[35] In fact, as we saw in the preceding chapter, Goeze blamed Lessing for contrasting the inner truth of the Christian religion and the biblical tradition as if they were opposites. According to Goeze, Lessing's statement about the difference between the two is nothing but "empty words." Hence he asks the following question: "Where does he wish to obtain the knowledge of the inner truth of the Christian religion if not from the scriptural traditions, or from the writings of the evangelists and apostles, in proper connection with the writings of the Old Testament?"[36] Goeze evidently has misgivings about the idea of the inner truth of religion. He fears that such inner truth, when separated from the historically given and objective foundations for the biblical traditions, may lapse into subjective religion or arbitrary religious subjectivity.

Against Goeze, however, Lessing boldly asserts:

> This inner truth is not a kind of wax nose (*wächserne Nase*) that every knave can mold as he likes to fit his own face. Where [do I] get the inner truth? From the Christian religion itself. That is why it is called *inner* truth, the truth that requires no authentication from without (*die Wahrheit, die keiner Beglaubigung von außen bedarf*).[37]

This statement makes it clear that for Lessing the inner truth of religion, insofar as we adhere to his intention, is a truth immanent in the religion itself. Its evidence consists primarily and solely in the object (subject matter) of the religion, and yet we are capable of feeling and experiencing this truth through personal commitment.

This point may be illustrated by reference to the *Parable* mentioned in chapter 3. According to the parable, there are only a few who find satisfaction in "working inside the palace" and are capable of saying, "It is enough that at every moment we learn that the most beneficent wisdom fills the entire palace, and that from this source nothing but beauty and order spread over the entire land."[38] More to the point, it is only these few who can truly understand the nobility and grandeur of the palace from within. In this parable, the nobility and grandeur of the palace are objective; they are independent of the subjective feeling of those who feel it noble and grand. But it is only when this nobility and grandeur are felt and experienced that the nobility and grandeur of the palace are understood as such. And who is it that can feel and experience these qualities? Neither observers, who are enchanted with its outward appearance, nor architectural connoisseurs, who show too much interest in the original plan, but only those who live and work inside the palace and experience that its design is consistent and that the palace is full of light.

In the "Editor's Counterpropositions," shortly before mentioning the "inner truth" of religion, Lessing observes in a remark we have quoted more than once: "For him it is simply a fact, this Christianity which he feels to be true and in which he feels blessed. When the paralytic experiences the beneficial shocks of the electric spark, does it worry him whether Nollet or Franklin or neither is right?"[39] In this case too, "the beneficial shocks of the electric spark" constitute a scientific phenomenon that can be verified objectively. The doctor can demonstrate with objective data how electric therapy is good for paralysis. The therapy is not efficacious because it makes the paralytic feel good. Its efficacy is essentially independent of how the patient feels about it. Nevertheless, no one can understand the beneficial shocks of the electric spark better than the paralytic who feels and experiences them.

To help the reader understand Lessing's concept of the "inner truth" of religion, we would like to cite, in support of this concept, H. Richard Niebuhr's well-known theory of "inner history." According to Niebuhr, there are two kinds of history: "history as lived" and "history as seen." He brilliantly explains the distinction by taking as an example "a man who has been blind and who has come to see."

> A scientific case history will describe what happened to his optic nerve or to the crystalline lens, what technique the surgeon used or by what medicines a physician wrought the cure, through what stages of recovery the patient passed. An autobiography, on the other hand, may barely mention these things, but it will tell what happened to a self that had lived in darkness and now saw again trees and the sunrise, children's faces and the eyes of a friend.[40]

Niebuhr therefore calls history as seen "outer history" and history as lived "inner history," stressing the importance of making a clear distinction between the two.[41]

Niebuhr's distinction between inner and outer history is not meant to devalue objective historical description. But implicit in his claim for the validity of inner history is that it is the patient, not the doctor, who actually feels or experiences the results of the cure or operation. Likewise, in Lessing the efficacy of the electric therapy is substantiated by the paralytic who undergoes it. And when the paralytic experiences the beneficial shocks of the electric spark, the question of who discovered electricity, or whose scientific theory is correct, is not of the least importance to the patient. What is important is the fact that he or she has been cured or is being cured. The same, Lessing holds, is true of religion. According to him, the truth of a religion is recognizable only when one participates in it from within, not when it is objectified in theory or doctrine.[42] This, in brief, is what Lessing means by his concept of the inner truth of religion.

This being the case, Lessing's idea of the inner truth of religion is by no means the "subjective religion" that Goeze attacks. Nor is it a truth of reason which, like mathematical truth, is capable of demonstration by strict methods and procedures. It is a truth based on the evidence of feeling, not on that of reason.

Why, then, does Lessing use such an ambivalent concept? In our opinion, which is based on Harald Schultze's judgment, Lessing, in view of biblical studies that used the modern, historico-critical method, shrewdly perceived the unworkability of Lutheran orthodoxy's theological apparatus. He adhered to the truth of the Christian religion, but wanted to substantiate its truth claim in a way different from the way of Lutheran orthodoxy. He sought to find the ultimate basis for Christian faith in the believer's inner experience and feeling, which were supposedly invulnerable to historical criticism. Thus he invented the problematic concept of the "inner truth" of religion.

If this interpretation is correct, it may be possible to regard Lessing's concept of the inner truth of religion as a harbinger of a direction in modern theology advanced in later years by Schleiermacher.

Genuine Christian Love

Lessing concluded *On the Proof of the Spirit and of Power* with the enigmatic words, "May all who are divided by the Gospel of John be reunited by the Testament of John. Admittedly it is apocryphal, this testament. But it is not on that account any the less divine."[43] To clarify these words, we need to consider *The Testament of John*, for this testament and Lessing's *On the Proof of the Spirit and of Power* form a set. In order to understand the real point of *On the Proof of the Spirit and of Power*, it is important to take a brief look at this small work, which takes the form of a dialogue between "he" and "I."

What is *The Testament of John*? According to Lessing, it is "John's last will," "the last remarkable words of the dying John, words he repeated over and over again."[44] That is why it is called his "testament." In the dialogue, the "he" seems to be a professional theologian. He asks about the source of *The*

Testament of John. The "I," who undoubtedly signifies Lessing, refers him to Jerome's *Commentary on Paul's Epistle to the Galatians,* chapter 6. From this text we learn that the blessed apostle and evangelist John stayed at Ephesus until his old age. Every day he spoke to the assembled community. At length he became so old that even with the assistance of his disciples he could hardly attend the assembly, but he would not neglect his ministry. He still wished to give his daily address to the community. Day by day his address became simpler and shorter. Finally, he reduced it to the words, "Little children, love one another." At first these words had a wonderful effect on the people who heard him, but as he only repeated the same words again and again, they eventually became bored and asked him, "But, Master, why do you always say the same thing?" John replied, "Because it is the Lord's command; because this alone, this alone, if it is done, is enough, is sufficient and adequate."[45]

From this anecdote it appears that what Lessing calls *The Testament of John* is summed up in the words "Little children, love one another" (*Kinderchen, liebt euch!*)[46]—the Christian commandment of love. Lessing contrasted *The Testament of John* to the Gospel according to John with its famous opening words, "In the beginning was the Word . . . " Of the two, Lessing attaches greater importance to *The Testament of John.*[47] This does not mean that he devalues the Fourth Gospel. On the contrary, the following statement shows that he held it in high esteem:

> It was only his [namely, John's] Gospel that gave the Christian religion its true consistency. We have only his Gospel to thank if the Christian religion, despite all attacks, has continued in this consistency and will probably survive as long as there are men who think they need a mediator between themselves and the Deity: that is, *forever.*[48]

There can be no question about the importance of the Gospel of John because, together with its teaching on the incarnation of the preexistent Logos or the divinity of Christ, it has played a decisive role in forming the doctrines of Christianity. In Lessing's eyes, however, it is also undeniable that the Gospel of John has been a remote cause of doctrinal oppositions and schisms. It is for this reason that John's command, "Little children, love one another," must be set alongside it. No, it must, rather, be placed before it. This is the context that makes understandable Lessing's wish that all who are divided by the Gospel of John may be reunited by *The Testament of John.*

The contrast between the Gospel of John and *The Testament of John* is, to use the terms Lessing employs in this tract, a contrast between "Christian dogmas" (*die christliche Glaubenslehren*) and "true Christian love" (*die wahre christliche Liebe*).[49] Lessing, as will now be evident, attaches priority to true Christian love. To be sure, the "priority of ethics over dogmatics" (*Priorität der Ethik vor der Dogmatik*)[50] is one of the basic characteristics of modern Protestant theology. But it does not follow that Lessing merely went along with this general tendency. We should, rather, remind ourselves once again of that famous letter which the twenty-year-old freelance journalist wrote to his pastor-father:

Time will tell whether I have respect for my parents, conviction in my religion, and morality in my path through life. Time will tell whether the better Christian is one who has the principles of Christian teaching memorized and on his tongue, often without understanding them, who goes to church, and follows all the customs because he is used to them; or whether the better Christian is one who has held serious doubts and, after examining them, has attained conviction, or at least is still striving to attain it. The Christian religion is not something to be swallowed blindly and taken in good faith from parents. Most of us simply inherit it from them, as we do their possessions, but our parents too show by their behavior the kind of honest Christians they are. As long as I see that one of the most important commandments of Christianity, "*Love thine enemy*," is observed no better than it is now, I shall continue to doubt whether those people who say they are Christians, really are Christians. (Letter to his father of 30 May 1749.)[51]

Here Jesus' command of love in Matt. 5:44 is declared to be "one of the most important commandments of Christianity." What is more, its observance, the practice of "genuine Christian love," is declared to be the hallmark of true Christianity. As we saw in chapter 2, this idea of Lessing's is impressively expressed in his earliest comedy *The Jews*. Further, as we shall see in chapter 5, the same idea manifests itself in his dramatic masterpiece *Nathan the Wise*. In its parable of the three rings, the modest judge gives the following counsel to three sons who are fighting with each other:

"Well, then! Let each aspire / To emulate his father's unbeguiled, /Unprejudiced affection! Let each strive / To match the rest in bringing to the fore / The magic of the opal in his ring! / Assist that power with all humility, / With benefaction, hearty peacefulness, / And with profound submission to God's will!"[52]

His counsel suggests that constant striving to emulate the father's unbeguiled, unprejudiced affection will demonstrate the genuineness of the ring in due course. In other words, the practice of genuine love proves the truth.

These observations show that for Lessing the quintessence of Christianity is to be found in the teaching and practice of genuine Christian love. John's words, "Because it is the Lord's command; because this alone, this alone, if it is done, is enough, is sufficient and adequate," carry weight. For, as indicated in yet another book by Jerome, a book that Lessing cites, John is the apostle "who leaned on the Lord's breast and drew the stream of teachings from the purest wellspring."[53] In any event, it is interesting and important not only for the interpretation of his thought but also for the study of European intellectual history to observe that Lessing thrust John's Christianity to the fore, the Christianity that emphasizes the supremacy of love. For in his last work, *The Education of the Human Race*, Lessing announces the coming of a new age, the age of the "new, eternal Gospel" promised in Revelation 14:6. In the early Christian churches, it should be noted, the apostle John was believed to be the author of all the Johannine literature, including Revelation.[54] In Lessing's day, only a small number of people held such a naive view, but the notion that the author of Revelation was a successor to the tradition of the apostle John was still deeply rooted among the people. This being taken into consideration, it might be conceivable that there was an essential connection between Lessing's emphasis on *The Testament of John* and his appeal to the "new, eternal Gospel" in the book of Revelation.[55]

The Authenticity of Lessing's "Ugly Ditch"

So far, in order to pursue the theological problem involved in Lessing's "ugly broad ditch," we have sought to shed light on the following topics: the validity of the proof of the spirit and of power, truths of history and truths of reason, appropriation of the truth, the inner truth of religion, and the quintessence of Christianity. We now return to Lessing's proposition that "accidental truths of history can never become the proof for necessary truths of reason" in order to reexamine this proposition in detail.

The reason Lessing's proposition and its metaphorical image of the "ugly broad ditch" have been discussed in Protestant theology over the past two centuries is that they accurately indicate the difficulty involved in the theological task of validating the truth claim of Christianity or of demonstrating the universal validity of the historical revelation. Lessing deplores the ugly broad ditch between accidental truths of history and necessary truths of reason, a ditch he cannot leap across no matter how often or how earnestly he tries. But why is there a "ditch" between the two truths? Why is the ditch "ugly"? How "broad" is it? Moreover, is Lessing's lament genuine? Impelled by such questions, we have thus far followed Lessing's discussion in *On the Proof of the Spirit and of Power*. Our examination showed that there was a subtle but very important change of subjects in Lessing's argument, a change carried out in a surreptitious, almost misleading, way. This change of subjects resulted in the ambiguities that cloak his famous image of the "ugly broad ditch." In my view, these ambiguities are also closely related to the obscurity of the terms he used. For the more we try to clarify what Lessing meant by "accidental truths of history" and "necessary truths of reason," the more ambiguous they become.

As pointed out earlier, Lessing's use of terms basically presupposes and follows the lines of thought laid down by Spinoza and Leibniz. But he also adds his own special nuances. For example, in *On the Proof of the Spirit and of Power*, when he mentions the prophecies fulfilled in the person of Christ, the miracles performed by Christ, the miracles performed in the primitive church by Christ's disciples, and not least the resurrection of Christ from the dead, it is evident from the context that these things belong to the "accidental truths of history." What is not evident is what he deems "necessary truths of reason." There is, in fact, some confusion as to this question. Lessing's argument leaves the impression that theological propositions, such as those on the consubstantiality of God and the Son or on the divine Sonship of the resurrected Christ, and "a very useful mathematical truth"[56] had been jumbled together promiscuously in the same bag. But should they not be differentiated? Should they not be separated into different categories? To be sure, mathematical truths belong to necessary truths of reason. But do theological propositions on God and Christ belong to the same category of truth? Do they not belong, rather, to the category of "revealed truths" (*geoffenbarte Wahrheiten*) and therefore to the truths of history—though in this case it would be inappropriate to call them "accidental."

Furthermore, Lessing uses the terms "historical truths" (*historische Wahrheiten*) and "truths of history" (*Geschichtswahrheiten*) as if they were virtually identical and interchangeable.[57] But should they not be distinguished?[58] As H. Richard Niebuhr's concept of "inner history" indicates, history has a dimension that cannot be illumined by ordinary history (*Historie*). Lessing undoubtedly knows this. He knows of historicity (*Geschichtlichkeit*) that cannot be dealt with by the science of history. But if he knows this, why, then, is he so careless in his use of these terms?

These questions inevitably lead us to discuss the concepts of revelation, reason, and history in Lessing. Since detailed analyses of these concepts will be undertaken in chapters 5 and 6, here we only plan to touch on the results of our considerations in an anticipatory way, saving for chapters 5 and 6 the grounds for these results. Our research will show that Lessing does not turn his back on supranatural revelation, that his concept of reason is fundamentally different from that of ordinary Enlightenment thinkers, and that a developmental concept of history mediates the opposition between revelation and reason. At any rate, Lessingian reason does not exclude revelation or faith but makes use of them for its own sake. To this extent, it may indeed be possible to speak of "the concept of religiously founded reason" (*der religiös fundierte Vernunftbegriff*)[59] or of the "devoutness of reason" (*Vernunftgläubigkeit*)[60] in Lessing.

Loosely related to these considerations is the question of what Lessing meant by "necessary." When he speaks of "necessary truths of reason," does the adjective "necessary" denote anything that is metaphysically necessary in the Leibnizean sense? That is to say, does "necessary" mean that "its opposite is impossible"? In my view, Lessing ostensibly follows the Leibnizean definition, but secretly incorporates into it a new existential meaning. To be concrete, Lessing means, it would seem, that I recognize a truth as necessary if it cannot be denied without contradicting my rationality, or if it is so convincing to my reason that I cannot oppose it. In a word, it connotes *what my reason discerns* as having the character of obligatoriness or binding force (*Verbindlichkeit*). If this is the case, the phrase "necessary truths of reason" in Lessing means not only "truths of reason" (*les vérités de raisonnement*) in the Leibnizean sense, but also *truths that my reason acknowledges as existentially obligatory or binding*. Only if the word "necessary" is understood in this way can we make sense of Lessing's proposition in *The Education of the Human Race* that "the development of revealed truths into truths of reason is absolutely necessary" (*die Ausbildung geoffenbarter Wahrheiten in Vernunftswahrheiten ist schlechterdings notwendig*).[61]

But here a new and difficult question arises. Lessing asserts that "accidental truths of history can never become the proof for necessary truths of reason."

Yet he also maintains that "the development of revealed truths into truths of reason is absolutely necessary." In other words, at the same time that he declares it impossible to proceed from "truths of history" to "truths of reason," he also declares it essential to develop "truths of history" into "truths of reason." Is this not a self-evident contradiction? Can these two propositions be compatible? If so, how are they related to each other?

True, it may be conceivable that it is this contradiction which gives rise to the "ugly broad ditch" and that for this very reason Lessing's lament over his inability to cross the ditch is all the more acute. But another view is possible, a view that removes the "ugly broad ditch" from the theological arena on the ground that it is merely fictitious. We find this sort of interpretation in Karl Barth's construal of Lessing.

Lessing's Problem and Peter's Problem

In his book *Protestant Theology in the Nineteenth Century*, Karl Barth presents a remarkably interesting and instructive interpretation of Lessing's theological thought. Barth's interpretation also contains several sharp criticisms. With regard to Lessing's "ugly broad ditch," for example, he observes:

> This lament about the impossibility of passing over from historical proof to revelation-faith is not, in fact, genuine. Lessing could perfectly well do without what he represented in those sentences as being inaccessible to him, and he wished to make it clear to the theologians that it is not only inaccessible but also superfluous for them, and that for the sake of their own cause they should give it up.[62]

Barth holds that Lessing knows how to build a bridge between "accidental truths of history" and "necessary truths of reason." For Lessing, "truths of history," when they are not merely accidental but convincing to a person, have become necessary truths, directly necessary to this person. They can thus become "truths of reason." That which is historical (*historisch*) denotes that which must first be made part of a person's own experience by investigation, and which is therefore not yet experienced by the person. Accordingly,

> historical truth as such, the truth that is in need of such investigation and is not yet part of my own experience, cannot be the legitimate and fully authorized messenger of the truth of revelation, that is, the truth which, being ultimately certain, necessarily imposes itself on my reason. A truth of history, if it were to have this significance for me, would have to come to me by other means, not as "accidental" and not as "historical" truth, not as requiring investigation by me, and thus not at all merely as truth that has been handed down, and by no means, further, in such a way that there should be any question at all of the problem of that "ugly broad ditch." It is impossible for a revealed religion that rests on human testimony to afford undoubted assurance in anything. There is, according to Lessing, another way.[63]

As the preceding quotation implies, Barth thinks that Lessing knows full well of "another way." In Barth's view, "experience" as Lessing interprets it is "the direct way from the truth of history to the *heart* (*Herz*) of the present-day person." Through *experience* "the historical element in Christianity assumes the power of proof for Christianity itself, and by way of the truth of history, becomes proof for the necessary truths of reason." After all, "the fact that this way exists," Barth insists, "is the positive side of that negative proposition. Lessing knows very well about the truths of history that can become proof for necessary truths of reason in this manner."[64]

The foregoing paragraphs summarize the main points in Barth's interpretation of Lessing's "ugly broad ditch." On the face of it, his interpretation may seem rather close to ours. In reality, however, his point of view is quite different from the one suggested by our research.

In the last analysis Barth takes what Lessing speaks of as miraculous power, experience, "the beneficial shocks of the electric spark" and the like as nothing more than "possibilities within history" (*innergeschichtliche Möglichkeiten*). Even Lessing's understanding of the "proof of the Spirit and of power" is in Barth's view merely "the realization of human possibilities." Hence Barth condemns Lessing for treating God as if he were something like "a fifth wheel on a carriage."[65]

Barth's basic stance is essentially what it was in his treatise "Lessing's Problem and Peter's Problem," written for the journal *Evangelische Theologie* in 1952 in commemoration of Ernst Wolf's fiftieth birthday.[66] Against the problem of "historical distance" (*die geschichtliche Distanz*) posed by Lessing's ugly broad ditch,[67] Barth raises "a completely different problem of distance" (*ein ganz anderes Distanzproblem*).[68] This is the problem of the distance between God and human beings. To be more precise, it is the problem of "the real distance" (*die eigentliche Ferne*) between God in heaven and human beings on earth. "There God is for the human being—here the human being is against God!" (*dort Gott für den Menschen—hier der Mensch gegen Gott!*). According to Barth, the problem that theology ought to tackle with utter seriousness is this problem alone. It is this problem, therefore, originally raised by Peter, that constitutes "the real problem" of theology. In comparison with this problem, the one of Lessing's ugly broad ditch is merely "a technical problem" and "a typically methodological problem."[69]

But this distance between God and us has already been overcome, Barth avers, by the incarnation of Jesus Christ. *Christus pro nobis tunc* is *Christus pro nobis nunc*. This simultaneity, however, inevitably brings us dread and fear. To avoid this dread and fear, we humans, instead of accepting the truth and reality of the reconciliation achieved by Jesus Christ, try to escape them as long as we can. The problem of Lessing's ugly broad ditch makes this dreadful simultaneity with Christ technically difficult and neutralizes it into the problem of a merely historical relationship. It thus helps us to evade the real problem, which Barth refers to as "Peter's problem."[70]

The paragraphs above give the gist of Barth's criticism of Lessing. We are prepared to acknowledge something worthy in Barth's sharp criticism. But his interpretation of Lessing's religious thought, though indeed excellent as a theological interpretation, strikes us as a bit forced because it is overwhelmingly colored by his own theology. For this reason we doubt that Barth's interpretation, as a proper study of Lessing, is adequate.[71] To give an example of its inadequacy, Barth takes the problem of Lessing's ugly broad ditch as no more than a problem of "historical distance." In his view it is a "temporal problem" (*Zeitproblem*) that differs from the religious problem. But it is incorrect to take Lessing's ugly broad ditch as involving no more than historical distance. For as Michalson's superb analysis shows, Lessing's ditch involves at least three dimensions: the "temporal ditch," the "metaphysical ditch," and the "existential ditch."[72] The "existential ditch," in particular, implies that Lessing's ugly broad ditch includes a religious dimension. The question of how a modern person can appropriate the religious message, often offensive to modern autonomous reason, without surrendering his or her intellect, is a religious problem par excellence for modern people.

In the end, despite our best efforts to clarify its meaning, Lessing's ugly broad ditch remains enigmatic. But this metaphorical image may attract us all the more strongly precisely because it continues to be enigmatic. In any event, everyone is invited to make an attempt to leap over this ditch. And only when we actually make such an attempt ourselves can we really understand the difficulty of crossing over Lessing's "ugly broad ditch."

5

Nathan the Wise and Lessing's "Ideal of Humanity"

With regard to Lessing's best-known dramatic work, Friedrich Schlegel once made the noteworthy comment: "*Nathan the Wise* is not only a continuation of his *Anti-Goeze*, a twelfth installment in the series, as it were; it is also, and it is indeed, a dramatized primer of higher cynicism."[1] This remark by one of the most prominent exponents of German romanticism suggests two important perspectives from which to interpret this classic work. In the first place, this dramatic masterpiece needs to be interpreted in close connection with, and as a prolongation of, Lessing's theological controversy with Goeze. In the second place, it also needs to be regarded as transcending the occasion that gave it birth, as representing the crystallization or embodiment of a universal idea.

Nathan the Wise was indeed, as Lessing himself admitted, a by-product of his controversy with Goeze. Accordingly, a proper understanding of the significance of this work requires us to have a clear idea of the course of the controversy. Conversely, to understand Lessing's theological position in the controversy fully and correctly, it is absolutely necessary that we pay full attention to the religious idea expressed in *Nathan the Wise*. For Lessing's statements in his controversy with Goeze—a controversy that the authorities brought to a premature end—were little more than a litany of bitter irony and sarcasm caused by his overreaction to Goeze's inquisitorial tone of censure. As a result, it is quite difficult to grasp Lessing's authentic theological ideas from the polemics of his anti-Goeze writings.

On the other hand, this dramatic work, said to be "a work produced by sheer reason," possesses a literary independence and a conceptual universality that hold good quite apart from the immediate context in which it came into being. Dilthey says of the idea of humanity that it "once made the hearts of the best people of our nation throb audibly in their breasts, but already by Herder's latter days, had became more and more threadbare."[2] It was this very idea of humanity that for the first time in German intellectual history took vivid and definite form in two of Lessing's best-known works, *Nathan the Wise* and *The Education of the Human Race*.

Our main task in this chapter will be to elucidate "Lessing's ideal" or his "new ideal of life"[3] as given poetic expression in *Nathan the Wise*, and to clarify the "new feeling for life" or "new worldview"[4] that emerge from this work. In carrying out this task, we will have to pay special attention both to the drama's immediate background, that is, Lessing's theological controversy with Goeze, and to the closely related work, *The Education of the Human Race.*

The Background and Main Theme of *Nathan the Wise*

As noted in chapter 1 and again in chapter 3, the posthumously published work by Reimarus that Lessing, as editor, issued under the title *Fragments from an Unnamed Author* caused a sensation in Germany. It evoked harsh counterarguments not only from the camp of Lutheran orthodoxy but also from that of liberal theology. This marked the beginning of the fragments controversy.

With the intervention of Johann Melchior Goeze, "the Inquisitor of Hamburg," the fragments controversy became the "Lessing-Goeze controversy," said to have been the bitterest theological dispute since the Reformation. Trivial misunderstandings led to personal hatred, causing the controversy to degenerate into a grudge fight. Goeze, judging that a continuation of this quarrel would be detrimental to his career and reputation, appealed to the government of Brunswick to step in and bring the controversy to a halt.

The government's decree entailed a change in Lessing's civil status. The censorship from which he had been free was now enforced. Moreover, on 17 August 1778 the government of Brunswick issued a circular notice saying that "as regards religious matters, he [that is, Lessing] is no longer allowed to have anything printed, here or elsewhere, whether under his real name or under assumed names, without prior permission of the Ducal Counsel of the Ministry."[5] Consequently Lessing had no prospect of continuing the theological battle. It was in this hopeless situation that he devised the idea of writing *Nathan the Wise.*

He first disclosed his plan in a letter of 11 August 1778 to his brother Karl:

> As yet I do not know what the outcome of my quarrel will be. But I would like to be prepared for any outcome. You know well that nothing is better than to have as much money as one needs. Last night I had a crazy idea. Many years ago I outlined a drama on a subject that has a certain analogy to these present controversies, little dreamt of then. If you and Moses think well of it, I shall have it printed by subscription, and you can print and distribute the enclosed announcement as soon as possible. . . . I do not wish to allow the real content of my announced piece to become known too early; but if you or Moses [Mendelssohn] want to know it, turn to Boccaccio's Decameron, Giornata 1, Novella 3: Melchizedek the Jew. I believe I have invented a very interesting episode for it, so the entire story should be a good read. And I certainly intend herewith to play a more wicked prank on theologians than if I were to write ten other fragments. If possible, answer me promptly.

> Gotthold[6]

In reply, Karl wrote: "Finish your *Nathan*! There will be no lack of subscribers. Our Moses, who has only today come back from a two-week trip, highly approves of your plan, I know; he has often found fault with you for not using your works in this way."[7] A week later, he conveyed Moses Mendelssohn's more measured advice: "Moses thinks that if you produce a piece that ridicules the foolishness of the theologians, they would have you where they want you. 'It is a comedy,' they would say; 'he has a great gift for mockery and for making people laugh. He is a Voltaire.' But if you stick to the tone that you promised to take in your last reply to Goeze, they could not get away with this evasion, however much they lay it on. You must write a dramatic piece, therefore, that has no relationship whatever to this dispute."[8] As this letter shows, Moses Mendelssohn feared that Lessing's overinvolvement in the barren theological controversy might lead to a waste of his literary talent.

Karl held a different opinion. In July 1778, when Lessing was deprived of his privilege of freedom from censorship, Karl encouraged him to write "a really funny epilogue" that would put an end to his quarrel with Goeze.[9] Now, however, he urges him to continue the theological controversy by writing a "theological comedy."[10] In the end, the wise elder brother, Gotthold, chose to follow not the inducement of his shallow-minded younger brother but the advice of his trusted friend.

This does not mean, however, that Lessing wanted to stop the controversy as such. It only means that he abandoned his earlier idea of presenting the theological controversy as a comedy. In a letter to his brother Karl dated 20 October 1778, Lessing indicated that what he wished to compose was to be not "a satirical piece, for the purpose of deserting the battlefield with scornful laughter" but "as touching a piece as I have ever created."[11] In any event, he says in another letter, he has made up his mind "to see whether one will even allow me to preach without molestation in my old pulpit, in the theater at least."[12]

The plot had been largely decided well before he became involved in the theological controversy with Goeze.[13] Nonetheless, the dramatic work thus produced was "more the fruit of the polemic than of genius."[14] As we have seen, Lessing himself, speaking of himself in the third person, characterized the work in the words "Nathan is a son of his approaching old age, [a son] whom the polemic helped bring to birth."[15]

In a first draft for his preface to *Nathan the Wise*, Lessing wrote: "Nathan's attitude toward *all* positive religion has always been mine."[16] This being the case, it is important that we consider the religious idea expressed in *Nathan the Wise* if we are to understand Lessing's idea of religion properly. It may be permissible, in this connection, to assume that Lessing's idea of religion is projected not only onto Nathan, the hero of the drama, but also onto various dramatis personae in one way or another. It may be that the Jewish philosopher Moses Mendelssohn was, as critics have often asserted, the real model for Nathan the Wise. This does not exclude the possibility, however, that Nathan is simultaneously a "Lessingian figure."[17] The truth is that Lessing, using as a model his old friend of nearly thirty years, Moses Mendelssohn, created in

Nathan an ideal person and breathed into this fictitious hero his own "ideal of humanity." The same holds true for Saladin, the only character borrowed from reality,[18] for the Patriarch of Jerusalem whose model is certainly Goeze, and for the dervish Al-Hafi, whose model is said to be Abraham Wulff, a merchant versed in mathematics who was a chess friend of Lessing.[19] It also holds true for the young templar, whose model, though difficult to identify, is recognizably an offshoot of Lessing. Nathan's adopted daughter Rachel can be regarded, we will see later, as "the first female representative of the new humanity."[20]

In the characters, words, and deeds of the various dramatis personae, we have to sense, then, Lessing's idea of humanity. But what is the subject of this drama? What place does it occupy in the history of German literature? According to H. A. Korff, Lessing's *Nathan the Wise* is the very first example of the German "literature of humanity" (*Humanitätsdichtung*) and "a great anthem to human friendship and brotherhood."[21] Dilthey seems to endorse this view of Korff's when he says:

> It was not this conflict [between free spirits and fanatically held orthodox faith] that constituted his theme, but rather how, in the midst of power struggles and fanatic religious opposition, free spirits emancipate themselves from the faith of their fathers. It is the theme of how they find themselves, discover within themselves an identical humanity, and form among themselves a spiritual solidarity.[22]

This being the case, our next task is to interpret, by a close analysis of the text, Lessing's idea of humanity and to inquire into its religious significance. The best and most appropriate way to achieve this purpose is to examine the parable of the three rings, which "was the starting point for the plot and stands at the center of the completed work."[23]

The Parable of the Three Rings

The parable of the three rings, as Lessing himself frankly admits, is an adaptation of Boccaccio's *Decameron*, Giornata 1, Novella 3. Yet it is not simply a matter of making use of this portion of the work of the Italian humanist, for in a masterly way Lessing adapted and reworked it at several important points.[24]

Lessing's parable of the three rings contains important hints and allusions to his own religious thought. It is therefore worth citing in full. We shall omit only Saladin's words and some insignificant expressions Nathan utters in relation to what Saladin says.

> In days of yore, there dwelt in eastern lands / A man who had a ring of priceless worth / Received from hands beloved. The stone it held, / An opal, shed a hundred colors fair, / And had the magic power that he who wore it, / Trusting its strength, was loved of God and men. / No wonder therefore that this eastern man / Would never cease to wear it; and took pains / To keep it in his household for all time. / He left the ring to that one of his sons / He loved the best; provid-

ing that in turn / That son bequeath to his most favorite son / The ring; and thus, regardless of his birth, / The dearest son, by virtue of the ring, / Should be the head, the prince of all his house . . .

At last this ring, passed on from son to son, / Descended to a father of three sons; / All three of whom were duly dutiful, / All three of whom in consequence he needs / Must love alike. But yet from time to time, / Now this, now that one, now the third—as each / Might be with him alone, the other two / Not sharing then his overflowing heart— / Seemed worthiest of the ring; and so to each / He promised it, in pious frailty. / This lasted while it might.—Then came the time / For dying, and the loving father finds / Himself embarrassed. It's a grief to him / To wound two of his sons, who have relied / Upon his word.—What's to be done?— He sends / In secret to a jeweler, of whom / He orders two more rings, in pattern like / His own, and bids him spare nor cost nor toil / To make them in all points identical. / The jeweler succeeds. And when he brings / The rings to him, the sire himself cannot / Distinguish them from the original. / In glee and joy he calls his sons to him, / Each by himself, confers on him his blessing— / His ring as well—and dies . . .

Scarce is the father dead when all three sons / Appear, each with his ring, and each would be / The reigning prince. They seek the facts, they quarrel, / Accuse. In vain; the genuine ring was not / Demonstrable;—/ almost as little as / Today the genuine faith . . .

As we have said: the sons preferred complaint; / And each swore to the judge, he had received / The ring directly from his father's hand.— / As was the truth!— And long before had had / His father's promise, one day to enjoy / The privilege of the ring.—No less than truth!— / His father, each asserted, could not have / Been false to him; and sooner than suspect / This thing of him, of such a loving father: / He must accuse his brothers—howsoever / Inclined in other things to think the best / Of them—of some false play; and he the traitors / Would promptly ferret out; would take revenge . . .

Thus said the judge: unless you swiftly bring / Your father here to me, I'll bid you leave / My judgment seat. Think you that I am here / For solving riddles? Would you wait, perhaps, / Until the genuine ring should rise and speak?— / But stop! I hear the genuine ring enjoys / The magic power to make its wearer loved, / Beloved of God and men. That must decide! / For spurious rings can surely not do that!— / Whom then do two of you love most? Quick, speak! / You're mute? The rings' effect is only backward, / Not outward? Each one loves himself the most?— / O then you are, all three, deceived deceivers! / Your rings are false, all three. The genuine ring / No doubt got lost. To hide the grievous loss / To make it good, the father caused three rings / To serve for one . . .

The judge went on, if you'll not have my counsel, / Instead of verdict, go! My counsel is: / Accept the matter wholly as it stands. / If each one from his father has his ring, / Then let each one believe his ring to be / The true one.—Possibly the father wished / To tolerate no longer in his house / The tyranny of just one ring!—And know: / That you, all three, he loved; and loved alike; / Since two of you he'd not humiliate / To favor one.—Well then! Let each aspire / To emulate his father's unbeguiled, / Unprejudiced affection! Let each strive / To match the rest in bringing to the fore / The magic of the opal in his ring! / Assist that power with all humility, / With benefaction, hearty peacefulness, / And with profound submission to God's will! / And when the magic powers of the stones / Reveal themselves in children's children's children: / I bid you, in a thousand thousand years, / To stand again before this seat. For then / A wiser man than I will sit as judge / Upon this bench, and speak. Depart!—So said / The modest judge.[25]

That is the full story of what is called the parable of the three rings. It is a story to be expressed on stage in the form of vivid dialogue between Nathan and Saladin. Accordingly, as Stuart Atkins cautions us, the parable is not to be treated as if it were "an independent text properly printed as such in anthologies of German verse." It is "actually a discontinuous text in a larger dramatic context."[26] Hence, he says, to understand the parable of the rings properly, "both the occasion of its telling and the larger design of the drama in which it is told must be kept in mind."[27]

The immediate occasion for Nathan's telling this parable is a cunning trick that Saladin has played on him. Suffering from a shortage of funds because the national treasury is close to the end of its resources, the Sultan Saladin, who regards himself as the "Reformer of the world and of the law," is taken in by a scheme proposed by his sister, Sittah. At Sittah's suggestion, he stoops to "insipid wiles." The trick is to ask a question that is almost impossible for a Jew to answer and to extort money from the wealthy Jewish merchant in exchange for pardoning him for not answering. So Saladin calls Nathan to his palace and asks the following question: "Since you're accounted wise: / Then tell me, pray—what faith, or moral law, / Has most appeal for you?"[28] On hearing Nathan answer "I am a Jew," Saladin immediately continues:

"And I a Mussulman. / The Christian stands between us.—Of these three / Religions only one can be the true one.—/ A man like you does not remain where chance / Of birth has cast him: if he so remains, / It's out of insight, reasons, better choice. / Well, then! such insight I would share with you. / Let me the reasons know, which I have had / No time to ponder out. Reveal to me / The choice determined by these reasons plain—/ Of course in confidence—that I as well / May make your choice my own . . . "[29]

Nathan is startled by this unexpected question since he had expected Saladin to ask him for money. Granted a moment to think it over, Nathan asks himself:

"H'm! h'm!—how strange!—I'm all confused.—What would / The Sultan have of me?—I thought of money; / And he wants—truth. Yes, truth! And wants it so—/ So bare and blank—as if the truth were coin!—/ And were it coin, which anciently was weighed!—/ That might be done! But coin from modern mints, / Which but the stamp creates, which you but count / Upon the counter—truth is not like that! As one puts money in his purse, just so / One puts truth in his head? Which here is Jew? / Which, I or he?—But stay!—Suppose in truth / He did not ask for truth!—I must admit, / Suspicion that he used the truth as trap / Would be too small by far.—Too small?—What is / Too small for one so great?— That's right, that's right: / He rushed into the house incontinent! / One knocks, one listens, surely, when one comes / As friend.—I must tread warily!—But how?—/ To be a Jew outright won't do at all.—/ But not to be a Jew will do still less. / For if no Jew, he might well ask, then why / Not Mussulman?—That's it! And that can save me! / Not only children can be quieted / With fables.—See, he comes. Well, let him come!"[30]

This monologue, presented immediately before the scene in which Nathan tells Saladin the parable of the three rings, shows that the parable is produced in order to evade Saladin's baffling question. Just as the father in the parable had a jeweler make two rings so indistinguishable from the original that "the genuine ring was not / Demonstrable," so too there is "almost as little" possibility of demonstrating today which of the three religions—Judaism, Christianity, or Islam—is "the genuine faith."[31] This is what Nathan means to suggest by the parable.

Growing angry at Nathan's shrewd subterfuge, Saladin presses him for an answer: "You mean this as / The answer to my question? . . . / The rings!—Don't trifle with me!—I should think / That those religions which I named to you / Might be distinguished readily enough. / Down to their clothing; down to food and drink!"[32]

Nathan responds to Saladin's specious objection with this profound counterargument.

> "In all respects except their basic grounds.—/ Are they not grounded all in history, / Or writ or handed down?—But history / Must be accepted wholly upon faith—/ Not so?—Well then, whose faith are we least like / To doubt? Our people's, surely? Those whose blood / We share? The ones who from our childhood gave / Us proofs of love? who never duped us, but / When it was for our good to be deceived?—/ How can I trust my fathers less than you / Trust yours? Or turn about.—Can I demand / That to your forebears you should give the lie / That mine be not gainsaid? Or turn about. / The same holds true of Christians. Am I right?"[33]

An important theological assertion is contained in these words, not to mention important implications for the content of the parable of the three rings. This assertion may be characterized as a thesis regarding the grounds for the truth claim of a historical religion and the demonstrability of this claim. Indeed, Saladin's inquiry, the occasion for the parable, implicitly calls into question the grounds for the truth claim of a historical religion: "Of these three / Religions only one can be the true one.—/ A man like you does not remain where chance / Of birth has cast him: if he so remains, / It's out of insight, reasons, better choice. / . . . such insight I would share with you. / Let me the reasons know. . . . Reveal to me / The choice determined by these reasons plain." But Nathan's answer is that all historical religions can be distinguished "in all respects except their basic grounds" because they are "grounded all in history." Just as the genuineness or spuriousness of the three rings is not objectively demonstrable, so there is no possibility of rational proof that any one of the three religions—Judaism, Christianity, or Islam—is the true one.

The sentence to be lifted up for special attention here is "A man like you does not remain where chance / Of birth has cast him." Of particular importance is the expression "where chance / Of birth has cast him" (*wo der Zufall der Geburt / Ihn hingeworfen*). The question Saladin asks is: from what insight (*Einsicht*), for what reasons (*Gründen*), and by what choice (*Wahl*) has Nathan come to have his own faith rather than remaining where the "chance of birth" had cast him. This is precisely the question of the relationship between the historically accidental and the rationally necessary. It is evident that Lessing's famous thesis that "accidental truths of history can never become the proof for necessary truths of reason"[34] is implicitly suggested here.

Accordingly, we wish to examine Lessing's religious thought more closely, especially the idea of humanity that finds metaphorical expression in the parable of the three rings. As we do so, we intend to keep in mind his proposition as to "accidental truths of history" and "necessary truths of reason."

The Truth Claim of a Historical Religion in the Interim

The first point to notice when we read the parable of the three rings as a story is that the biblical view of history as a dramatic movement that proceeds from beginning to end is implicitly presupposed as a general framework. The premise that underlies the beginning of the story is the prehistory (*Urgeschichte*) in which man stands in close relationship with God.

According to the story, a man of ancient times who dwelt in eastern lands received a ring of priceless worth from the hand of God. This ring, adorned with an opal that radiated a hundred beautiful colors, had the magical power to make its bearer, if he wore it trusting in the strength of the stone, beloved of God and men. But with the passage of time, confusion arose. It turned out that there were actually three rings, each of which was alleged to be the original, genuine ring—though only one was supposed to be the true one. Faced with this unacceptable situation, each of the three bearers, insisting that the one in his possession was the only genuine ring, eventually went so far as to file a suit against the other two bearers. At the bar, however, no solution was forthcoming. "The modest judge" (*der bescheidne Richter*) left the final judgment to "a wiser man" (*ein weisrer Mann*) who would sit as judge on the bench when "a thousand thousand years" had passed. In other words, the question as to which of the three rings is the true one would find an answer only at the end of history. This shows that Lessing has basically presupposed the biblical or Judeo-Christian view of history as the general framework for his parable of the three rings.

In this historical framework, the present time is an "interim" between the beginning and the end of history. In the beginning, history knows no confusion or conflict because it has only one true ring that originates from God himself. At the end of history, one of the three rings will be demonstrated to be the true ring, thus putting an end to confusion and conflict. Thus unity and uniformity characterize both the beginning and the end of history, whereas plurality and disunity are characteristic of the interim. Everything in the interim is ambiguous and equivocal. For this very reason, the effort to demonstrate the truth by seeking out the facts is futile. The method of objective demonstration is useless because wheat and tares are inseparably mixed together in the present. As a result, it is quite impossible to make a decisive judgment about anything in this interim period of history.

Thus the "modest judge," fully aware of existing in this interim, gives up any attempt at "solving riddles" from the outset, gives up any attempt to determine the genuineness or spuriousness of the rings. He knows how far his discerning eye can see. In other words, he knows the limits of human reason. As a result, all he can do is to give "counsel, instead of verdict." But since it is necessary to make a preliminary or penultimate judgment as to the matter under dispute, the criterion for judgment must be sought in the magical power of the ring itself.[35] So he says, "But stop! I hear the genuine ring enjoys / The magic power to make its wearer loved, / Beloved of God and men. That must decide! / For spurious rings can surely not do that!" This criterion shows, however, that none of the three sons can meet the requirements for making the magic power of the ring reveal itself because they are all fighting each other. Each one lives for himself, loves himself first of all, so "the magic power to make its wearer loved, / Beloved of God and men" fails to show itself. To quote the modest judge's words, "The rings' effect is only backward, / Not outward? Each one loves himself the most? / O then you are, all three, deceived deceivers (*betrogene Betrieger*)!" This implies that the loving father might have deceived his beloved sons. But this too is impossible!

Is there any way out of this dilemma? According to the counsel of the modest judge, the only interim solution is to vindicate the claim for the genuineness of the ring by one's own religious and moral conduct. So the judge counsels the three as follows:

> "Accept the matter wholly as it stands. / If each one from his father has his ring, / Then let each one believe his ring to be / The true one . . . Let each aspire / To emulate his father's unbeguiled, / Unprejudiced affection! Let each strive / To match the rest in bringing to the fore / The magic of the opal in his ring! / Assist that power with all humility, / With benefaction, hearty peacefulness, / And with profound submission to God's will!"

In short, since it is impossible to demonstrate objectively the genuineness or spuriousness of the rings, the only way left for us is to strive, trusting in the goodwill of the bestower, to make ourselves worthy of being loved by God and men.

When we interpret the parable of the three rings in this way, we can see that this masterly fable accurately reflects Lessing's basic position in his theological controversy with Goeze. It is not without reason that *Nathan the Wise* is often called his *Anti-Goeze*, no. 12. As noted above, the original question that Saladin raised was which one of the three religions—Judaism, Christianity, or Islam—is the true religion. His question implicitly presupposes not only that "Of these three / Religions only one can be the true one" but also that the truth of the one true religion, whichever it may be, is demonstrable.

To begin with the second presupposition, Lessing clearly asserts through this parable that the truth claim of a historical religion cannot be objectively demonstrated. Just as the two extra rings the father ordered from the jeweler were so similar to the original that no one could tell which of the three rings was the genuine one, so in the case of Judaism, Christianity, and Islam, it is impossible to demonstrate that any one of the three is the genuine faith. The reason, as stated above, is that in this interim period of history, everything is ambiguous and equivocal. As Lessing puts it in another work, within history "truth moves under more than one form" (*Die Wahrheit rühret unter mehr als einer Gestalt*). To put it another way, all historical truths are partial and restricted and therefore to some extent untrue. In his epigraph to *The Education of the Human Race* Lessing cites Augustine's dictum, "Haec omnia inde esse in quibusdam vera, unde in quibusdam falsa sunt," words that will occupy us again in chapter 6 and that certainly relate to this way of thinking about historical truths.

How, then, does Lessing regard Saladin's first presupposition? He too thinks that "only one [religion] can be the true one"—but in a sense that differs from Saladin's idea. That is to say, Lessing does not think, as Saladin did, that among Judaism, Christianity, and Islam, only one is the true religion. The true religion in Lessing's sense is a religion that transcends all of the historical religions and yet underlies the truth of each. It is a religion based on real and universal humanity. Such a religion is not only one and universal; it also unifies people into a fellowship. In a word, it is Lessing's "religion of humanity."

If we interpret the parable of the three rings faithfully, it is true that only one of the three rings is genuine. The other two are fakes, no matter how closely they resemble the original. To this extent, there is no justification for the judge's conjecture that "Yours rings are false, all three. The genuine ring / No doubt got lost. To hide the grievous loss, / To make it good, the father caused three rings / To serve for one." Though we cannot discern it, one genuine·ring does exist among the three. When applied to the issue at stake, it might seem that the proper way to reason would be to hold that only one of the three historical religions is the true one, the other two being false. But this is certainly not correct reasoning from the standpoint of the parable. No careful reader of the story will be led to this conclusion. For the magic power of the opal in the genuine ring does not reveal itself so long as he who is lucky enough to possess it is fighting with his brothers as to the genuineness or spuriousness of the ring. Even though he has the genuine ring, he is not loved by God and men. But what will happen to one who has received a fake ring, "believ[ing] his ring to be / The true one," if he aspires "to emulate his father's unbeguiled, / Unprejudiced affection?" Will he not be loved by God and men? And if this be true, what, then, about the magic power of the ring? Is not such power a matter of indifference?

The real difficulty with the parable of the three rings lies at this point. But is "the magic power" (*die geheime Kraft*) of an opal set in a ring such a "magic or supernatural power" (*Zauberkraft*) that it will work automatically regardless of the bearer's personality or mode of life? It was said of the stone that it had "the magic power that he who wore it, / *Trusting* its strength, was loved of God and men" (italics added). In other words, a voluntary faith from the human side is the sine qua non of the effectiveness of the ring's miraculous power. To be so bold as to use a misleading term, a kind of *synergism* is presupposed from the outset.

In addition, the fake rings are "in all points identical" with the genuine ring, so no one, not even the owner of the original, can tell which are fake. Ought they not to have, then, magic powers similar to those of the original ring? If we think of the matter this way, we have to conclude that magical powers will disclose themselves even in the case of the two sons who received fake rings so long as they, in full compliance with the judge's counsel, strive to emulate the father's unbeguiled, unprejudiced love. On this view, synergism holds good even for the bearers of the fake rings.

Nathan and the Education of Humanity

So far, we have focused exclusively on the parable of the three rings. But in order to grasp the cardinal point of the religious thought that finds poetic expression in *Nathan the Wise*, it is necessary to take into consideration not only the parable of the three rings but also the entire work at the center of which the parable stands. A rough sketch of the play as a whole will be of some help here.

The setting for the play is Jerusalem at the time of the Crusades. Each character in the play represents, in one way or another, Judaism, Christianity, or Islam. A fire breaks out in the house of the Jewish merchant Nathan while he is away on business. His daughter, Rachel, narrowly escapes being burned to death, but is rescued thanks to a young Christian templar who happened by. This templar had originally been sent from Europe as a crusader. Arrested by Islamic troops, he had been condemned to the scaffold, but his life had been spared by a special pardon from the Sultan Saladin because the templar closely resembled Saladin's missing brother, Assad. Since then, he had been staying in Jerusalem as a free prisoner of war. Influenced by Daya, Nathan's fanatic Christian housemaid, Rachel at first yearns for the young man in a white mantle who had rescued her from the fire as if he were an angel sent from heaven. But her fantastic dreams are corrected by Nathan when he returns home. To the young man who had saved his beloved daughter, Nathan expresses his hearty thanks. The templar, for his part, though at first taking a somewhat contemptuous attitude toward Nathan, is deeply impressed by the noble personality and deep insight of the Jewish merchant. At the same time, his hitherto suppressed feeling for Rachel suddenly turns into burning love.

About this time Saladin, faced with a financial crisis in the national treasury, succumbs to his sister Sittah's idea of summoning the rich and wise Nathan to the palace as part of a trick. At his sister's suggestion, he reluctantly stoops to asking Nathan a question that will be almost impossible for a Jew to answer, thus hoping to frighten him into paying money so as to be pardoned for not answering Saladin's question. Nathan shrewdly evades the trap by telling the Sultan the parable of the three rings. Deeply moved by Nathan's virtuous and wise character, Saladin humbly bows to him and begs his pardon for the insipid wiles he had attempted. Nathan and Saladin thus become comrades, bound together by trust and friendship.

Meanwhile, the tale-telling Daya informs the templar that Rachel is not Nathan's real daughter but an adopted daughter who, having been born into a Christian family, had been baptized into Christianity at birth. Angry at the news that Nathan had reared a baptized Christian child as a Jewess, the templar grows distrustful of her foster father Nathan. In deep distress and fury, the templar consults with the Patriarch of Jerusalem. The matter is thus on the verge of developing into a major religious scandal.

The Patriarch, who takes pride in being the protector of Christianity, embarks on a personal investigation of Nathan with a view to bringing this unforgivable Jew to the Inquisition and burning him at the stake. But the ways of heaven are inscrutable. As the drama evolves, all the curtains covering the back of the stage are removed one by one until hidden truths eventually reveal themselves all at once. It turns out that the templar is the son of Saladin's younger brother, Assad, and the elder brother of Nathan's adopted daughter, Rachel. The drama has a happy ending with mutual embraces and kisses on the part of the Jew, the Christians, and the Muslims.

The governing idea central to the plot is, as most scholars agree, the idea of "humanity" (*Humanität, Menschlichkeit*). Each character in the play has a status and temperament that correspond to the degree or manner in which he or she embodies this idea.[36] The central character is, of course, Nathan the Wise. He is "the figure who embodies this humanity in the most comprehensive, most serene, and purest form."[37] His mind is free of prejudice, his heart "open unto every virtue, / With every beauty perfectly attuned."[38] He treats every individual as a person and of his own accord does away with every kind of prejudice caused by religious and racial differences. Thus "Nathan's greatness lies in his humanity."[39] This fair and upright quality is reflected in his words: "I know as well / That all lands bear good men."[40] Again, "What is a folk? / Are Jew and Christian sooner Jew and Christian / Than man? How good, if I have found in you / One more who is content to bear the name / Of man!"[41] In the play, Nathan plays the role of an "educator" (*Erzieher*) who, himself embodying the highest idea of humanity, teaches this idea to others through his noble personality and conduct.

The Sultan Saladin is a stalwart and large-minded man who embodies nearly as noble a humanity as Nathan does, though as yet he is not completely free from arrogance and whim.[42] This nobility appears clearly in his words to the templar: "Would you remain with me? Here at my side?—/ As Christian, Musselman, all one! In cloak / Of white, in Moslem robe; in turban, or / In Christian cowl: just as you will. All one! / I never have required the selfsame bark / To grow on every tree."[43] Thus Saladin has already reached a high stage of humanity, a stage only once removed from Nathan. Through personal encounter with the Jewish wise man, he is to be raised to the highest level of humanity.

Other characters in the play, with the exception of Daya and the Patriarch of Jerusalem, all have something to do, in varying degrees, with the ideal of humanity. The templar, with his youthful impetuosity and one-track mind, is sometimes driven by his passions to extremes. But he also has it in him to take a more universally human stance, ridding himself of the Christian prejudices imbued in him since birth.

> "The Templar loves indeed—the Christian loves / The Jewish maid indeed.—Well! What of that?—/ In this the Land of Promise—hence to me / Of Promise likewise to eternity!—I've rid myself of many a prejudice.—/ What would my Order have? As Templar, I / Am dead; was from that moment dead to it, / Which made me prisoner to Saladin. / That head which he gave back, was it my own?—/ No, it's a new one, ignorant of all / That was impressed on that one, bound it fast.—/ And better, too, for my paternal heaven / More suitable. I feel that now . . . "[44]

As the above quotation shows, the templar is quite ready to be raised to a higher humanity by Nathan and Saladin.

Nathan's adopted daughter, Rachel, is, so to speak, his artistic masterpiece[45] and an excellent product of his education.[46] Nathan sowed in her soul "the seeds of reason" (*Samen der Vernunft*)[47] and "taught this child not more or less of God / Than reason would require."[48] In Nathan's words, Rachel "was born / And reared to be of any faith and house / The ornament."[49] According to Fittbogen, Rachel is "already a step beyond Nathan" because "Nathan had to work out his way for himself, only gradually growing beyond his old faith, whereas Rachel stands 'beyond' every positive religion" from the outset. In this sense, she is said to be "the first female representative of the new humanity, completely unhindered from the restraints of any positive religion."[50]

The dervish Al-Hafi and the Christian friar, playing supporting roles, are not opposed to the genuine idea of humanity but stand in somewhat different relationships to it. "Al-Hafi embodies inwardness without its moral purification into humanity."[51] The friar, or lay brother, by contrast, is "an ironic figure, [ironic] in his mixture of shrewdness and simplicity, and in his dependence on external authority, on the one hand, and on simple moral conscience, on the other."[52] These two subordinate characters, though embodying the idea of humanity to some extent, still lack the moral purification essential to genuine humanity.

Finally, some mention must be made of the two characters who stand far removed from, or completely outside, the idea of humanity. The fanatically Christian housemaid Daya is an example of misguided humanity. She is still far from living by this ideal. Nevertheless, it is not yet utterly hopeless to guide her toward a better direction through education and irony. The Patriarch of Jerusalem, on the contrary, exists completely outside the idea of humanity. He is an incarnation of authoritarian faith and intolerance, qualities diametrically opposed to the idea of humanity. Nathan's efforts to teach him real humanity will be of no avail.[53]

On the basis of the preceding analysis, we have to ask, finally, what constitutes the real substance of the idea of humanity that the characters in the play embody in varying degrees. To be succinct, what is humanity anyway?

According to the formulation by Benno von Wiese, humanity is "first, emancipation from its historical existence; second, elevation to spiritual personality; third, optimism as to worldview and view of life." Moreover, "in these three characteristics are embodied the three basic ideas of the Enlightenment: suprahistorical validity, autonomous reason, and a harmonious picture of the world."[54] In itself, Wiese's characterization of humanity is correct, to be sure. But this alone is not enough to express the Lessingian idea of humanity. The depth of Lessing's idea can hardly be comprehended by such a general characterization. We need to clarify, therefore, the salient features of the reason exemplified by the wise Nathan. Our next task, then, is to explain the essence of Nathanian reason.

The Essence of Nathan's Reason

The depth dimension in the idea of humanity that Lessing wanted to express in this play seems implied by the last two words of its title, *Nathan the Wise*. The wise man, understood literally, is the man who possesses wisdom (*Weisheit*). What, then, is wisdom? What is Nathan's wisdom like? Why do people call him "the wise man"?[55]

In order to think about these questions, it will be helpful to examine some interesting material provided in a dialogue between Nathan and Saladin in Act 3, Scene 5.

> *Saladin:*   You say you're Nathan?
> *Nathan:*   Yes.
> *Saladin:*   Wise Nathan?
> *Nathan:*   No.
> *Saladin:*   If you don't say it, yet the people do.
> *Nathan:*   May be; the people!
> *Saladin:*   Yet you don't suppose
>   That I am scornful of the people's voice? —
>   I long have had a wish to know the man
>   Whom they call wise.
> *Nathan:*   And if it were in scorn
>   They called him so? If to the people "wise"
>   Were nothing more than "shrewd"? and shrewd were he
>   Who knew his interest well?
> *Saladin:*   Of course you mean
>   His genuine interest?
> *Nathan:*   Why then indeed
>   Most selfish were most shrewd. And shrewd and wise
>   Were one.
> *Saladin:*   I hear you prove what you'd deny. —
>   Mankind's true interests, to the folk unknown,
>   Are known to you; at least you've tried to know them;
>   You've pondered them; and that alone produces
>   The wise man.
> *Nathan:*   As each thinker thinks he is.
> *Saladin:*   Enough of modesty! For when one longs
>   To hear dry reason, constant modesty

Is sickening. (*He jumps up.*) Let's come to business, Jew.
But with sincerity![56]

The foregoing dialogue shows that Nathan does not think of himself as a wise man. According to him, it is only that the people call him so, and among the people, reputation is often expressed ironically. One may well discern a trace of cynicism in Nathan's utterance. The extreme humility that provokes Saladin's antipathy might seem to come from this cynicism.

In my view, however, Nathan's humility springs from a deeper source. In the conversation between Nathan and the friar in Act 4, Scene 7, the secret source of Nathan's existence becomes manifest. "[To] you alone I'll tell it. / To simple piety alone I'll tell it. / Since that alone can understand the deeds / God-fearing man can force himself to do."[57] With this introductory remark, Nathan begins to disclose to the friar a secret that he has never before spoken of to anyone.

According to Nathan's confession, his wife and seven sons were burned to death by Christians a few days before he made up his mind to adopt and nurture Rachel. Three days and nights he lay in dust and ashes, weeping bitter tears. He argued with God, stormed, became enraged, and cursed himself and the entire world. He swore that he hated all Christians, that he would never be reconciled with them. But in the midst of his despair and fury, he gradually regained his reason and became calm enough to obey what he wisely discerned as God's decree. In his own words:

"But bit by bit my reason found return. / With gentle voice it spoke: 'And yet God is! That too was God's decree! Up then, and come! Now practice what you long have understood; / And what is scarcely harder to perform / Than just to comprehend, if you but will. / Arise!'—I stood and cried to God: I will! / If Thou wilt, then I will!—Then you dismounted / And handed me the child, wrapped in your cloak."[58]

What Nathan the Jew had long understood in his head was nothing other than the supreme commandment of Christianity, the command to "Love thine enemy!" The way he put it into practice was to adopt an orphan baby of Christian parents and bring her up with genuine love and abundance of heart. That orphan child was, of course, Rachel. This action by the pious Jew accounts for the friar's exclamation: "O Nathan, Nathan! You're a Christian soul! / By God, a better Christian never lived!"[59]

Nathan had been visited by calamities that may well remind us of the tragic difficulties that befell the "blameless and upright" man in the Book of Job.[60] But gradually learning to cope, he regained his originally "cool, quiet reason" (*kalte, ruhige Vernunft*).[61] The gentle voice of his reason said to him, "And yet God is!" Of the tragic event that seemed so absurd and nonsensical in human eyes, his reason said, "That too was God's decree!" It then encouraged him to practice what he had long understood intellectually, what a later age would speak of as Good Samaritanism. He obediently followed his inner voice and determined to take his first step as a new self. From that moment, however, his volition is no longer merely autonomous volition. It is a volition that wishes to hearken to God's antecedent volition and conform to it. Nathan's words, "I will! / If Thou wilt, then I will!" (*Ich will! / Willst du nur, daß ich will!*), suggest that he, having lost everything and having wandered in the depths of despair, becomes a new, "theonomous" self, or more precisely, an "autotheonomous" self.[62]

From these considerations it is clear that Nathan, contrary to the generally held view, is not an autonomous person of the modern type. By the same token, his reason is not mere autonomous reason in the modern sense. The starting point of everything for Nathan as a wise man consists in the duplex or multiplex structure of volition, a structure implied in his words, "I will! / If Thou wilt, then I will!"[63] This may also be called a structure of autonomy buttressed by theonomy, a structure in which the divine volition is hidden behind the human but precedes and underlies it. Borrowing Troeltsch's term, we propose to call this the "autotheonomous" structure of volition.

In any case, Nathan's reason is, first and foremost, "hearkening reason" (*eine vernehmende Vernunft*).[64] It signifies "the ability to hearken to, and immediately become aware of, what is given by God."[65] Accordingly, it is not a self-centered reason that turns its back on God and shuts itself up within itself. Instead, it is "believing reason" (*glaubende Vernunft*) that opens itself to God and hearkens to admonitions from above. To borrow Hans Baumgartner's term but use it in a somewhat different way, it is "boundary reason" (*Grenzvernunft*) that is fully aware of its own limitations.[66] This kind of reason is what Ingrid Strohschneider-Kohrs calls "reason as wisdom" (*Vernunft als Weisheit*).[67] Johannes von Lüpke asserts that "Nathan's wisdom is based on reason that has become aware of its own limitations."[68] It appears, therefore, that Nathan's reason is not only fully aware of its own limitations but also conforms to the decrees of the deity who transcends his reason. Yet Nathan's reason is at the same time Lessing's. It seems indisputable, therefore, that this kind of "reason as wisdom" forms the essential core of Lessingian reason.[69]

Be that as it may, it is quite natural that a wise man like Nathan, possessing this "reason as wisdom," must admonish himself against "overstepping the limits" (*Grenzüberschreitungen*).[70] Though his modest and humble attitude irritated Saladin, for Nathan as a man of wisdom this attitude was perfectly natural. In this connection, it may be helpful to call attention to the fact that the judge in the parable of the three rings, through whom Lessing expresses his own opinion, is called "the modest judge" (*der bescheidne Richter*). As we have already seen, this judge too is a very wise man. Nevertheless, he does not venture to solve riddles by himself but leaves the final solution to the discretion of a wiser judge (*ein weiserr Mann*). This enables us to glimpse the Nathanian, and therefore Lessingian, understanding of existence.

So far we have observed, from our own viewpoint, Lessing's idea of humanity as it finds poetic and literary expression in *Nathan the Wise*. Though limited in scope, our observation demonstrated that Lessing's idea of humanity as "a new ideal of life" is suffused with deep piety. Far from being a bare affirmation of and praise for human nature as it stands, his new ideal of life constitutes a new form of Christian piety that sees life oriented to humanity as a correlate of life oriented to God. Distancing himself from the traditional Christianity that Goeze represented, Lessing, considering himself a "beloved bastard of a noble, gracious lord" (*lieber Bastard eines großen, gnädigen Herrn*),[71] strove to go back to the wellspring of Christianity and draw fresh water from it.[72] *Nathan the Wise* is undoubtedly the most brilliant literary product of, or better, an authentic monument to, such striving. And what glitters most brilliantly in this monumental work is the idea of humanity.

But Lessing did not stop short with this immortal work. He also wanted to give philosophical expression to what he had expressed poetically. This led him to produce his theological and religious-philosophical manifesto, *The Education of the Human Race*. Our next task, therefore, will be to explicate this book as clearly as possible on the basis of the results attained in this chapter.

6

Lessing's Basic Thought in *The Education of the Human Race*

In a tribute to the memory of Lessing, his senior by fifteen years, the romantic poet Johann Gottfried Herder, another advocate of "the ideal of humanity," made a significant comment about Lessing's last prose work: "It is well that Lessing completed his career with *a confession of faith* [that is, his alleged confession of Spinozism] and a booklet on *The Education of the Human Race*. For all its exaggerated hypotheses, the latter is a work that many theologians might wish to have written."[1] As this comment suggests, Lessing's *The Education of the Human Race* (1780) is widely regarded as a work that offers important clues to his theological and religious-philosophical thought.

According to Helmut Thielicke, who provided one of the most penetrating theological interpretations of Lessing's philosophy of religion in this century, "an intrinsically well-rounded system of . . . thought undoubtedly lies in *The Education of the Human Race*. For many reasons, therefore, it is recommended for the analysis of Lessing's esoteric theology, that is, his normative attitude in the conflict between religious faith in the transcendent and adhesion to the immanent."[2] Paul Tillich, another theologian, endorses this view when he says that one can perceive in this work "the most genuine spirit of Lessing, a really Lessingian mode of thought and speech."[3] Judging from the comments of these two theologians, we can safely assert that *The Education of the Human Race* is the manifesto of Lessing's theological and religious-philosophical thought.

Though full of antithetical statements, hypothetical assertions, mere hints, and the intentional concealment of some truths, this small book, composed of one hundred brief paragraphs, is a pithy expression of the results of Lessing's lifelong quest in pursuit of theology and philosophy of religion.[4] It can be read as containing his final convictions—or at least some clues as to what those convictions were. Accordingly, it is undoubtedly one of the most important works we have for discerning some of the key ideas in his "esoteric" theology.

Furthermore, this work is regarded by many as "the foundation of a modern philosophy of religion and the beginning of a deeper observation of history."[5] From this point of view, it is sometimes characterized as inaugurating the great idealist philosophy of Germany. Wilhelm Lütgert, for example, maintains:

The idealist philosophy of history begins with Lessing's *The Education of the Human Race*. By sketching a historical worldview, he stepped over the horizon of the Enlightenment. Through this attempt, he belongs to the fathers of German idealism. He knew no such thing as reason that is the same and complete at all times. Instead, by understanding history as a developmental process of reason, he drew reason into history. He was the first man to apply the concept of development to history. Lessing's philosophy of history is religious and theological. The authentic core of history for him is the history of religions.[6]

This is an eloquent statement as to the significance of *The Education of the Human Race* for the history of ideas in early nineteenth-century Germany. It does not mean, however, that Lessing's basic thought as contained in this work is so evident that no special effort is needed to discern it. Quite the contrary. In fact, it is not too much to say that the ambiguity of his philosophy of religion, notorious for its ironical expressions and paradoxical assertions, reaches its climax in this, his final work. The difficult problem of the "exoteric" and "esoteric" with which every Lessing scholar has been confronted reaches its acme here. Consequently, proper understanding of the work calls for hard and painstaking labor. It is a task of grasping Lessing's real intentions and identifying the esoteric convictions hidden under, or behind, the exoteric statements. The subtle maneuvers and tricks Lessing has employed will easily mislead the superficial reader who is unable to fathom Lessing's innermost spirit. As a result, this work has given rise to diametrically opposed interpretations, causing Lessing the theologian or Lessing the philosopher of religion to remain enigmatic to the present day.

Our main task in this chapter, therefore, is to unravel the basic thought of Lessing's philosophy of religion as contained in his *The Education of the Human Race*. We embark on this task by undertaking a detailed reading and comprehensive interpretation of the German original.

Basic Features of *The Education of the Human Race*

It has already been shown that Lessing's thought is eminently polemical, antithetical, "gymnastic," and hypothetical.[7] This is especially true of *The Education of the Human Race*, where his mode of thought and description has been characterized as highly "fragmentary, antithetical, hypothetical-tactical—and in every respect pedagogical."[8] According to Martin Haug, "we may often regard Lessing's apparent propositions as actually no more than hypotheses."[9] It may safely be said, moreover, that by the very nature of how it came into being, this work is "a batch of 'counterpropositions'" (*ein Stück der "Gegensätze"*).[10] What, then, were the propositions to which the counterpropositions were opposed? These, needless to say, were the radical propositions advanced by Reimarus, the anonymous writer whose manuscripts Lessing had published under the title *Fragments from an Unnamed Author*.

It was Eastertime 1780, one year before Lessing's death, that *The Education of the Human Race* appeared in book form. The first half, however, (paragraphs 1 through 53) had already appeared three years earlier, appended to the *Fragments* as part of the "Editor's Counterpropositions." When he published the first half, Lessing did not reveal that he himself was the author of these paragraphs, but pretended that they had been borrowed from "a small essay in handwritten form" that had been circulating "among a certain circle of friends for a few years."[11] The first half was originally issued to enunciate the assertions with which the editor proposed to counter the unnamed author's fourth fragment. At least this part, therefore, may be characterized as Lessing's counterpropositions to Reimarus's proposition "that the books of the Old Testament were not written to reveal a religion."

Reimarus's line of argument is consistent with his rationalistic presuppositions. On his view, a "revealed religion" is "a supernatural beatific religion" that must contain among its essential doctrines three tenets: (1) "immortality of the soul," (2) "future reward and punishment in an everlasting life," and (3) "the union of devout souls with God in ever-greater glorification and beatitude."[12] As this definition shows, Reimarus's basic position is generally that of deism. According to the rationalistic conception of religion derived from the English deists, what has been revealed must be true, but only what accords with reason is true. A revealed religion, therefore, must be both true and reasonable; that is, it must contain all the fundamental truths of rational religion. These fundamental truths are the concept of God, the obligation to do the good and be rewarded for doing so, and the immortality of the soul. As unflinching historico-critical study shows, however, the Old Testament does not contain the doctrine of the immortality of the soul, nor does it know anything of reward and punishment in an afterworld. Consequently, the religion of the Old Testament lacks two of the essential characteristics of rational religion. Because of this lack, it cannot be in accord with reason, and therefore cannot be revealed. This, in brief, is Reimarus's argument.

Over against Reimarus's bold assertion, Lessing, in his "Editor's Counterpropositions," offers his own argument. To be sure, he agrees with Reimarus on subjecting the biblical accounts to radical historical criticism, and he subscribes to Reimarus's conclusion that the doctrine of the immortality of the soul is lacking in the Old Testament. Taking a step beyond Reimarus, Lessing even goes so far as to advance the bold conjecture that the books of the Old Testament, or the Jewish people before the Babylonian captivity, did not have "the true conception of the One." That is to say, he suggests that genuine monotheism, said to be the primary element of rational religion, was lacking in the first stage of Old Testament religion. Nevertheless, he resolutely rejects Reimarus's conclusion "that the books of the Old Testament were not written to reveal a religion." What made Lessing's seemingly paradoxical view possible was a brand new idea, alien both to Lutheran orthodoxy and to deistic rationalism. Though deistic rationalism objected to Lutheran orthodoxy, particularly with regard to the doctrine of verbal inspiration, these two ways of thinking were at one in their implicit premise. Both presupposed that revealed religion must *always* contain the rational truths of God's unity and of the immortality of the soul. Lessing, in contrast, contends that revelation does *not* necessarily contain *all* the content of rational religion *from the outset*. If we assume, he argues, that human reason develops slowly and gradually, and that truths now evident to all were once difficult for most people to understand, it follows that *all* the contents of rational religion need not be fully revealed from the first. Would it not be wiser to think that some truths, rather than being revealed all at once, were held in reserve at the early stages when human reason was still undeveloped, still too immature to grasp rational truths? If this assumption is correct, what Reimarus criticizes as the "unreasonable" (*nichtvernünftig*) aspects of the Old Testament can also be taken as signifying "not yet reasonable" (*noch-nicht-vernünftig*). In this case, they need not be understood as "contrary to reason" (*contra rationem*). Accordingly, they do not prove that the books of the Old Testament are contrary to revelation.[13]

The paragraph above gives the gist of the "counterpropositions" (*Antithese*) that Lessing formulated in opposition to Reimarus's "propositions" (*These*). To buttress his assertions without revealing himself as the author, he produced an excerpt from a handwritten form of what later became *The Education of the Human Race*. Three years later, he used this excerpt to form the first fifty-three paragraphs of *The Education of the Human Race*. We turn now to an examination of the structure of this book.

Basic Structure of *The Education of the Human Race*

The Education of the Human Race is a small book of precisely one hundred paragraphs. The first fifty-three paragraphs, forming one section of the "Editor's Counterpropositions," are presented as a "foretaste" (*Vorschmack*).[14] The remaining forty-seven paragraphs were added when *The Education of the Human Race* was published in book form. By slightly modifying Martha Waller's structural divisions,[15] we can divide the book into six main parts, some with several subdivisions. The six parts and their subdivisions are as follows:[16]

A. Editor's Preface
B. Basic Theses Concerning the Relationship between Revelation and Education (§§1–5)
C. Primitive History (§§6–7)
D. Jewish History (§§8–50)
   1. The Jews before the Babylonian Captivity (§§8–33)
     a) The Israelite in Egypt (§§8–10)
     b) The Jewish Idea of God (§§11–15)
     c) Moral Laws (§§16–17)
     d) Vindication of Jewish History (§§18–33)
   2. The Jews after the Babylonian Captivity (§§34–50)
     a) The Concept of God (§§34–41)
     b) The Beginning of the Doctrine of the Immortality of the Soul (§§42–46)
     c) The Old Testament Scriptures as the First Primer (§§47–50)

E. History of Christianity (§§51–75)
   1. Transition (§§51–57)
   2. The Person and Teaching of the Christ (§§58–61)
   3. Propagation of Christianity (§§62–63)
   4. The New Testament Scriptures as the Second, Better Primer (§§64–67)
   5. Demonstrations that the Doctrines of the New Testament Are Rational (§§68–75)
       a) References to Doctrines Already Proved to be Rational (§§68–72)
       b) Demonstration that Doctrines Regarded as Suprarational Are Actually Rational (§§73–75)
           (a) The Doctrine of the Trinity (§73)
           (b) The Doctrine of Original Sin (§74)
           (c) The Doctrine of Redemption (§75)
F. "A New Eternal Gospel" for the Third Age (§§76–100)
   1. Transition: The Significance of Developing Revealed Truths into Rational Truths (§§76–80)
   2. Ethics of the "Eternal Gospel" (§§81–86)
   3. Comments on the Enthusiasts of the Thirteenth and Fourteenth Centuries (§§87–90)
   4. The "Eternal Gospel" and the Idea of Reincarnation (§§91–100)
       a) Faith in Providence as the Basis for the Idea of Reincarnation (§§91–93)
       b) Hypotheses for Reincarnation (§§94–100)

No matter how the one hundred paragraphs are divided, what is of crucial importance is the basic thesis, contained in the first few paragraphs, concerning the relationship between revelation and education. (It should be noted that the theses on these topics, in addition to being hypotheses, are also antitheses!) The remaining paragraphs are merely illustrations or applications of the basic thesis with regard to Jewish history in the Old Testament age and to Christian history in the New Testament age.

Because assertions in later paragraphs depend on the basic assertions of the first few paragraphs, we must focus our energies on analysis of these basic assertions. Before doing so, however, we should first give attention to the epigraph placed at the beginning of the book and also to the "Editor's Preface," both of which were added when all paragraphs had been finished and the book was about to be published. They provide, in our view, an important perspective from which to understand the book correctly.

Lessing's Historical Position

Most of Lessing's writings during the period of the fragments controversy open with a citation in Latin or Greek taken from the church fathers or from ancient writers. *The Education of the Human Race* likewise opens with a quotation from one of the classical languages. Taken from Augustine's *Soliloquies* 2, 10, the citation reads: "Haec omnia inde esse in quibusdam vera, unde in quibusdam falsa sunt."[17] What significance does this epigraph have for understanding the content of Lessing's discussions in the book? Is it a mere embellishment with no particular meaning at all?

According to Eckhard Heftrich, Lessing's use of classical phrases for epigraphs was not merely a matter of conformity to the custom of the day, nor was it merely for the purpose of showing off his erudition. In choosing an epigraph, says Heftrich, Lessing presupposes "the erudite reader who, like himself, sees not merely the isolated sentence but also knows, or looks for, the context in which the sentence originally stands."[18] It is only to such a reader, he goes on, that it matters whether the cited phrase is faithful to the original text and context, or whether the original meaning is slightly altered or intentionally skewed. How is it, then, with Lessing's citation from Augustine? As Heftrich sees it, "With this motto, Lessing seemingly refers to the authority of Augustine; in reality, however, he twists the sentence of this authority, expecting that the reader will recognize and understand what lies behind this twisting of the original meaning."[19]

In this connection, it will be helpful to inquire into the nature of Augustine's *Soliloquies*. This is a work comprising a fictitious dialogue between the author and "Reason." The dialogue centers on the locus of truth and its absoluteness, to which the immortality of the soul is closely related. Reason, by heaping up roundabout arguments, endeavors to convince the author that truth is eternal and the soul immortal. It induces the author to consider what separates the false from imitation, implying that a man painted on a canvas or an actor on the stage is in some respects true and in other respects false. It suggests to him "that all these things are in certain aspects true, by this very thing that they are in certain aspects false." Reason then asks him the following question: "Wherefore, if it avails some things that they be somewhat false in order that they may be somewhat true; why do we so greatly dread falsity, and seek truth as the greatest good?" To this rhetorical question the author's answer is: "We ought . . . to seek that truth, which is not, as if laid out on a bifronted and self-repugnant plan, false on one side that it may be true on the other." Satisfied with this answer, Reason eventually declares: "High and Divine are the things which thou requirest."[20]

Heftrich, after comparing the original context and the new, comes to the conclusion that Lessing is here trying to sever Augustine's phrase from its original context in order to make it serve his own "model for thinking about history" (*ein Denkungsmodell von Geschichte*).[21] Willi Oelmüller seems to concur when he says—quite aptly, in our view—that Lessing has transformed Augustine's phrase into one that connotes "historical ambivalence" (*die geschichtliche Ambivalenz*).[22] Lessing has twisted the meaning, Oelmüller avers, to make the phrase imply that "the present *still* belongs to the second age, yet *already* belongs to the third."[23] That is to say, the citation from Augustine turns out to be instrumental to the famous theory that Lessing espouses in the latter part of the book, the theory of the "Three Ages of the World."

The question that arises most acutely here is that of the "*locus* of truth" (Ort *der Wahrheit*) and the "point of view" (*Gesichtspunkt*) from which truth is sought.[24] This inevitably leads to the further question as to the "position" or the "standpoint" (*Standort*)[25] of the author of *The Education of the Human Race*. Where does he stand? The "Editor's Preface" has much to do with this question. There Lessing states:

> I have published the first half of this essay in my *Contributions*. Now I am in a position to give the remainder.
>
> The author has set himself upon a high eminence from which he believes it possible to see beyond the limits of the allotted path of his present day's journey. But he does not call away from his road any wanderer hastening home whose one desire is to reach his night's lodging. He does not ask that the view which enchants him should also enchant every other eye.
>
> And so, I would suppose, he may be allowed to stand and wonder where he stands and wonders. Would that from the immeasurable distance which a soft evening glow neither entirely conceals nor wholly reveals to his gaze, he could bring some guiding hint, for which I have often felt myself at a loss!
>
> This is what is in my mind. Why are we not more willing to see in all positive religions simply the process by which alone human understanding in every place can develop, and must still further develop, instead of either ridiculing or becoming angry with them? In the best world there is nothing that deserves this scorn, this indignation we show. Are religions alone to deserve it? Is God to have part in everything except our mistakes?[26]

It is to be noted, first of all, that Lessing is posturing here as if he were no more than an editor (*Herausgeber*). He is pretending that the editor, or "I" (*ich*), and the author (*Verfasser*) are quite different persons.[27] Why did he contrive this fictitious construction?[28] Was the fabrication due to a desire to be consistent with what he had once said to Johann Albert Reimarus? For to this trusted friend he had said, "*The Education of the Human Race* was [written] by a good friend, who is fond of making various hypotheses and systems for the pleasure of tearing them to pieces again."[29] Or was it rather the case that he did not wish to present this book as his own work because it consisted largely of hypothetical counterassertions to the assertions of other thinkers? Such motives may have played a role, but there seems to have been yet another reason. Our conjecture is that Lessing's fabrication of an anonymous author had something to do with the structure of Augustine's *Soliloquies*, a fictitious dialogue between Augustine and Reason. That is to say, it is a dialogue that takes place within Augustine's mind and is therefore a monologue. Erwin Quapp seems to endorse our conjecture when he says, "The fiction of an [anonymous] author is . . . a figure necessary for an inner dialogue."[30]

Let us examine, then, the content of the editor's preface. The author claims to stand on "a high eminence" that is "beyond the limits" of the historical horizon of his contemporaries. From this height he "believes it possible to see" what is still invisible to them or hidden from them. The view and knowledge now available to him are superior to those that have hitherto prevailed. But he does not insist that his newly acquired view and knowledge be recognized as *objectively* and *absolutely* superior; neither will he force them on others. He is remarkably humble. He merely "believes" that he can see "something more" (*etwas mehr*) than what is currently accessible to the limited view of his contemporaries. "He does not ask that the view which enchants him should also enchant every other eye." And so, he modestly suggests, "he may be allowed to stand and wonder where he stands and wonders." That is to say, his contemporaries, still confined within the ordinary knowledge of the time, should not be allowed to prevent him from pursuing the new knowledge dawning upon him!

Yet no matter how high it may be, and what a superior view it may command, the place where the author stands is still a point within history. The consummation of history lies at an "immeasurable distance" from the place he now stands; it must be looked forward to and awaited in the future.[31] Accordingly, as "a soft evening glow is neither entirely concealed from nor wholly revealed to his gaze,"[32] so the whole truth to be manifested at the consummation of history is neither fully revealed to nor entirely concealed from him. Thus the author's position, to use Oelmüller's term again, is one of "historical ambivalence." This implies that truth as known in the present is ambiguous (*zweideutig*). It is in this sense that Lessing, in his epigraph, cites Augustine's words from the *Soliloquies*: "All these things are in certain aspects true, by this very thing that they are in certain aspects false."[33]

Nonetheless, Lessing entertains a secret expectation: the expectation that the author might possibly "bring some guiding hint, for which I have often felt myself at a loss!" The guiding hint is that the history of the human race, especially the history of religions, may be seen as the locus of a process whereby human reason is educated, developed, and brought to completion. This expectation, this hint, will help us to examine the arguments Lessing presents in this book.

Revelation as the Education of the Human Race

The main section of the book begins with the seemingly innocuous proposition that "what education is to the individual man, revelation is to the whole human race" (§1). This is followed by the supplementary proposition that "education is revelation coming to the individual man; and revelation is education which has come, and is still coming, to the human race" (§2). Lessing then asserts the great advantage to theology of conceiving revelation as the educating of the human race. "Whether it can be of any advantage to the science of instruction to consider education from this point of view I will not here inquire; but in theology it may unquestionably be of great advantage, and may remove many difficulties, if revelation be conceived of as an education of the human race" (§3).

Lessing then sets forth the sensational proposition: "Education gives man nothing which he could not also get from within himself; it gives him that which he could get from within himself, only quicker and more easily. In the same way too, revelation gives nothing to the human race which human reason could not arrive at on its own; only it has given, and still gives to it, the most important of these things sooner" (§4). This categorical proposition is accompanied by the hypothetical assertion: "And just as in education, it is not a matter of indifference in what order the powers of a man are developed, as it cannot impart to a man everything at once; so also God had to maintain a certain order and a certain measure in his revelation" (§5).

It is not too much to say that the assertions of greatest importance in *The Education of the Human Race* are contained in these first five propositions. The question we must begin with is whether it is appropriate to conceive revelation in analogy to education as Lessing is doing. It should be noted, in this connection, that the idea of conceiving revelation in analogy to education is not original with Lessing. He is by no means the first to interpret God's salvation history as God's education of the human race. According to Karlmann Beyschlag, a historian of Christian doctrine, the expression "the education of the human race" originates with the phrase "humani generis recta eruditio," found in Augustine's *De Civitate Dei*, book 10, chapter 14.[34] But the idea itself goes back to the New Testament, especially the apostle Paul. The most conspicuous example is Galatians 3:24: "ὥστε ὁ νόμος παιδαγωγὸς ἡμῶν γέγονεν εἰς Χριστόν" (RSV: "So that the law was our custodian until Christ came"). Similar ideas or expression can be found here and there in the New Testament.[35] Moreover, the idea of "the education of the human race" has been taken over by apostolic fathers, apologists, and eminent church fathers of antiquity such as Irenaeus, Tertullian, Clement of Alexandria, and Origen.[36] "Throughout the patristics," says Hans Liepmann, "this line of thought can be pursued further, of course, and especially beyond Augustine into the ·Scholastics."[37] In the High Middle Ages, this idea came to be combined with the individual believer's personal development in faith and was generally accepted in this combined form. The reformer Martin Luther also referred to it. In the seventeenth and early eighteenth centuries, we can find this line of thought in Johannes Coccejus, the father of "federal theology," and in such Pietists as Bengel, Oetinger, and Zinzendorf. Piepmeier puts it more generally: "For the theology of the Enlightenment, the idea of the education of the human race combined with accommodation theory was fundamental."[38] This being the case, Lessing, with his thorough knowledge of contemporary theology as well as of patristics, must have been quite familiar with the idea of the education of the human race.

Given this state of affairs, it appears that neither the conception of revelation as analogous to education nor the idea of the education of the human race is in itself unique to Lessing. If there is anything new in Lessing's adventure of ideas, it must be due to fresh content poured into the old vessel of the education of the human race. This novel content can be identified as the idea of the development of human reason, an idea already suggested in §5, where Lessing says, "just as in education, it is not a matter of indifference in what order the powers of a man are developed." The powers of a man, however, cannot be developed all at once (*auf einmal*), but must be developed step by step from the ground up. Yet once the gradual development of human powers (including human reason) is assumed, the idea of revelation as educating human reason is forced, in turn, to undergo substantial change. To reveal things that human reason is unprepared to receive would be "the same fault in the divine rule as is committed by the vain schoolmaster who chooses to hurry his pupil too rapidly and boast of his progress, rather than thoroughly to ground him" (§17). On this view, God would have to reveal himself slowly, and by degrees, in accordance with the degree of development in human reason. Accommodation theory, as Enlightenment theology employed it for biblical interpretation, might seem to imply a similar conclusion.[39] Lessing is probably the first, however, to have conceived and given bold expression to the idea of divine revelation as "progressive revelation" (*die fortschreitende Offenbarung*).[40]

To conceive of the idea of revelation after the model of education would seem to involve a grave difficulty. For education can only bring out latent talent or capacity; it cannot develop what does not at least potentially exist. If revelation is viewed in this light, the question arises as to whether revelation can do anything more than to help human reason develop what it is already endowed with by nature. Furthermore, revelation modeled on education implies something else. In the case of education, the educator has to accommodate himself or herself to the level of those being educated. And when they have fully developed their latent talents or capacities, they will eventually do without their educator. This being the case, will not revelation modeled after education eventually become useless? As noted above, §4 audaciously declares, "Education gives man nothing which he could not also get from within himself; it gives him that which he could get from within himself, only quicker and more easily. In the same way too, revelation gives nothing to the human race which human reason could not arrive at on its own; only it has given, and still gives to it, the most important of these things sooner."

But is revelation that "gives nothing to the human race which human reason could not arrive at on its own" worthy of the name? Lessing once asked, "What, then, is a revelation that reveals nothing?"[41] The question implies that it is because it reveals something that the term "revelation" applies. And only that which transcends the bounds of human reason can reveal something. The suspicion arises, therefore, that the revelation Lessing advocates for the education of the human race in §4 is merely an exoteric expression by which to camouflage the immanent development of human reason. On the face of it, Karl Aner seems quite right when he declares that "in Lessing the supernaturalness of 'revelation' is mere appearance."[42]

The crucial question with regard to Lessing's concept of revelation is whether revelation in the Lessingian sense is worthy of divine, transcendent revelation, or whether it is merely another name for immanently developing human reason. Most Lessing scholars, in discussing *The Education of the Human Race*, concentrate on the question of the relationship between the transcendence of divine revelation and the immanence of human reason. As mentioned earlier, however, diametrically opposed interpretations are numerous. Most researchers have reached a conclusion similar to that proposed by Aner,[43] whereas such scholars as Helmut Thielicke and Otto Mann maintain the transcendent nature of Lessing's concept of revelation.[44] For our part, we wish to examine this question without prejudgment by meticulously reading the original text and interpreting it against the background of our survey in the preceding chapters.

Revelation and Reason: (1) The Old Testament Age

In order to gain a firm grasp of the relation between divine revelation and human reason in *The Education of the Human Race*, we propose to extract the essence or outline of Lessing's arguments from the text, setting to one side merely rhetorical statements and unimportant details. We begin by summarizing paragraphs 6 through 53.

Human reason was at first immature and imperfect. "Even though the first man was furnished at once with a conception of the One God; yet it was not possible that this conception, freely imparted and not won by experience, should subsist long in its clearness. As soon as human reason, left to itself, began to elaborate it, it broke up the one immeasurable into many measurables" (§6) and treated each of them as divine. "Hence naturally arose polytheism and idolatry." Accordingly, "for . . . many millions of years human reason would have been lost in these errors, . . . had it not pleased God to afford it a better direction by means of a new impulse" (§7). So God "selected an individual people for his special education; and that the most rude and the most ferocious, in order to begin with it from the very beginning" (§8). "This was the Hebrew people" (§9). "To this rude people God caused himself to be announced at first simply as 'the God of their fathers'" (§11). With miracles God "led them out of Egypt and planted them in Canaan" (§12). "Demonstrating himself to be the mightiest of all, . . . he gradually accustomed them to the idea of the One" (§13).

But "this conception of the One" was far inferior to "the true transcendental conception of the One" (§14). This accounts for the fact that the Hebrew people "so often abandoned their one God, and expected to find the One . . . in some other god belonging to another people" (§15). "But of what kind of moral education was a people so raw, so incapable of abstract thoughts, and so entirely in their childhood, capable?" They were capable of "none other but such as is adapted to the age of children, an education by rewards and punishments addressed to the senses" (§16).

Because the Israelite as yet "envisaged nothing beyond this life," "as yet God could give to his people no other religion, no other law than one through obedience to which they might hope to be happy, or through disobedience to which they must fear to be unhappy." Therefore, they "knew of no immortality of the soul; they yearned after no life to come." Nevertheless, had God revealed these things "when their reason was so little prepared for them," it would have been "the same fault in the divine rule as is committed by the vain schoolmaster who chooses to hurry his pupil too rapidly and boast of his progress, rather than thoroughly to ground him" (§17).

But "to what purpose," then, was this education of the Jewish people? Lessing replies: it was "that in the process of time he might all the better employ particular members of this nation as the teachers of all other peoples." God was "bringing up in them the future teachers of the human race." "These were Jews, these could only be Jews, only men from a people which had been educated in this way" (§18).

"When the child by dint of blows and caresses had grown and was now come to years of understanding, the Father sent it of a sudden into foreign lands: and here it recognized at once the good which in its Father's house it had possessed, and not been conscious of" (§19). "While God guided his chosen people through all the degrees of a child's education, the other nations of the earth had gone on by the light of reason. The most part had remained far behind the chosen people. Only a few had got in front of them" (§20). But the fact that a few heathen nations "hitherto seemed to be ahead of the chosen people even in the knowledge of God" serves to "prove nothing against a revelation." "The child of education begins with slow but sure footsteps; it is late in overtaking many a more happily placed child of nature; but it *does* overtake it; and thenceforth can never be overtaken by it again" (§21).

Likewise, "the fact that the doctrine of immortality . . . is not to be found in [the Old Testament], but is wholly foreign to it, and all the related doctrine of reward and punishment in a future life" proves "just as little against the divine origin" (§22) of the books of the Old Testament. For "a primer for children may fairly pass over in silence this or that important piece of the science or art which it expounds, when the teacher considers that it is not yet suitable for the capabilities of the children for whom he was writing." But even such a primer "must contain absolutely nothing which bars the way to the knowledge which is held back, or which misleads the children away from it. Rather, all the approaches towards it must be carefully left open" (§26). In the same way, "the doctrines of the immortality of the soul, and future recompense, might be fairly left out" of "the writings of the Old Testament, those primers for the Israelitish people" (§27).

As yet the Israelite people as a whole did not entertain the slightest thought of the immortality of the soul or of a life to come. "It was impossible that daily experience should confirm" these doctrines, "or else it would have been all over, for ever, with the people who had this experience, so far as all recognition and reception were concerned of the truth as yet unfamiliar to them" (§30). Rather, "an Israelite here and there [may] directly and expressly have denied the immortality of the soul and future recompense, on the grounds that the law had no reference to it." The denial of these doctrines by an individual Israelite, however, "did not arrest the progress of the common reason, and was in itself, even, a proof that the nation had now taken a great step nearer to the truth." For "to think over an idea about which before no one troubled himself in the least, is half-way to knowledge" (§31).

Furthermore, "it is a heroic obedience to obey the laws of God simply because they are God's laws . . . even though there be an entire despair of future recompense, and uncertainty respecting a temporal one" (§32). "A people educated in this heroic obedience towards God" must be "destined" and be "capable beyond all others of executing divine purposes of quite a special character" (§33).

As yet the conceptions that the Jewish people held of their God "were not exactly the right conceptions" of the one, eternal God. "However, now the time was come for these conceptions of theirs to be expanded, ennobled, rectified, to accomplish which God availed himself of a perfectly natural means" (§34). They "began, in captivity under the wise Persians, to measure him against the 'Being of all Beings,' such as a more disciplined reason recognized and worshipped" (§35). "Revelation had guided their reason, and now, all at once, reason gave clearness to their revelation" (§36). "This was the first reciprocal influence which these two (reason and revelation) exercised on one another." And for God "such a mutual influence" was "far from unbecoming" (§37).

The Jewish people, sent into foreign lands, saw other peoples who were better off both intellectually and morally, and asked themselves, in confusion, "Why do I not know that too? Why do I not live so too? Ought I not to have learnt and acquired all this in my Father's house?" Thereupon they again "sought out its primer, which had long been thrown into a corner, in order to push the blame on to the primer." But they discovered that "the blame [did] not rest upon books, but the blame [was] solely [their] own, for not having long ago known this very thing, and lived in this very way" (§38). "The Jews, by this time, through the medium of the pure Persian doctrine, recognized in their Jehovah not simply the greatest of all national deities, but God" (§39).

"Thus enlightened respecting the treasures which they had possessed without knowing it, they returned, and became quite another people" (§40). "The theologians have tried to explain this complete change in the Jewish people in different ways." But it is only explicable when one "presupposes the exalted ideas of God as they now are" (§41). No doubt, "the Jews became better acquainted with the doctrine of immortality among the Chaldeans and Persians. They became more familiar with it, too, in the schools of the Greek philosophers in Egypt" (§42). Since the doctrine of the immortality of the soul did not correspond to their scriptures, however, "previous exercising was necessary, and as yet there had been only *hints* and *allusions*" (§43) in their scriptures. "Such exercises, allusions, hints" constitute "the *positive* perfection of a primer," while the quality of "not putting difficulties or hindrances in the way to the truths that have been withheld" comprises "its *negative* perfection" (§47).

"But every primer is only for a certain age. To delay the child, that has outgrown it, longer at it than was intended, is harmful." For the only profitable way "to be able to do this" would be to "insert into it more than there is really in it, and extract from it more than it can contain." One "must look for and make too much of allusions and hints; squeeze allegories too closely; interpret examples too circumstantially; press too much upon words." Yet this "gives the child a petty, crooked, hairsplitting understanding: it makes him full of mysteries, superstitions, full of contempt for all that is comprehensible and easy" (§51). These were "the very way in which the Rabbis handled *their* sacred books" and "the very character" that "they thereby imparted to the spirit of their people!" (§52). "A better instructor must come and tear the exhausted primer from the child's hands—Christ came!" (§53).

The arguments outlined above contain nothing in particular to cavil at from a Christian standpoint, but represent, rather, an excellent "apologetic of revelation." This apologetic offers a formidable refutation to Reimarus's caustic criticism of the Christian understanding of revelation.

To recapitulate, "human reason, left to itself" (*die sich selbst überlassene menschliche Vernunft*) (§6), lapsed into the errors (*Irrwege*) of polytheism and idolatry quite "naturally." "Had it not pleased God to afford it a better direction by means of a new impulse," it "would have been lost in these errors" for some millions of years (§7). God selected "the most rude and the most ferocious" people for his special education, "in order to begin with it from the very beginning" (§8). This was the deliberate decision of a wise schoolmaster who knew how important it was "thoroughly to ground" (§17) his pupil. God did not commit the folly of imparting everything at once (§5). "To reveal . . . things, when [human] reason was so little prepared for them," would have been to commit the same fault as that committed by "the vain schoolmaster who chooses to hurry his pupil too rapidly and boast of his progress" (§17). God chose to guide human reason to higher truths "gradually" (*allmählig*) (§13). When the Jewish people "by dint of blows and caresses had grown and was come to years of understanding," he sent them "of a sudden" (*auf einmal*) into foreign lands. There they recognized "at once" (*auf einmal*) the good which they had possessed in their homeland, but had not been aware of (§19). While God guided the Jewish people "through all the degrees of a child's education," the other nations of the earth had gone on "by the light of reason." Though most of these nations had remained "far behind" the chosen people, a few nations had got "in front" of them (§20). But these few nations, if more advanced even in the knowledge of God, "prove nothing against a revelation." "The child of education begins with slow but sure footsteps; it is late in overtaking many a more happily placed child of nature; but it *does* overtake it; and thenceforth can never be overtaken by it again" (§21).

The conception of God that the Jewish people had hitherto entertained was not as yet "the true transcendental conception of the One" (*der wahre transzendentale Begriff des Einigen*). But now the time had come for their conception of God to "be expanded, ennobled, rectified" (§34). During the Babylonian captivity, they began to measure God against the "Being of all Beings" (*das Wesen aller Wesen*) that "a more disciplined reason" (*eine geübtere Vernunft*) recognized and worshiped (§35). "Revelation had guided their reason, and now, all at once, reason gave clearness to their revelation" (§36). This was "the first reciprocal influence" (*der erste wechselseitige Dienst*) that reason and revelation exercised on one another. Such "a mutual influence" (*ein gegenseitiger Einfluß*) between the two was, in God's eyes, "becoming" (§37). The Jewish people "became better acquainted with the doctrine of immortality among the Chaldeans and Persians," and also "in the schools of the Greek philosophers in Egypt" (§42). Though the immortality of the soul had not been expressly taught in the Old Testament, there was some "previous exercising," there were some "allusions" and "hints" to this doctrine in the Old Testament books (§§43–47). The Old Testament had "all the good qualities of a primer both for children and for a childlike people" (§50). But because every "primer" (*Elementarbuch*) is only for a certain age, it would do harm if the child who had outgrown it were kept at it longer than was intended (§51). So Christ came as "a better instructor" (*ein beßrer Pädagog*) in order to "tear the exhausted primer from the child's hand" (§53).

Thus far, the arguments in *The Education of the Human Race* seem far from offensive to Christian theology. The essential qualities of divine revelation, its *precedence, preeminence,* and *generating power* over against human reason, are firmly maintained. That is to say, divine revelation guides, educates, stimulates, and energizes human reason. Of the two, it is divine revelation that takes the initiative. Guided, inculcated, and motivated by revelation, human reason continues to grow and develop until it eventually begins, "all at once" (*auf einmal*), to "give clearness" (*erhellen*) to what revelation has alluded to or hinted at. This final "clearness" that human reason gives to revelation, however, is not accomplished by human reason alone; it is a *cooperative* achievement, brought about through the "reciprocal influence" of human reason and divine revelation. This is the "synergism" pointed out in the preceding chapter. So if Lessing had stopped with §53, not a few Christian theologians, including the ancient church fathers who suggested the idea of the education of the human race, would have agreed with him, perhaps even applauded him. But he did not stop here. We turn, in the next three sections, to the more controversial arguments he presents in paragraphs 54 through 100.

Revelation and Reason: (2) The New Testament Age

Here again, let us examine Lessing's arguments before we attempt a critical appraisal.

"That portion of the human race which God had wished to embrace in one plan of education, was ripe for the second great step" (§54). That is to say, that portion of the human race "had come so far in the exercise of its reason, as to need, and to be able to make use of, nobler and worthier motives for moral action than temporal rewards and punishments, which had hitherto been its guides. The child has become a youth. Sweetmeats and toys have given place to an awakening desire to be as free, as honoured, and as happy as its elder brother" (§55). It was now "time that another *true* life to be expected after this one should gain an influence over the youth's actions" (§57). So Christ was "the first *reliable, practical* teacher of the immortality of the soul" (§58). He taught us to judge inner and outer actions in accordance with eternal norms. "To preach an inward purity of heart in reference to another life, was reserved for him alone" (§61). "His disciples have faithfully propagated this teaching" (§62). "If, however, they mixed up this one great truth together with other doctrines whose truth was less enlightening, whose usefulness was less considerable," it could not be otherwise. Instead of blaming them for this, one should "rather seriously examine whether these very commingled doctrines have not become a new directing impulse for human reason" (§63).

It is clear from our experience that the New Testament scriptures "have afforded, and still afford, the second, better primer" for the human race (§64). They "have occupied human reason more than all other books, and enlightened it more" up to the present day, "were it even only through the light which human reason itself put into them" (§65). "It would have been impossible for any other book to become so generally known among such different nations." The fact that people of such completely diverse modes of thought have turned their attention to one and the same book has indisputably "assisted human reason on its way more than if every nation had had its *own* primer specially for itself" (§66). It was therefore "most necessary that each people should for a time consider this book as the *non plus ultra* of their knowledge" (§67).

What is "of the greatest importance now" is to proceed with caution. "You who are cleverer than the rest, who wait fretting and impatient on the last page of the primer, take care! Take care that you do not let your weaker classmates notice what you are beginning to scent, or even see!" (§68). "Until these weaker fellows of yours have caught up with you, it is better that you should return once more to this primer, and examine whether that which you take only for variations of method, for superfluous verbiage in the teaching, is not perhaps something more" (§69).

"You have seen in the childhood of the human race, in the doctrine of the unity of God, that God makes immediate revelations of mere truths of reason, or has permitted and caused pure truths of reason to be taught, for a time, as truths of immediate revelation, in order to promulgate them the more rapidly, and ground them the more firmly" (§70). "You learn in the childhood of the human race the same thing, in the doctrine of the immortality of the soul. It is *preached* in the second, better primer as revelation, not *taught* as a result of human reason" (§71). "As we by this time can dispense with the Old Testament for the doctrine of the unity of God, and as we are gradually beginning also to be less dependent on the New Testament for the doctrine of the immortality of the soul," so there might be mirrored in the Bible "also other truths of the same kind, which we are to gaze at in awe as revelation, just until reason learns to deduce them from its other demonstrated truths, and to connect them with them" (§72).

The first thing to notice in the above arguments is that Christ, referred to as "a better instructor" (*ein beßrer Pädagog*) in §53, is now expressly defined as "the first *reliable, practical* teacher of the immortality of the soul" (*der erste zuverlässige, praktische Lehrer der Unsterblichkeit der Seele*) (§§58–60). He was the first "to preach an inward purity of heart in reference to another life" (§61), and "his disciples have faithfully propagated this teaching" (§62). The New Testament scriptures, even if thought to include some less enlightening and less useful doctrines, "have become a new directing impulse (*ein neuer*

Richtungsstoß) for human reason" (§63). Thus they "have afforded, and still afford, the second, better primer" for the human race (§64). Lessing stresses the fact that the New Testament scriptures "have occupied human reason more than all other books, and enlightened it more" (§65).

But the cardinal question is whether it is theologically adequate to regard the New Testament scriptures as "the second, better primer" for the human race. This question is central, no matter how greatly it is stressed that the New Testament scriptures are superior to those of the Old Testament. The issue at stake becomes manifest in §68 and following. As expected, Lessing begins to speak of "you who are cleverer than the rest, who wait fretting and impatient on the last page of the primer" and of "your weaker classmates" (§§68–69), thus suggesting both the possibility and the necessity of advancing from "truths of immediate revelation" (*unmittelbare geoffenbarte Wahrheiten*) to "mere truths of reason" (*bloße Vernunftswahrheiten*) (§§70–72). To demonstrate this possibility, he presents his own rational reinterpretation of Christian doctrines, such as the doctrine of the Trinity, of original sin, and of redemption, all of which have been regarded as "truths of revelation" (§§73–75).

According to Lessing, "the development of revealed truths into truths of reason, is absolutely necessary, if the human race is to be assisted by them" (*die Ausbildung geoffenbarter Wahrheiten in Vernunftswahrheiten ist schlechterdings notwendig, wenn dem menschlichen Geschlechte damit geholfen sein soll*). For "when they were revealed they were certainly not truths of reason, but they were revealed in order to become such." To put it parabolically, "they were like the 'facit' said to his boys by the mathematics master; he goes on ahead of them in order to indicate to some extent the lines they should follow. . . . If the scholars were to be satisfied with the 'facit,' they would never learn to do sums, and would frustrate the intention with which their good master gave them a guiding clue in their work" (§76). If we were to judge solely by the foregoing paragraphs, we could safely conclude that Lessing's conception of revelation and reason is basically on the same path as that of Hegel, who insists that religious "representation" (*Vorstellung*) should be developed and transformed into a philosophical "concept" (*Begriff*).

What makes the matter extremely puzzling, if not hopelessly complicated, is that in the very same breath Lessing sets forth the following proposition: "And why should not we too, by means of a religion whose historical truth, if you will, looks dubious, be led in a similar way to closer and better conceptions of the divine Being, of our own nature, of our relation to God, which human reason would never have reached on its own?" (§77). This proposition clearly attests to the limitations of human reason and suggests that some knowledge is available only through revelation. This being the case, §77 seems to stand in diametrical opposition to §4, where it was asserted that "revelation gives nothing to the human race which human reason could not arrive at on its own; only it has given, and still gives to it, the most important of these things sooner." Is this not a sheer contradiction? Or if these two propositions are not mutually contradictory but are supposed to hold true together, how, then, do they relate to each other? This is precisely the question that has tortured Lessing scholars. Faced with this difficult question, most scholars have condensed Lessing's entire argument in *The Education of the Human Race* into the apparent contradiction between §4 and §77. So simplistic a treatment of the problem, however, would seem to miss the real point that Lessing apparently intended to make by juxtaposing these contradictory propositions. We propose, therefore, to follow to the last letter, and as meticulously as possible, the arguments he presents.

According to Lessing, these "speculations" (*Spekulationen* or *Vernünfteleien*) that he tried out experimentally on "the mysteries of religion" have never "done harm or been injurious to civil society"; but they are unquestionably "the most fitting exercises of the human reason that exist, just as long as the human heart, as such, is capable to the highest degree of loving virtue for its eternal blessed consequences" (§§78–79). The goal at which the exercises of the human reason aim, he asserts, is "to attain its perfect illumination, and bring out that purity of heart which makes us capable of loving virtue for its own sake alone" (§80). "Or," he asks himself, "is the human species never to arrive at this highest step of illumination and purity?—Never?" (§81). Such a suspicion is entirely out of the question. It would be blasphemous to suspect that nature is not "to succeed with the whole, as art succeeded with the individual" (§84). "No! It will come! it will assuredly come! the time of the perfecting, when man, the more convinced his understanding feels about an ever better future, will nevertheless not need to borrow motives for his actions from this future; for he will do right because it *is* right, not because arbitrary rewards are set upon it" (§85).

Lessing's arguments come to their climax when he speaks, in the end, of "a new, eternal gospel" (*ein neues ewiges Evangelium*). Before considering this important topic, however, we had better reexamine his arguments thus far and point out some problems.

The first point open to theological criticism is Lessing's view of Christ as a teacher of the human race. Though Christ is referred to as "a *better* instructor" and "the first *reliable, practical* teacher of the immortality of the soul," it is undeniable that his conception of Christ as an ideal moral teacher has something in common with Enlightenment theology's shallow, moralistic view of Christ. But we must also admit that the point he is trying to make here is not concerned with Christology proper. In the face of Reimarus's deistic and rationalistic criticism as well as his radically historical criticism, the point with which Lessing is concerned centers, rather, on the reaffirmation of Christian revelation by means of the postulated idea of the education of the human race. We would do him an injustice, therefore, if we were to speak of his Christology solely on the basis of these hypothetically formulated propositions.

The next question, touched upon earlier, is whether it is possible and permissible to develop or deepen revealed truths into truths of reason. The Christian theologian would reject such an attempt as presumptuous; the speculative philosopher, however, would assuredly recommend it as a task that must be carried out. In any case, there is no doubt that Lessing was proceeding in a direction that moved from revelation to reason. His aforementioned proposition that "the development of revealed truths into truths of reason, is absolutely necessary, if the human race is to be assisted by them" is certainly its most explicit indication. Yet we must notice here that this proposition is not a categorical but a hypothetical one. We tend to be dazzled by the main clause and its insistence that "the development . . . is absolutely necessary" without giving full attention to what follows. It is important to consider the conditional clause, "if the human race is to be assisted by them." What, then, does this conditional clause imply?[45]

In our interpretation, the conditional clause means that revealed truths, if fully understood and appropriated by the human race, become essential to its development toward perfection. In other words, revealed truths must not remain extraneous truths coming from without; they must become intrinsic to the human race. They are to be appropriated so as to be part of humanity. Thus understood, what is at issue in this proposition is the "appropriation" (*Aneignung*) of revealed truths. If this interpretation is correct, then the proposition can be paraphrased as follows: the development of revealed truths into truths of reason is absolutely necessary for us, *if they are to be appropriated by the human race in such a way as to promote the development of humanity*. Thus paraphrased, the proposition evokes no objection. For revealed truths, if we are to appropriate them, must become truths that are internally intelligible to us. This meaning of revealed truths is precisely what Lessing intends by the phrase "mere truths of reason."

A "New Eternal Gospel" and the Completion of the Human Race

The fact that Lessing's *The Education of the Human Race* is still a subject for research and discussion is due not so much to its importance for the philosophy of religion or the philosophy of history as to the "new, eternal gospel" that he made famous in this book. For he is generally regarded as the thinker who has rendered the greatest service to "the rediscovery of the eternal evangel."[46]

Having mentioned "the time of the perfecting" in §85, Lessing declares that "it will assuredly come! the time of a new, eternal gospel, which is promised to us in the primers of the New Covenant itself!" (§86). This implies that the time of the perfecting is the time of "a new, eternal gospel" and that the coming of such a time is promised in the books of the New Testament. In fact, there is mention of an "eternal gospel" (εὐαγγέλιον αἰώνιον; evangelium aeternum) in Revelation 14:6.

At any rate, Lessing jumps from the New Testament age directly to the enthusiasts of the thirteenth and fourteenth centuries in order to make some comments about them. According to him, "perhaps even some enthusiasts of the thirteenth and fourteenth centuries had caught a glimmer of this new eternal gospel, and only erred in that they predicted its arrival as so near to their own time" (§87). What is more, "perhaps their 'Three Ages of the World' were not so empty a speculation after all," says Lessing, "and assuredly they had no bad intentions when they taught that the new covenant must become as antiquated as the old has become. There remained with them the same economy of the same God. Ever, to put my own expression into their mouths, ever the selfsame plan of the education of the human race" (§88).

It is generally taken for granted that Lessing had in mind here the Calabrian abbot Joachim of Fiore and the radical Franciscan spiritualists influenced by his ideas. The surprising thing is, however, that no mention of Joachim of Fiore occurs anywhere in Lessing's works. Moreover, it is not clear whether Lessing had ever read Joachim's works at all. Christian Gross, one of the editors of the Hempel edition of Lessing's works, was the first to assert that in §87 Lessing made implicit reference to Joachim of Fiore. Gross made this assertion in the editor's notes to volumes 14 through 17, volumes he edited in 1873–74. Since then, Gross's surmise has gained wide recognition in the academic world. But it remains unclear as to exactly how much Lessing knew about Joachim of Fiore and, if he did know something, through what channel he came to know about Joachim's theory of the "Three Ages of the World."[47]

Be that as it may, it is certain that from the very outset Lessing conceived *The Education of the Human Race* in terms of a Joachim-like scheme of three ages of the world. According to this theory of the tripartite development of history, the New Testament must become as antiquated as the Old Testament has become, and in its place there must someday begin a new age of the eternal gospel. Lessing has incorporated into this scheme of historical development his original idea of the necessary development of revealed truths into truths of reason. "You who are cleverer than the rest, who wait fretting and impatient on the last page of the primer" (§68) could be taken as meaning Lessing himself. In any event, when he says, "Take care that you do not let your weaker classmates notice what you are beginning to scent, or even see," this exhortation certainly has to do with the coming of "the time of a new eternal gospel."

What is novel, then, in his espousal of the new, eternal gospel? It is undoubtedly his characterization of this gospel as the attainment of "perfect illumination" (*die völlige Aufklärung*) and "purity of heart" (*die Reinigkeit des Herzens*) which is capable of loving virtue solely for its own sake.

Admittedly, there are some scholars who object to this generally held view. Heinz Bluhm, for example, relativizes the novelty of Lessing's concept when he says:

> The answer to the question raised in this treatise, whether Lessing's conception of the eternal gospel is new, must therefore be as follows. Lessing's concept of the eternal gospel is *new* only insofar as Lessing has given an *ethical* definition of Joachim of Fiore's commonly held idea of *evangelium aeternum* and has thereby provided it with solid content. Yet the higher morality propagated by Lessing as of the eternal gospel itself is—contrary to the opinion widely held in German circles today—*not new*.[48]

Christoph Schrempf, from a different perspective, also poses an objection to the idea of novelty in Lessing's higher morality. From Schrempf's point of view, the higher morality Lessing espoused is characterized by naiveté. But a morality characterized by naiveté, Schrempf maintains, is exactly what Jesus Christ proclaimed and practiced. Accordingly, the Lessingian higher morality should be called "a second naiveté" (*eine zweite Naivität*). But, says Schrempf, Lessing's misunderstanding of Jesus's ethics makes his relationship to Christianity somewhat awkward.[49] Bluhm's and Schrempf's criticisms of Lessing's idea of a "new, eternal gospel" appear to raise important questions, but we must press on to the question of its relation to enthusiasm.

As Lessing puts it, "Some enthusiasts of the thirteenth and fourteenth centuries had caught a glimmer of this new, eternal gospel." The only mistake they made is that "they predicted its arrival as so near to their own time." "They were," he says, "premature. They believed that they could make their contemporaries, who had scarcely outgrown their childhood, without enlightenment, without preparation, at one stroke men worthy of their *third age*" (§89). He goes on:

> And it was just this which made them enthusiasts. The enthusiast often casts true glances into the future, but for this future he cannot wait. He wants this future to come quickly, and to be made to come quickly through him. A thing over which nature takes thousands of years is to come to maturity just at the moment of his experience. For what part has he in it if that which he recognizes as the best does not become the best in his life time? Does he come again? Does he expect to come again? It is strange that this enthusiasm is not more the fashion, if it were only among enthusiasts. (§90)

We can see here Lessing's attitude toward enthusiasts (*Schwärmer*). According to him, the enthusiasts often see truly into the future, but they are too impatient to wait calmly for its arrival. They want what they have glimpsed, what nature takes thousands of years to realize, to materialize immediately. Lessing is not fond of this enthusiastic impatience. He is a man of farseeing wisdom and patience. "Until these weaker fellows of yours have caught up with you, it is better that you should return once more to this primer, and examine whether that which you take only for variations of method, for superfluous verbiage in the teaching, is not perhaps something more" (§69). As this statement shows, Lessing as the educator of the human race impressed on the fretful and impatient the importance of "waiting" (*Warten*).[50] He is distrustful of the notion that his immature contemporaries could be made, "without enlightenment, without preparation, at one stroke men worthy of [the] *third age*." Looking forward to the dawning of a new age, he calmly waits for the moment to take a step forward.[51]

"Go thine inscrutable way, Eternal Providence! Only let me not despair of thee because of this inscrutableness. Let me not despair of thee, even if thy steps appear to me to be going backward. It is not true that the shortest line is always straight" (§91). "Thou hast on thine eternal way so much that thou must concern thyself with, so much to attend to! And what if it were as good as proved that the great, slow wheel, which brings mankind nearer to its perfection, is only set in motion by smaller, faster wheels, each of which contributes its own individual part to the whole?" (§92).

These two paragraphs most clearly demonstrate Lessing's "faith in providence" (*Vorsehungs-Glaube*).[52] It is true that referring to God's providence, even when it had no special religious meaning, was a common practice in the age of the Enlightenment. But Lessing's reference to God's providence in these paragraphs is to be distinguished from the common practice.[53] These paragraphs express Lessing's own deep religious piety and mature wisdom. The protagonist's words in *Nathan the Wise* 4/7, "If Providence demands her at my hands / Again—I shall obey," can be regarded as connoting Lessing's own faith in providence.[54] In any event, it would be safe to assume that Lessingian reason, backed by this faith in providence, is of a dimension that differs completely from the shallow reason characteristic of the Enlightenment, reason that takes it for granted that "the shortest line is always straight." For Lessingian reason, being wise enough to discern that eternal providence has "so much that thou must concern thyself with," is also backed by a piety capable of accepting with serenity the slow and winding course of inscrutable providence.[55]

The Idea of Reincarnation

In the concluding portion of *The Education of the Human Race* there are eight paragraphs that will astound the reader. Without prior guidance, nearly every reader will find it hard to understand why these timeworn hypothetical propositions were included in this book.

"It is so! Must every individual man—one sooner, another later—have travelled along the very same path by which the race reaches its perfection? Have travelled along it in one and the same life? Can he have been, in one and the selfsame life, a sensual Jew and a spiritual Christian? Can he in the selfsame life have overtaken both?" (§93). "Surely not that! But why should not every individual man have been present more than once in this world?" (§94). "Is this hypothesis so laughable merely because it is the oldest? Because human understanding, before the sophistries of the Schools had dissipated and weakened it, lighted upon it at once?" (§95). "Why may not even I have already performed all those steps towards my perfection which merely temporal penalties and rewards can bring man to?" (§96). "And, once more, why not all those steps, to perform which the prospects of eternal rewards so powerfully assist us?" (§97). "Why should I not come back as often as I am capable of acquiring new knowledge, new skills? Do I bring away so much from one visit that it is perhaps not worth the trouble of coming again?" (§98). "Is this a reason against it? Or, because I forget that I have been here already? Happy is it for me that I do forget. The recollection of my former condition would permit me to make only a bad use of the present. And that which I must forget *now*, is that necessarily forgotten for ever?" (§99). "Or is it a reason against the hypothesis that so much time would have been lost to me? Lost?—And what then have I to lose?—Is not the whole of eternity mine?" (§100).

The issue at stake here, to use science of religion terms, is the question of "metempsychosis" (*Seelenwanderung*) or "reincarnation" (*Reinkarnation*). Why, then, does such a modern intellect as Lessing bring up this hypothesis that seems absurd to the modern mind? This question is all the more urgent because Lessing brings up this "oldest" hypothesis immediately after he has declared the opening of the third age, the age when the human race is to reach its highest level of illumination and purity and thereby attain perfection. The answer, as Paul Tillich has aptly pointed out, is that Lessing took very seriously the ideal of human perfection. In other words, the ideal of human perfection demanded of him the idea of reincarnation.[56]

The question that inevitably arises when the idea of perfection is taken seriously is: how can every generation and every individual not belonging to the age of consummation participate in the ideal of perfection? Are they not shut out from perfection because they do not belong to the third age? If all past generations are merely steps to a goal of perfection that only the last generation can attain, what significance does the entire course of human development have for each of these generations? If they are destined to live, fight, and suffer solely for the benefit of the last generation, is not this destiny too cruel and too unfair to all generations except the last? And even if we are fortunate enough to live in the age of consummation, is not life too short for us to attain perfection?

Such questions arise, says Paul Althaus by way of criticism, only when we presuppose a moralistic worldview.[57] Christian theology has traditionally sought to solve these difficult questions by proclaiming otherworldly salvation alone. That is to say, it has taught that human perfection, or salvation, was attainable in the next world. There is no room for the idea of reincarnation in Christian theology when eschatology is preached in such a way as to annul the moral order of the world.[58] But how will it be once dogmatic presuppositions for otherworldly salvation have collapsed? According to Tillich, there will then be only two possible alternatives. One is the path indicated by Hegel. According to this path, the problem is solved by asserting that "not [individual] personality but the objective spirit is realized in history." This alternative entails the difficulty that it devalues the individual personality and its perfection. The second possible solution is "Lessingian." It would solve the problem by assuming that each person is capable of returning to this world often enough that he/she may participate in the perfection of history as a whole. This is exactly what Lessing suggests with his problematic idea of reincarnation.[59]

It is true that neither alternative harmonizes with orthodox Christian doctrine. But Tillich argues that the Lessingian solution is more Protestant than the Hegelian. On Tillich's view, Lessing's idea of reincarnation does not go beyond the confines of myth and hypothesis. Nevertheless, in this dubious form "Lessing has given expression to a fundamental Christian truth, the unconditional value of the individual, on the ground of humanism."[60] Hence Tillich draws the remarkable conclusion: "So in this question [of reincarnation] too, Lessing stands as the great representative of a Christian humanism."[61] By and large, this conclusion of Tillich's seems justifiable. In any event, we basically agree with his interpretation of Lessing's idea of reincarnation.

To sum up, Lessing's idea of reincarnation is integral to his espousal of the education of the human race. He introduces hypothetical propositions about the reincarnation of the human soul because he takes seriously the question of how each individual can take part in the ideal of human perfection. Conceiving human history as an educational process that leads toward perfection, he deems it incumbent on each and every person to tread the same path by which the human race reaches perfection. How, then, is it possible for past generations to participate in the future consummation? And no matter how blessed and privileged one may be, is it possible to take all the steps necessary to perfection in one lifetime? Is not one life too short and limited for the attainment of such a sublime goal? These questions have induced Lessing to postulate that one should be able to exist in the world more than once.

It is clear, therefore, that Lessing's idea of reincarnation and the Buddhist doctrine of transmigration, though similar in appearance, are quite different in nature. The Buddhist doctrine of transmigration is a negative and pessimistic thought ruled by karma or the higher law of cause and effect, whereas the idea of reincarnation that Lessing holds is a positive and progressive thought demanded by the ideal of the perfection of human personality. Accordingly, Ernst Benz is quite right when he asserts: "By contrast, in Lessing a completely new, positive evaluation of reincarnation comes to the fore; namely, the thought of progressive perfection of the human person in a series of reincarnations."[62]

It would be improper, however, to take Lessing's idea of reincarnation *dogmatically* (δογματικῶς), since he puts it forward only *gymnastically* (γυμναστικῶς), or as a mental exercise.[63] His espousal of this idea does not go beyond the limits of a hypothesis. It may be suggested that it is in order to make this hypothetical character clear that he poses the idea of reincarnation in interrogative form.

A Dialectical View of Revelation and Reason

Thus far, we have sought to comprehend the spectrum of Lessing's religious-philosophical thought in his last book, *The Education of the Human Race*. As our detailed reading of the original text has shown, Lessing was unmistakably a many-faceted thinker whose mode of thought was multidimensional and highly flexible. Quite a number of previous studies, sacrificing the multidimensional richness of his ideas, have put Lessing in a straitjacket, only to expose him to sharp criticism from their own viewpoints. To avoid this kind of one-sided, arbitrary interpretation, we have sought to adhere to our principle of understanding a thinker from the original text. We have tried to reproduce Lessing's subtle arguments as faithfully and exhaustively as possible while at the same time giving attention to previous studies and, when necessary, making critical comments about them. To repeat such criticisms here is needless. What should be done here, rather, is to offer our concluding reflections, focusing attention on the most important point in his argument as a whole. The most important question to be raised and answered here is that of the relationship, in Lessing's thought, between divine revelation and human reason, or between the transcendent and the immanent.

As we have seen, Lessing's arguments had their starting point in his hypothetical conception of revelation as the education of the human race. This concept was intended to serve as a counterassertion (*Antithese*) to Reimarus's naturalistic dissolution of revelation. Lessing sought a way to overcome the antithetical opposition between revelation and reason, an opposition that had become almost unbridgeable in the eighteenth century. He found a possible solution in the concept of "development" (*Entwicklung*) and introduced this concept into the traditional dichotomy between revelation and reason. It might be possible, he thought, to achieve a dynamic mediation between the two if revelation were conceived, on the education model, as developing step by step toward a goal. But what goal? What objective will revelation conceived after the educational model attain? One can hardly avoid coming to the conclusion that Lessing himself came to.

> Education gives man nothing which he could not also get from within himself; it gives him that which he could get from within himself, only quicker and more easily. In the same way too, *revelation gives nothing to the human race which human reason could not arrive at on its own; only it has given, and still gives to it, the most important of these things sooner.* (§4, italics added)

This conclusion is logically inevitable when one posits the idea of the education of the human race. But this is merely a hypothetical conclusion, because its major premise, revelation as the education of the human race, is itself a hypothesis. Accordingly, §4 is a hypothetical proposition.

The following facts, however, cannot be denied. Human reason has a tendency to transform the one immeasurable into many measurables (§6). Human reason would have been lost in errors, had it not been for God's revelation (§7). What positive religion has taught as revelation has functioned as a directing impulse for human reason (§§7, 63) and has enlightened human reason more than anything else (§65). From these undeniable historical facts, the following puzzling proposition can be taken as an inference: "And why should not we too, by means of a religion whose historical truth, if you will, looks dubious, be led in a similar way to closer and better conceptions of the divine Being, of our own nature, of our relation to God, which human reason would never have reached on its own?" (§77). As can be seen from the fact that it is posed in interrogative form, this proposition too is a hypothetical one.

In the past, researchers have found these two hypothetical propositions so contradictory that no bridge could be established between them. To solve the problem, they have set forth a variety of interpretations, only to find that these interpretations merely amplified and expanded the original contradiction. Let us set aside nonessential things and present the matter simply so as to make the controversial issue clear. It then appears that the essential contradiction has to do with the relationship between two propositions, which we shall call Proposition A and Proposition B. Proposition A states that "revelation gives nothing to the human race which human reason could not arrive at on its own; only it has given, and still gives to it, the most important of these things sooner" (§4). Proposition B asserts that revelation leads us to "closer and better conceptions of the divine Being, of our nature, of our relation to God, which human reason would never have reached on its own" (§77). Which, then, is Lessing's authentic opinion, Proposition A or Proposition B? The majority of Lessing scholars have upheld Proposition A. They regard Lessing as an immanentist who does not believe in the transcendent revelation of God. Hence all his statements and utterances about God and divine revelation are declared to be mere exoteric teachings. A minority of Lessing scholars, however, insist that Proposition B represents Lessing's authentic opinion. They regard Lessing as a transcendentalist who holds fast to Christian or theistic faith.

For our part, we side with the theistic interpretation that regards Lessing as a thinker who upholds faith in the transcendent, but on grounds somewhat different from those presented by such interpreters as Helmut Thielicke and Otto Mann. First of all, we deem the either/or choice between §4 and §77 senseless. Both propositions, as pointed out earlier, are "gymnastic" *hypotheses* proposed by this thinker "who is fond of making various hypotheses and systems for the pleasure of tearing them to pieces again."[64] It is therefore impossible to grasp Lessing's decisive assertions here. Moreover, it is hard to imagine that such a wise and clever man as Lessing would have overlooked the contradiction between these two propositions. We think it more probable that he *intentionally* posited this apparent contradiction himself. Our conjecture is that he deliberately set forth these diametrically opposed propositions in order to suggest that the relationship between revelation and reason should be considered not in a static and unilateral way, but in a more dynamic and multilateral manner. If this conjecture is correct, Lessing's wisdom as an educator was undoubtedly at work here. In any event, Lessing's conception of the relationship between revelation and reason is dialectical. And dialectic is a method of systematic reasoning or critical investigation that begins with the juxtaposition of opposed or contradictory ideas and seeks to overcome this opposition or contradiction by attaining a higher synthesis between them.[65]

Dialectically, then, how does Lessing conceive of the relationship between revelation and reason? For the sake of argument, we shall emphasize only a few important paragraphs.

A: "Revelation had guided their reason, and now, all at once, reason gave clearness to their revelation" (§36). This proposition is a descriptive statement based on historical facts related to Jewish people of the Old Testament age.

B: "When they were revealed they were certainly not truths of reason, but they were revealed in order to become such. They were like the 'facit' said to his boys by the mathematics master; he goes on ahead of them in order to indicate to some extent the lines they should follow in their sums" (§76). This proposition is sheer hypothesis.

C: "The development of revealed truths into truths of reason is absolutely necessary, if the human race is to be assisted by them" (§76). This is a hypothetical proposition that formulates the logical conclusion to be drawn from B.

In all these propositions, revelation precedes human reason. Human reason is guided by and seeks, or must seek, revelation. And at some point in history, human reason catches up, or must catch up, with revelation. Thus revealed truths become, or must become, truths of reason. This is what can clearly be deduced from Lessing's utterances, no matter what hypothetical assertions they may involve.

But the really important question is whether revelation becomes useless, whether human reason can be autonomous after human reason has caught up with revelation and revealed truths have thus become truths of reason. Scholars who interpret *The Education of the Human Race* in immanentist terms declare that this is precisely what Lessing intended to assert. But never did he express such a contention.

Lessing's basic standpoint is implied in the following noteworthy dictum: "Let everyone tell what *seems* to him to be truth; and let *the truth itself* be entrusted to God!" (*Jeder sage, was ihm Wahrheit dünkt, und* die Wahrheit selbst *sei Gott empfohlen!*).[66] Another famous dictum is this: "If God held all truth in his right hand and in his left everlasting striving after truth, so that I should always and everlastingly be mistaken, and said to me, 'Choose,' with humility I would pick the left hand and say, 'Father, grant me that. Absolute truth is for thee alone.'"[67] Both dictums point in the same direction.

In the last analysis, judging from all of Lessing's statements, we consider Lütgert's formulation of Lessing's conception of the relationship between revelation and reason as most fitting. Lütgert says, "He does not know a completely free self-development [of human reason], even if revelation [in him] is little more than the trellis by which the human race grows."[68] Wilhelm Windelband appears to endorse this judgment when he says, "he [Lessing] does not yet know the concept of self-development. . . . Accordingly, the only thing that later philosophers could add to the Lessingian principle was the dissolution of the concept of revelation and the endeavor to conceive the history of religions as the self-development and self-revelation of the human spirit."[69] In any case, one thing is clear: Lessing's thought by no means rules out the concept of transcendent revelation.

Up to this point we have striven to analyze Lessing's dialectical understanding of revelation and reason on the basis of a careful reading of the original German text. In consequence, we have confirmed that the concept of revelation continues to be valid in his thought. This fact compels us, however, as Johannes von Lüpke contends, to reconsider the age in which Lessing lived, generally regarded as an age of "moral autonomy" (*die sittliche Autonomie*).[70]

As is well known, Immanuel Kant saw the goal of enlightenment in "man's release from tutelage," that is, in deliverance from "man's inability to make use of his understanding without direction from another." The motto of enlightenment, he maintained, was to be, "Have courage to use your own reason!" His goal, therefore, was to attain autonomy for human reason.

For Lessing, however, such a definition of enlightenment was clearly insufficient. For from his point of view, "to deliver oneself from instruction by another, can also be a sign of refusal to come of age."[71] The highest stage of "perfect illumination" and "purity of heart" is, as Lessing sees it, the stage at which we are "capable of loving virtue for its own sake" (§80) and "will do the right because it *is* right" (§85). The ordinary concept of autonomy would certainly be inadequate for expressing the ideal of Lessingian reason. As we asserted in the preceding chapter, Lessingian reason is, in essence, a "religiously grounded concept of reason" (*die religiös fundierte Vernunftbegriff*).[72] Correspondingly, the ideal of autonomy he envisioned is an autonomy backed by awareness of its own limitations. In other words, such autonomy is a mature autonomy, capable of confessing that absolute truth is for God alone. An autonomy of this sort may well be called "autotheonomy" (*Autotheonomie*).[73]

In conclusion, we can aver that the ideal of Lessingian enlightenment is the attainment of an "autotheonomy" in which "autonomy is at the same time theonomy." In order to attain such a goal, revealed truths must not remain unintelligible truths that are only to be believed, but must become truths of reason that are intrinsic to human reason. And only when revealed truths thus become truths of reason can human reason find certitude and repose in God.

7

Lessing's "Spinozism"

For the student of Western philosophy today, it is simply a matter of common sense that the most important philosophical event to take place during the 1780s and 1790s was the appearance of Immanuel Kant's three critiques: the *Critique of Pure Reason* (1781; 2d ed., 1787), the *Critique of Practical Reason* (1788), and the *Critique of Judgment* (1790). But the common sense of the present is not always that of the past. Much to our surprise, at the time it came into being, Kant's critical philosophy was not taken to be an epoch-making philosophical event. It took four or five years from the time of its publication for the *Critique of Pure Reason* to draw the attention of the reading public.[1]

By contrast, the "Spinoza controversy" (*Spinoza-Streit*), in which Moses Mendelssohn and Friedrich Heinrich Jacobi fought over the question of who should assume the deceased Lessing's mantle, was an entirely different matter. According to Hermann Timm, "in connection with the pros and cons of the matter, there entered into the consciousness of contemporaries [the awareness of] a change in eras. There is no event of comparable influence in modern intellectual history."[2] This controversy eventually engaged almost all the best minds of late eighteenth-century Germany. Wizenmann, Herder, Goethe, Hamann, Reinhold, Kant and other eminent thinkers took part. It led to what is known as the "pantheism controversy" (*Pantheismusstreit*), which in turn gave rise to the "Spinoza renaissance."[3] The Jewish philosopher, who had been treated like "a dead dog" (*ein todter Hund*)[4] for over a hundred years due to misunderstanding and slander, was now cordially welcomed and extolled as "Benedictus," or "the blessed." The philosophy of Spinoza thus resurrected was to give rise, in the course of time, to the great German idealist philosophy as represented by Fichte, Schelling, Hegel, and Schleiermacher.[5]

Apart from the revival of Spinozism, the pantheism controversy posed "the dilemma of a rational nihilism or an irrational fideism,"[6] a central problem that occupied Fichte, Schelling, Hegel, Kierkegaard, and Nietzsche. Consequently, as Beiser pertinently states, "It is indeed no exaggeration to say that the pantheism controversy had as great an impact upon nineteenth-century philosophy as Kant's first *Kritik*."[7] In any event, the pantheism controversy is "one of the most significant debates for the emergence of a modern view of the world and one that considerably shook the self-confidence of the German Enlightenment."[8]

As mentioned above, the pantheism controversy, which is so important for the history of modern German philosophy, originated in the Spinoza controversy that began soon after Lessing's death between Mendelssohn and Jacobi over Lessing's theological and/or religious-philosophical convictions. The immediate cause was that Jacobi, soon after Lessing's death, disclosed the content of private conversations he had held with Lessing during his last years. According to what Jacobi alleged in his *Concerning the Doctrine of Spinoza, in Letters to Herr Moses Mendelssohn (Über die Lehre des Spinoza in Briefen an den Herrn Moses Mendelssohn)*, Lessing confided to him his secret allegiance to "Spinozism." Hence the focus of the dispute between Mendelssohn and Jacobi was Lessing's alleged Spinozism. The burning question was that of how Lessing's Spinozism should be interpreted.[9]

From the start, however, three dimensions of the question were involved in the pantheism controversy. From "the biographical issue of Lessing's Spinozism," the central issue gradually shifted to "the exegetical question of the proper interpretation of Spinoza" and eventually to "the problem of the authority of reason" as such.[10] To use Heinrich Scholz's words, the pantheism controversy, while involving many thinkers, shifted its center of gravity "from Lessing to Spinoza and from this to the worldview of rationalism."[11] Since telling the whole story of the pantheism controversy[12] would be too big a topic for us here, the discussion to follow will be restricted to a consideration of Lessing's "Spinozism."

The rationale for this restriction is that quite apart from the development of the pantheism controversy, it is a task of the highest importance for an appraisal of Lessing's theological and religious-philosophical thought as a whole to interpret the allegedly "Spinozistic" confession that Jacobi claimed to have heard in conversation with him. As Vallée pertinently states, "Indeed Spinozism has been the Trojan horse [which,] introduced into Lessing's works . . . [shakes] the citadel of his thought."[13] It is no exaggeration to say that the loss of Lessing's prestige or the vindication of his honor hinges on how one interprets his ἓν καὶ πᾶν.

The Beginning of the *Pantheismusstreit*

On 15 February 1781, when he died at the age of fifty-two, Lessing left behind a great number of fragments and unfinished manuscripts. Among them, those in the fields of theology and philosophy were of special value. When his younger brother Karl edited and published them after a few years in several volumes of Lessing's collected works,[14] people were amazed at the breadth and depth of his interests in theology and philosophy of religion. To the surprise of the general public, however, Jacobi, who had held private conversations with Lessing during the last years of his life, imputed to him the disgrace of being a Spinozist, though no clear avowal of Spinozism could be found even in these posthumous works. The story thus evolves dramatically, the dramatis personae being two of Lessing's oldest friends, Moses Mendelssohn and Elise Reimarus, and a newly emergent friend, Jacobi, who claimed to be "the legitimate heir and spokesman for Lessing."[15]

Shortly after Lessing's death, the Jewish philosopher Moses Mendelssohn, who "had lived with him in intimate friendship for over thirty years, had unceasingly sought with him the truth, had conversed with him repeatedly, by letter and face to face, on those important [religious-philosophical] matters,"[16] determined to "write something on the character of our Lessing."[17] He set about preparing for this task, but poor health prevented smooth progress. Meanwhile, Elise Reimarus, a close friend of Lessing for some fifteen years and through him a good friend of Mendelssohn as well, brought him unexpected news. By letter she informed him that that Jacobi, knowing that Mendelssohn intended to write a work commemorating Lessing, had sent her the following message:

> I was not able to answer your letter by return post because I wanted to tell you something of great importance: about our Lessing's thinking toward the end of his life, and that Mendelssohn might be so instructed, should you find it appropriate. -- You know perhaps, and if you do not know, I confide it to you here *sub rosa*, that in his final days Lessing was a firm . . . Spinozist. It is conceivable that Lessing may have expressed this view to others; in that case, it would be necessary for Mendelssohn, in the memorial he intends to dedicate to him, either to avoid certain matters totally or at least to treat them with the utmost caution. Perhaps Lessing expressed himself to his dear Mendelssohn as clearly as he did to me; or again, perhaps not -- because he had not conversed with him for a long time and wrote letters only with reluctance. It is a matter for your discretion, my dear and trusted friend, whether or not you wish to disclose any of this to Mendelssohn; but for now I can write in no greater detail.[18]

At that time, being a "Spinozist" was considered almost the same as being an atheist or a blasphemer (*Gotteslästerer*).[19] Jacobi's bombshell announcement that "Lessing in his final days was a firm Spinozist" was therefore a great shock to Lessing's old friends.

Perceiving the great importance of the information she had received from Jacobi, Elise Reimarus immediately wrote Mendelssohn to inform him of what Jacobi had communicated to her as "Lessing's secret."[20] Mendelssohn was deeply perturbed by Elise's letter. In great shock and disturbance he asked himself, "Was Lessing a Spinozist? Did Jacobi hear the same from Lessing himself? What precisely was their state of mind when that confidence passed between them?"[21] Through Elise, because of her personal acquaintance and correspondence with Jacobi, he asked Jacobi the following questions: "Did Lessing come right out and say: I believe Spinoza's system to be true and well founded?" "Which system [of Spinoza's did he mean]?" "Is it the one propounded in his *Tractatus theologico-politicus*, or the one in his *De principiis philosophiae cartesianae*, or the one Ludovicus Mayer circulated under Spinoza's name after his death?" "Did Lessing . . . understand the system with the mis-understanding of a Bayle or with the better understanding of some others?" and so forth.[22] At this time Mendelssohn thought that if Lessing had concurred with another person's system of thought without qualification, he would either have been distraught or made paradoxical assertions, half jokingly or from caprice.[23]

In response to Mendelssohn's request for greater detail of his conversations with Lessing, Jacobi sent the Jewish philosopher, by way of Elise as before, a minute report of about thirty-six pages in quartos on 4 November 1783. This report, however, contained such unexpected material that Mendelssohn was first shocked, then became indignant.[24] Contrary to his initial assumption, it was not "a mere retailing of anecdote," or "something which a visiting traveller might possibly have passed on to him,"[25] but "the sum total of those . . . intimate conversations"[26] with Lessing which Jacobi had had the good fortune to enjoy. There could be no doubt of the authenticity of Jacobi's report. It became abundantly clear to Mendelssohn that Jacobi was by no means the "amateur at philosophy" he had assumed, but "a man who has made thinking his chief business and who possesses the strength to throw off the reins and go his own way."[27] Mendelssohn felt himself greatly humiliated and even grew angry that Lessing, his closest friend for many years, seemed to have "concealed his real system from [him] . . . his most esteemed friend," while "another mortal," on short acquaintance, "was being made privy to Lessing's great secret."[28]

Stunned by Jacobi's report, Mendelssohn asked himself, "Did Lessing deem me unworthy of his confidence? Was I, in his eyes, so philosophically weak and immature of mind that he concealed the real heart of his esoteric philosophy in order not to rob me of my Jewish conviction?" Whatever the answer to these questions, the heart of the Jewish philosopher, who had deemed himself Lessing's oldest, most intimate, and most esteemed friend, was deeply hurt by such humiliating thoughts. This hurt, this humiliation on Mendelssohn's part, as our consideration will shortly reveal, was precisely what Jacobi intended.[29] Consequently, the dispute between Mendelssohn and Jacobi, occasioned by "a trap"[30] that Jacobi laid for Mendelssohn, was from the very start destined to lead to an unhappy end.

The Spinoza Conversations between Lessing and Jacobi

According to Jacobi's report, his conversations with Lessing[31] began when he showed the author of *Nathan the Wise* Goethe's unpublished poem "Prometheus."[32] Since this poem is important for the argument to follow, the English translation is here cited in full.

Prometheus (1773)

Cover your heaven, Zeus, / With cloudy vapors / And like a boy / Beheading thistles / Practice on oaks and mountain peaks— / Still you must leave / My earth intact / And my small hovel, which you did not build, / And this my hearth / Whose glowing heat / You envy me.

I know of nothing more wretched / Under the sun than you gods! / Meagerly you nourish / Your majesty / On dues of sacrifice / And breath of prayer / And would suffer want / But for children and beggars, / Poor hopeful fools.

Once too, a child, / Not knowing where to turn, / I raised bewildered eyes / Up to the sun, as if above there were / An ear to hear my complaint, / A heart like mine / To take pity on the oppressed.

Who helped me / Against the Titans' arrogance? / Who rescued me from death, / From slavery? / Did not my holy and glowing heart, / Unaided, accomplish all? / And did it not, young and good, / Cheated, glow thankfulness / For its safety to him, to the sleeper above?

I pray homage to you? For what? / Have you ever relieved / The burdened man's anguish? / Have you ever assuaged / The frightened man's tears? / Was it not omnipotent Time / That forged me into manhood, / And eternal Fate, / My master and yours?

Or did you think perhaps / That I should hate this life, / Flee into deserts / Because not all / The blossoms of dream grew ripe?

Here I sit, forming men / In my image, / A race to resemble me: / To suffer, to weep, / To enjoy, to be glad— / And never to heed you, / Like me!

As he handed Lessing the copy of Goethe's "Prometheus," Jacobi joshingly said, "you have so often given offence that you will not mind taking offence for once."

Lessing: (*After reading the poem and returning it to Jacobi*) I take no offence; I long ago became acquainted with it first hand.
Jacobi: You know the poem?
Lessing: I have never read the poem; but I find it good.
Jacobi: I find it good too, in its way; otherwise I would not have shown it to you.
Lessing: That's not what I mean. . . . The point of view in which the poem is cast is my own point of view. . . . The orthodox concepts of the divinity are no longer for me; I cannot stand them. *Hen kai Pan*! [= One and All] I know naught else. That is also the tendency in this poem; and I must admit, I like it very much.
Jacobi: Then you would indeed be more or less in agreement with Spinoza.
Lessing: If I am to call myself by anybody's name, then I know none better.
Jacobi: Spinoza is good enough for me; nevertheless, there is scant benefit . . . to be found in that name.
Lessing: Well fine, if that is what you think! . . . And yet . . . are you aware of a better one?[33]

In the meantime, a third person enters the room, so they go to the library. The next morning, when Jacobi returns to his room to dress after breakfast, Lessing follows him in. As soon as the servants have left, Lessing begins:

Lessing: I came to talk with you about my *Hen kai Pan*. You looked startled yesterday.
Jacobi: You surprised me and I felt confused. Dismay it was not. I certainly did not expect to find you a Spinozist or pantheist; and still less did I

	expect that you would put it to me directly and so frankly and clearly. I had come chiefly in the hope of receiving your help against Spinoza.
Lessing:	Then you really do know him?
Jacobi:	I believe as probably only very few have.
Lessing:	Then there is no help for you. Why don't you become his friend openly? There is no other philosophy but the philosophy of Spinoza.
Jacobi:	That may be true. For if a determinist wants to be consistent, he must become a fatalist; all else will follow as a matter of course.
Lessing:	I can see we understand each other. That makes me the more eager to hear from you what you consider to be the *spirit* of Spinozism; I mean the spirit which possessed Spinoza himself.
Jacobi:	Probably it was none other than is found in the time-honoured phrase *a nihilo nihil fit* [= nothing is made out of nothing] which Spinoza contemplated, applying more abstract concepts than did the philosophising Cabbalists and others before him. When using those more abstract concepts, he found a *something out of nothing* to be posited by anything that originated within the infinite, no matter what metaphors or words one might use to express it, or by each and every change within the infinite. And so he rejected any *transition* from the infinite to the finite [= creation]; he rejected transient causes altogether, be they secondary or remote. In the place of the emanating One he posited an Ensoph that was *immanent* only; an inherent cause of the world, eternally unchangeable *in itself*, which, taken together with all that followed from it, would be One and the Same.[34]

At this point in the conversation, Jacobi unfolds his interpretation of Spinoza's philosophy, asserting that it denies free will, divine providence, and the personal God. Lessing, after hearing Jacobi's interpretation, speaks out again:

Lessing:	Let us not quarrel over our credo.
Jacobi:	Quarrel, certainly not. But my credo is not to be found in Spinoza. *I believe in an intelligent personal first cause of the world.*
Lessing:	Oh! all the better! Now I am going to hear something quite new.
Jacobi:	Do not rejoice too soon. I extricate myself from the affair by a *salto mortale* and you do not usually take great pleasure in somersaults.
Lessing:	Say not so; provided I am not required to follow suit. And anyway you will soon land back on your feet. If it is not a secret, I insist on hearing what you have to say.
Jacobi:	You could always learn the trick from me. The whole matter consists in my arguing from fatalism directly against fatalism and all that is connected with it.[35]

Their conversation then shifts to the question of freedom. Here too we find an interesting exchange of opinions. Jacobi asserts that the most important concept is that of "final cause" (*Endursache*). For if there were no final cause, we could not help, in his opinion, denying freedom and becoming fatalists. If fatalism is right, moreover, the thinking faculty can do nothing but observe.

Noticing that Jacobi has a strong desire for free will, Lessing counters him by saying, "I have no craving for free will" (*ich begehre keinen freyen Willen*).

According to him, it is "human prejudice" to "consider the idea as primary and supreme, and want to derive everything from it."

On hearing this, Jacobi says that Lessing's thought is more extreme than Spinoza's.

Jacobi: You are going further than Spinoza. *Understanding (Einsicht)* was everything to him.

Lessing: Only as far as *human beings* are concerned! He was, however, far from considering as the best method our wretched way of acting according to intentions and of giving the idea pride of place.[36]

After this interesting exchange of opinions on the issue of freedom, Lessing directs his attention to Jacobi's "personal, extra-mundane divinity" (*Ihre persönliche extramundane Gottheit*). Endeavoring to see what kind of philosophical proof Jacobi intends to offer for such a divinity, he anticipates what Jacobi will say, and in order to lead the discussion forward, cleverly brings forward his hypothetical assertion that Leibniz was a Spinozist.

Jacobi heartily agrees with Lessing's assertion and develops a lengthy, pedantic argument as to the fundamental agreement between Leibniz and Spinoza. To crown his argument, he goes so far as to say, "To grasp Spinoza requires too long and persistent an effort of the mind. Anyone for whom a single line of the *Ethics* remains obscure has not really grasped him. . . . Few will have enjoyed such peace of mind or so celestial an understanding, as he reached through the crystal clarity of his mind."[37] Yet even with this high appraisal of Spinoza, and with all his pedantic knowledge of Spinozism, Jacobi nevertheless declares, on his honor, that he is not a Spinozist.[38]

On hearing this flat denial, Lessing cuts in:

Lessing: If you follow your philosophy, you ought indeed, on your honour, to turn your back on all philosophy.

Jacobi: Why turn my back on all philosophy?

Lessing: If you don't, you are a total sceptic.

Jacobi: On the contrary, I draw back from a philosophy that makes a total scepticism necessary.

Lessing: But where do you go from there?[39]

This question primes the pump for further discussion. During the course of the discussion, Jacobi's argument reaches its climax. Referring to a statement by Spinoza, Jacobi declares that, though not a Spinozist, he will "follow the light which, Spinoza says, illumines both itself and the darkness." For, he says, "more that [*sic*] any other philosopher" Spinoza has led him "to believe firmly that certain things cannot be explained; things that we therefore cannot disregard but must take as we find them." It follows, Jacobi contends, that a person "who does not attempt to explain the inexplicable, but simply to know the line of demarcation where the inexplicable begins, simply to recognize its presence, has created within himself the maximum space for the harbouring of human truth."[40]

Dissatisfied with Jacobi's explanation, Lessing presses him for a further, more satisfactory explanation.

Lessing: Words, words, my dear Jacobi! The line you wish to draw cannot be drawn. And besides, you are giving free rein to nonsense, fancies, blindness.

Jacobi: I think, it is possible to find such a line of demarcation. To *draw* it is not my intent, simply to discover the one already there and let it be. As far as nonsense, fancies, blindness are concerned . . .

Lessing: They find their dwelling wherever confused concepts prevail.

Jacobi: They are even more at home wherever *deceitful* concepts prevail. There we find enthroned the blindest, the most foolish, not to say the most stupid of beliefs. For if anyone ever becomes infatuated with a certain type of explanation, he will accept blindly all conclusions following from it; he is powerless to resist the compulsion for consistency, even if that consistency means he must needs stand on his head.

. . . In my own judgment a scholar's greatest merit is to unveil, to reveal *existence (Daseyn zu enthüllen, und zu offenbaren)*. . . . To explain is for him simply a means, a pathway to an end . . . the proximate, but never the ultimate goal. His ultimate goal is that which cannot be explained: whatever is insoluble, whatever is immediate, whatever is simple.[41]

Restraining Jacobi from developing his pedantic view, Lessing makes the ironical remark:

Lessing: Good, very good! That's all very helpful to me; but it does not help me in the same fashion. All in all, I find your *salto mortale* not bad and I can see how a man with a head on his shoulders might have to turn a somersault in order to get moving ahead. Take me with you if that is possible.

Jacobi: If you will just jump onto this springboard from which I am launched . . . , that's all you need to do.

Lessing: Even to do that would entail a leap I may no longer ask of my old legs and my muddled head.[42]

The statements cited above give a rough outline of the philosophical conversations that Lessing, in his last years, is said to have had with Jacobi.

Jacobi and Spinozism

Personal contact between Lessing and Jacobi began, incidentally, on 18 May 1779 when Lessing, in token of thanks for a complimentary copy of *Woldemar* from Jacobi, sent him a copy of his newly published *Nathan the Wise*. Deeply moved by this gift, Jacobi wrote a lengthy letter of thanks on 20 August 1779, expressing his wish to pay a visit to Lessing when he next traveled to Wolfenbüttel. Having received a cordial invitation, he visited Lessing's home in Wolfenbüttel for the first time from 5–11 July 1780. He then had good opportunity to engage Lessing in long and heated discussions on metaphysical topics.

About a month later (according to Scholz's assumption), presumably between August 10th and 15th, he again met Lessing both in Brunswick and in

Halberstadt (where Lessing had business to attend to) and had another opportunity to engage him in metaphysical discussions.[43]

The first question we have to ask here has to do with Jacobi's intention in visiting Lessing at this time. In order to clarify his motive, we direct our attention to his remark, "I had come chiefly in the hope of receiving your help against Spinoza." This clearly shows that Jacobi sought out Lessing not to converse about general topics in literature, philosophy, and religion, but for the definite purpose of discussing the specific topic of Spinozism. But why this particular topic? And why seek help from Lessing? In my view Frederick Beiser has an accurate grasp of the matter and of the circumstances. I propose, therefore, to follow his account.

According to Beiser, Lessing was "a deeply symbolic figure for Jacobi" and was essentially "a vehicle for Jacobi's criticisms of the Berlin *Aufklärer*, and in particular Mendelssohn."[44] Since his early days, Jacobi had been disdainful of the Berlin *Aufklärer*. In his eyes the Enlightenment thinkers of the Berlin circle represented "a form of intellectual tyranny and dogmatism." These thinkers behaved as if they were the guardians of tolerance and free thought. In his view, however, they were in reality hypocrites who were "willing to forfeit their intellectual ideals for the sake of compliance with the moral, religious, and political status quo." Although they championed "the ideals of radical criticism and free inquiry," they easily abandoned these ideals and acquiesced in the Establishment as soon as "they seemed to threaten the foundation of morality, religion, and the state." In the final analysis, they were *Popular-philosophen* who, Jacobi thought, aimed at practical or utilitarian ends, such as "the education of the public, the promotion of the general welfare, and the achievement of a general culture." But he wondered whether philosophy could serve two masters: reason and the public. With regard to philosophy he asked, "Can it be both critical and practical, both rational and responsible, both honest and useful?" Is the purpose of philosophy "truth or the general happiness?" Is it not an illusion to think, as the Berlin *Aufklärer* do, that philosophy supports morality, religion, and the state? On the contrary, is it not true that free inquiry, when pursued to its limits without restraint, inevitably leads to skepticism? And is it not always the case that "skepticism erodes the very foundation of morality, religion, and the state?"[45]

Guided by such ideas, Jacobi sought to teach the Berliners the lesson that philosophy could not serve both truth and the public. For this purpose, he conceived the notion of "preparing for them the eighteenth-century equivalent of hemlock: namely, the bitter pill of Lessing's Spinozism."[46] For in his eyes Lessing represented "the very antithesis of the *Berliner Geist*" and was "the only courageous and honest thinker of the *Aufklärung*." That is to say, "he alone had the courage to pursue inquiry for its own sake, despite the consequences; and he alone had the honesty to take criticism to its tragic conclusion without moral or religious scruples."[47] To put it in Jacobian terms, "Lessing was the only man with the honesty to admit the consequences of all inquiry and criticism: atheism and fatalism."[48] But such atheism and fatalism are, in Jacobi's view, the quintessence of Spinozism. Thus despite his remark that "I certainly did not expect to find you a Spinozist or pantheist," it is quite possible that Jacobi, from the outset, suspected Lessing of being a Spinozist and took him in by means of shrewd, leading questions.[49] If this observation is correct, then we can say that Jacobi used "the figure of Lessing to criticize the Berlin establishment."[50]

The next question to be considered is that of Jacobi's relationship to Spinozism. To put it in a nutshell, it is, as Vallée says, "a love-hate relationship."[51] Jacobi's vivid and empathetic presentation of Spinozism can easily give us the impression, the false impression, that he speaks "in Spinoza's stead."[52] For example, the following previously cited words can be taken as an indication both of Jacobi's high esteem for Spinoza and of his pedantic knowledge of Spinozism:

> To grasp Spinoza requires too long and persistent an effort of the mind. Anyone for whom a single line of the *Ethics* remains obscure has not really grasped him. . . . Few will have enjoyed such peace of mind or so celestial an understanding as he reached through the crystal clarity of his mind.[53]

Nevertheless, Jacobi's attitude toward Spinoza is extremely paradoxical. To use Heinrich Scholz's formulation, Jacobi's conclusion is that "Spinozism is, according to its form, a system of consistent rationalism and, according to its content, atheism."[54] For what reasons, then, and by what method of argument was Jacobi led to this conclusion? If, moreover, Spinozism is a form of atheism, why does he praise Spinoza so much, even going so far as to say, "I love Spinoza"?[55]

In Jacobi's view, reason by itself cannot grasp the transcendently infinite. At most, all it can do is to conceive the infinite within the world. Nevertheless, rationalists seek to grasp and explain everything in terms of reason. Rationalism, when it pursues its ideal to the limit, inevitably ends up in pantheism. What happens to Spinoza is nothing but an example of how rationalism, through being self-consistent, ends up as a form of pantheism. Thus the true character of Spinozism is consistent rationalism. But the immanent "infinite substance" in Spinoza and the truly infinite (the personal God who creates and presides over the world) are alike only in appearance.[56] To be sure, Spinoza speaks of God. But to identify God with blind necessity or nature as Spinoza did is nothing but "the deification of the world" (*Weltvergötterung*).[57] Even if a somewhat euphemistic term like "cosmo-theism" (*Kosmotheismus*)[58] is used, "the personal extramundane divinity" is in fact denied. For Jacobi, consequently, in the final analysis Spinozism is atheism.

Jacobi's method of argument, illustrated above, seems forced. In any event, his assertion that Spinozism as a consistent rationalism represents the destiny and the problems of every rationalism in an extreme form, and that Leibniz-Wolffian philosophy and the Berlin *Aufklärung* are less consistent than Spinozism, lead, in the end, to the same dilemma of which he accused Spinozism. Does not Jacobi's position turn, of necessity, into anti-philosophy? Does philosophy itself not become impossible if, and to the extent that, one holds to Jacobi's presuppositions? When Lessing said to Jacobi, "If you follow your philosophy, you ought indeed, on your honor, to turn your back on all philosophy," he implied precisely these questions.

Since our task here is not to discuss Jacobi's philosophy or his understanding of Spinozism, we must be content to refer to other scholars' studies on this point.[59] The most important thing to observe is that Jacobi used Spinozism as a springboard for his "philosophy of faith" (*Glaubensphilosophie*). His criticism of Spinozism as a thoroughgoing rationalism served as the fulcrum from which his *salto mortale* was to be converted into his fideistic philosophy.[60] Hence his understanding of Spinoza and Spinozism is dubious. Indeed, David Bell passes a rigorous judgment on Jacobi's understanding of Spinoza. He says:

> Spinoza is thus no more than an instrument used by Jacobi as part of his grand scheme to discredit rationalism and replace it with his own "science of ignorance." . . . Jacobi's interpretation of Spinoza must therefore ultimately be seen as part of his own philosophy of faith, implacably opposed to the *Aufklärung.* . . .
>
> In the last resort, then, Jacobi's view of Spinoza must be seen to be severely limited. Spinoza simply plays the part of a weapon in his campaign against the *Aufklärung*.[61]

However that may be, it is clear that a correct understanding of Lessing's confession of "Spinozism" requires meticulous and painstaking analysis. First of all, one has to uncover Jacobi's real intention in disclosing "Lessing's secret" to Mendelssohn. Then one must investigate whether the content of their conversations has not been biased or distorted by Jacobi's own "philosophy of faith." And if there is any possibility that the content of their conversations as reported by Jacobi has been biased or distorted, his report should not be accepted at face value. Instead, one needs to discount Jacobi's account wherever this is the case. Before setting about this task, however, we should attend to what Mendelssohn has to say.

Mendelssohn and "Refined Pantheism"

We have already seen how Mendelssohn reacted to the "apple of discord" (*Zankapfel*) that Jacobi hurled at him at an early stage of their controversy. He declared it an outrage that Jacobi would brand Lessing "a Spinozist, an atheist, and a blasphemer." His friend Lessing, the author of *Nathan the Wise*, was, rather, a "great and respected champion of theism and of the religion of reason."[62]

But when he realized that there was little room for doubt as to the authenticity of Jacobi's account, Mendelssohn sought to make Jacobi's poisonous apple as innocuous as possible. He did so by interpreting Lessing's alleged "Spinozism" in a harmless way.[63] For this purpose, and before Jacobi's account had been made public, he published a book, *Morning Hours, or Lectures on the Existence of God* (*Morgenstunden oder Vorlesungen über das Dasein Gottes*). In this book he discussed the problem of Spinozism and pantheism in three chapters, and in the last chapter, Lessing's worldview. He thus made full use of the information confidentially supplied by Jacobi, but did not mention his source at all.[64]

In these lectures, the theist Mendelssohn draws a clear line between theism and pantheism, particularly as to the God-world relationship. According to him, theists make a sharp distinction between God and the world, maintaining that God (the infinite One) has brought the world (the finite Many) into being, while pantheists deem God and the world identical, asserting that God is one and all, infinite and finite at the same time. Hence Mendelssohn says:

> Accordingly, we separate God from nature and ascribe an extramundane exist-
> ence to God just as we ascribe an extradivine existence to the world. On the
> other hand, the adherents of the aforesaid pantheism, with which we have to do
> here, assume that there is no extradivine existence at all. But their presupposition
> is that the ideas of the infinite, by reason of their necessity, obtain a sort of exist-
> ence in God himself, [an existence that] at bottom is intimately united with his
> existence.[65]

Thus Mendelssohn insists on the fundamental difference between theism and pantheism. He does not, however, force us to choose between them. For the problem that divides them has to do with an extremely subtle metaphysical speculation devoid of practical consequence. Instead, he suggests that theism and pantheism, in the end, might possibly draw nearer to each other than people generally deem possible. There can be a position, he suggests, that affirms the immanence of the world in God without abandoning the basic convictions of theism (the createdness of the world by God's free act of creation and its objective existence outside God). He calls such a position "refined pantheism" (*der geläuterte Pantheismus, der verfeinerte Pantheismus*) and stresses its "harmlessness" and "compatibility with religion and morality."[66] His concept of refined pantheism, however, lacks further elaboration and gives us the impression that it is a mere artifact brought forth so as to exonerate Lessing from the charge of Spinozism.[67] In any event, having thus laid the foundation for his discussion of Lessing's worldview, Mendelssohn asserts that "Lessing envisaged pantheism in the totally refined manner I have ascribed to him" and that "he was on his way to link pantheistic concepts even with positive religion."[68] His conclusion is that Lessing's worldview, as a refined pantheism, is "totally compatible with the truths of religion and morality."[69]

In these assertions we can discern Mendelssohn's intention to defend his deceased friend from slander and abuse. That is to say, he presented an argument that would make nonsense of Jacobi's branding of Lessing as a Spinozist and atheist. He intended to minimize any bad effects and shape public opinion in a way that would be favorable to his friend, even if his adversary should disclose to the public the content of his conversations with Lessing. But his intention was defeated because Jacobi, doubting Mendelssohn and suspecting that he would do what he did, published the content of the conversations as a book entitled *Concerning the Doctrine of Spinoza, in Letters to Herr Moses Mendelssohn.* He took this action mainly out of fear of being forestalled by the Jewish philosopher. Adding insult to injury, he also broke his promises to

Mendelssohn and to Elise Reimarus by putting into print private letters from them without their permission, hoping that his appeal to the public would justify bringing their letters to light.[70] Bitterly resentful of this unforgivable action, Mendelssohn, old and sick though he was, took up his pen and completed in great haste a manuscript *To the Friends of Lessing* (in German). Wishing to have it published as soon as possible, he hurried to the publisher on 31 December 1785 in freezing Berlin weather without an overcoat. This was a reckless and imprudent action for one who was said to have been the model for Nathan the Wise. On returning home, he took to his bed and passed away on the morning of 4 January 1786.[71]

Mendelssohn's posthumous work *To the Friends of Lessing*, which became his swan song, contains superb appraisals of Lessing that only he could have made. One cannot read it without being touched by their extraordinarily deep friendship. In this moving piece, Mendelssohn acutely takes note of Jacobi's secret intention in confiding to him the content of his private conversations with Lessing. According to him, Jacobi's true intention is nothing other than "to lead his fellow-men, who have lost their way in the arid wastes of speculation, back to the straight and narrow path of *faith*"[72] or "to retreat to the shelter of faith."[73] For this purpose Jacobi has, in Mendelssohn's eyes, labeled Lessing a Spinozist and is now using him as a weapon in his own campaign against the Berlin Enlightenment circle. In other words, branding Lessing a Spinozist was merely a means to the end of fighting against the adherents of reason. Thus Mendelssohn proclaims that Jacobi's secret intent was to convince him of the following lessons: "Speculative reason, when consistent, leads perforce to Spinozism," and "once someone has reached the precipitous peaks of metaphysics, there is no recourse but to turn one's back on all philosophy and plunge headfirst into the depths of faith."[74]

It is clear, therefore, that Mendelssohn has his own interpretation for what he has discerned of Jacobi's secret intention and underlying antagonism. Furthermore, he calls attention to Lessing's innate perversity and roguish playfulness, traits which he, through his long years of friendship with Lessing, was better acquainted with than anyone else. He thus raises a serious question as to whether Lessing's alleged Spinozism was "a joke or a philosophy" (*Schäckerey oder Philosophie*).[75] To this extent, Mendelssohn's attempt to vindicate his deceased friend against the charge of being a Spinozist may be considered successful in a general way.

In any event, the question Mendelssohn raises has something to do with the extremely difficult question of γυμναστικῶς and δογματικῶς, or of "the esoteric" and "the exoteric," which confronts every student of Lessing.[76] Since this is so, the problem of how we should take Lessing's "Spinozistic confession" is indeed formidable. Heinrich Scholz remarks, "Jacobi has understood Lessing much too dogmatically. He has overlooked the antithetical, the hypothetical, and the humorous—three infinitely important factors for Lessing—in Lessing's expressions and thereby, in a certain sense, has mystified himself."[77] Be that as it may, to correctly understand Lessing's "Spinozism" calls for a more in-depth, full-scale investigation.

Lessing's *Hen kai Pan*

So far, we have gained some idea of the nature of the philosophical conversations between Lessing and Jacobi, conversations which, when their content was disclosed, gave rise almost immediately to the "Spinoza controversy" between Mendelssohn and Jacobi and, eventually, to the "pantheism controversy" that engaged almost all the best minds of late eighteenth-century Germany. We have seen that the controversy between Mendelssohn the Jewish philosopher and Jacobi the "poet-philosopher of Goethe's era" (*Philosoph und Literat der Goethezeit*)[78] is, in the last analysis, a dispute between two different interpretations of Lessing's worldview. Mendelssohn depicts Lessing as a representative of a "rational theism" similar to his own and identifies his worldview as one of "refined pantheism." Jacobi, on the other hand, portrays this rational theism as nothing more than "an exoteric veil" (*eine exoterische Hülle*) for Lessing's esoteric Spinozism.

Seen in this light, the dispute can be said to center on the issue of whether Lessing is a rational theist or a Spinozist.[79] Our analysis so far, however, does not permit us to tell which of these two interpretations is the more probable, or whether both are wrong. In our view, Mendelssohn and Jacobi alike interpret Lessing a bit too one-sidedly. In particular, it would be a mistake to swallow Jacobi's account whole and to speak without further ado of Lessing's "Spinozism." Instead, one needs to attend to the minute details of the Lessing-Jacobi conversations, particularly to Lessing's remarks, and examine them carefully, paying full attention to their original context.

First of all, it is important to observe that it was not Lessing but Jacobi who first brought up the name of Spinoza. When Jacobi showed Lessing Goethe's poem "Prometheus"[80] and asked him what he thought of it, Lessing indicated that he was in sympathy with the poem and indeed that the viewpoint it expressed was his own. Then he added, "The orthodox concepts of the divinity are no longer for me; I cannot stand them. *Hen kai Pan*! I know naught else." On the face of it, Jacobi was greatly surprised at Lessing's "unexpected" answer. But as mentioned above, this answer of Lessing's was precisely what he had expected and precisely what he had intended to draw from him. Happy to hear such an answer, Jacobi mentioned Spinoza's name for the first time: "Then you would . . . be more or less in agreement with Spinoza."

In this connection the questions to be considered here are these: (1) why did Jacobi show Goethe's poem "Prometheus" to Lessing? (2) can Goethe's poem be regarded as an expression of Spinozism? and (3) does Lessing's ἕν καὶ πᾶν signify Spinozism as Jacobi assumes?

As to the first question, we cannot help thinking that Jacobi took Goethe's unpublished poem to Lessing with a specific intention. As suggested above, if it is the case that Jacobi suspected Lessing of being a Spinozist from the very outset, we have to assume that Jacobi had some ulterior motive for taking the poem with him when he visited Lessing. We conjecture that Jacobi, having intuitively caught the scent of Spinozism in Goethe's poem, wanted to prove through Lessing that his intuition was correct and, if all went well, to worm out of Lessing his secret allegiance to Spinozism. Jacobi's act of showing Goethe's poem to Lessing meant, according to this conjecture, that Jacobi was both testing the accuracy of his own intuition and trying to get at what he supposed was Lessing's Spinozism. Thus Goethe's "Prometheus" served, in two senses, as a litmus test for the existence of Spinozism.

What, then, was the result of his test? On the face of it, Lessing seems to have been so taken in by Jacobi's shrewd leading questions that he disclosed his secret allegiance to Spinozism. Jacobi's litmus test seems to have proved the accuracy of his intuition as poet-philosopher. But it would be hasty to jump to such a conclusion. For even judging from Jacobi's report alone, his conversations with Lessing disclose a slight but significant divergence on the point at issue between the two thinkers.

Having read the poem, Lessing remarked, "I take no offence; I long ago became acquainted with it first hand." On hearing these words, Jacobi wondered if Lessing was already familiar with the poem and asked, "You know the poem?" Lessing answered, "I have never read the poem; but I find it good." In this dialogue, a divergence as to the point at issue is already evident. The key to the divergence is implied by Lessing's words, "I long ago became acquainted with it first hand" (*ich habe das schon lange aus der ersten Hand*). But what is meant by the term "first hand" (*aus der ersten Hand*)? How could Lessing be acquainted with the poem *first hand* if he had never read it before? According to our conjecture, Lessing, without knowing who the author was, keenly perceived the spirit of the poem and expressed his sympathy with it. At the same time, he wanted to state that he was well acquainted with the classic source of the poem, namely, Aeschylus's work. Hence the term "first hand" may be taken as implying his familiarity with Aeschylus's classic tragedy.[81]

If this is so, it can safely be said that Lessing expressed his sympathy not with Spinozism but with the point of view, expressed in the poem, that goes back to *Prometheus Bound*. At this point, the second question becomes all the more acute. Was Goethe's poem "Prometheus" an expression of Spinozism? Was the author's viewpoint, which Lessing identified with his own, Spinozistic as Jacobi suspected?

With regard to this question, one can best let the author speak for himself. In his *Truth and Poetry*, part 3, book 15, Goethe says:

> The myth of Prometheus came to life in me. I tailored the old titanic garments to my size, and without further reflection began to write a play portraying the difficulties Prometheus experienced with Zeus and the new Olympian gods when he formed human beings on his own initiative, brought them to life with Minerva's help, and founded a third dynasty. And truly, the gods who were now ruling had every cause to complain, because they could be viewed as entities illegitimately inserted between the Titans and mankind. Set as a monologue into this singular composition is that poem which has won a significant place in German literature because it prompted Lessing to declare his views to Jacobi on some important points of philosophy and sentiment. It served as the tinder for an explosion which revealed and brought to discussion the most secret concerns of worthy men, concerns which, unknown even to them, slumbered in an otherwise very

enlightened society. The fissure was opened so violently that because of it, and some contingent occurrences, we lost one of our worthiest men, Mendelssohn.

Although, as actually happened, one can attach philosophical, indeed religious considerations to this subject matter, it really belongs to the realm of poetry. The Titans are the foil to polytheism, just as the devil can be viewed as the foil to monotheism. But neither the latter nor the one God to whom he stands in contrast is a poetic figure. Milton's Satan, gallantly as he is portrayed, remains in a disadvantageously subaltern position as he attempts to destroy the splendid creation of a superior Being. Prometheus, on the other hand, has the advantage of being able to create and form in defiance of higher beings. Also, it is a beautiful thought, one appropriate for poetry, to have human beings created, not by the supreme ruler of the world, but by a lesser figure who, however, is sufficiently worthy and important to do this because he is a scion of the oldest dynasty. And, in general, Greek mythology offers us an inexhaustible wealth of human and divine symbols.[82]

These words of Goethe show unmistakably that the poem "Prometheus" originally had nothing to do with Spinozism. According to Erich Trunz, editor of Goethe's *Werke*, Prometheus is both a mythical and a poetic figure: a demigod (*Halbgott*) in the Greek myth, on the one hand, and a genius enhanced to the level of myth, on the other. Consequently, it would be appropriate to regard the poem as a poetic expression of Goethe's "idea of genius" (*Geniegedanke*).[83] In other words, wishing to found the whole of his existence on "my productive talent" (*mein produktives Talent*) or "this natural gift" (*diese Naturgabe*), Goethe borrowed from Prometheus an old mythical costume in order to give poetic expression to his idea of the whole man.[84] The poem is intended to be, then, as Goethe himself makes clear, a poetic expression of "this trend toward the titanic-gigantic and earth-shaking" (*der titanisch-gigantische, himmelstürmende Sinn*).[85]

The great Goethe scholar H. A. Korff sees in this poem "the battle of man for his metaphysical freedom."[86] In his view, it expresses the spirit of the genius-poet Goethe, aware of something divine within himself, and it expresses "revolt against God out of the feeling of his own inner divinity."[87] Accordingly, it is a product of that spirit closely connected with the famous epigraph in part 4 of *Truth and Poetry*: "Nemo contra deum nisi deus ipse."[88] Since Korff makes a convincing case for the view that this new feeling of divinity, in which both intimacy with and revolt against God coexist, has some connection with "a pantheistic sense of the world,"[89] it might be possible to speak of a "Spinozistic" point of view in this poem. But this would be possible only by way of such a pantheistic detour—and even then, it would be more accurate to speak of a "pantheistic" rather than a "Spinozistic" point of view. In any event, our consideration shows that Goethe's "Prometheus" is not, in the first instance, a manifestation of Spinozism.

Our third question has to do with the relationship between Lessing's ἕν καὶ πᾶν and Spinozism. It will be recalled that on reading Goethe's poem (though strictly speaking, he did not know its author's name), Lessing expressed complete sympathy for its point of view, going on to say, "The orthodox concepts of the divinity are no longer for me; I cannot stand them. *Hen kai Pan!* I know naught else." And when Jacobi seized on these words with the comment, "Then you would . . . be more or less in agreement with Spinoza," the response Lessing made was, "If I am to call myself by anybody's name, then I know none better."

Judging from this dialogue alone, people may well be led to conclude that Lessing's ἕν καὶ πᾶν is a manifestation or confession of Spinozism. But since we have familiarized ourselves with Lessing's character and his peculiar mode of thinking, we need to be very careful here. For Lessing did not praise Spinoza as his philosophical mentor unconditionally. On the contrary, he qualified his agreement with Spinoza by saying, "If I am to call myself by anybody's name"—and did so only after Jacobi had introduced Spinoza's name. In addition, Spinoza, who had been treated as badly as "a dead dog," was for him a philosopher whose lost honor ought to be retrieved. At any rate, Lessing was not the sort of thinker who had no choice but to cling to a greater thinker's shirttail. As we have seen in the preceding chapters, he was an utterly independent thinker with his own style and logic. To cite Windelband's words again, Lessing was "the only creative mind in German philosophy between Leibniz and Kant."[90] In fact, Lessing was unwilling to agree completely even with the great German philosopher Leibniz, with whom he felt the most affinity and congeniality. It is unthinkable, therefore, that so independent a mind would have accepted Spinoza's philosophy without qualification.[91]

The words Lessing used when he resumed with Jacobi the conversation that had been broken off the day before are worth remembering. Instead of saying that he had come to talk about Spinozism, Lessing said, "I came to talk with you about *my* ἕν καὶ πᾶν" (italics added). The use of this personal pronoun "my" seems to point toward the correctness of our conjecture.

But how, then, are his words "There is no other philosophy but the philosophy of Spinoza" to be understood? These words too can be taken as expressing Lessing's peculiarly ironical attitude toward Jacobi, who took pride in his erudition with regard to Spinozistic philosophy. For it is not Lessing but Jacobi who develops a lengthy and pedantic interpretation of Spinozism in the succeeding discussion, and it is not Spinoza's philosophical system but "the spirit of Spinozism" (*der Geist des Spinozismus*)[92] that is of interest to Lessing. What is more, when Jacobi declares, "But my credo is not to be found in Spinoza," Lessing responds, "I sincerely hope that it is not to be found in any book."[93] For one who distinguished sharply between "letter" and "spirit" and attached greater importance to the spirit, this response is by no means insignificant.

On the basis of the foregoing observations, we venture to assert that the ἕν καὶ πᾶν of which Lessing spoke is not to be linked with Spinozism, as Jacobi sought to do, but should be interpreted independently of Spinozism. What, then, is Lessing's ἕν καὶ πᾶν? How is it to be interpreted? This is the problem to be taken up in the next section.

Lessing's Panentheism

The first thing to observe is that Lessing introduces his ἕν καὶ πᾶν as a concept that stands in antithesis to "the orthodox concepts of the divinity" (*die orthodoxen Begriffe von der Gottheit*). The simplest interpretation would be to take it as implying allegiance to the pantheistic worldview, which can be characterized by the motto ἕν καὶ πᾶν or ἕν πάντα. According to this interpretation, Lessing could no longer believe in Christian theism but would have to be an adherent of pantheism.

Yet here too we must proceed cautiously. For Jacobi himself elsewhere admits that Lessing never denied "a personal divinity" (*eine persönliche Gottheit*).[94] Furthermore, the meaning of "the orthodox concepts of divinity," which Lessing says he cannot stand, is not self-evident. Does he mean Christian theism as such, or alternatively, the orthodox Lutheran concept of God that prevailed in his age? Reinhard Schwarz conjectures that what Lessing denied is "the extramundane God" (*der außerweltliche Gott*) taught by Sigmund Jakob Baumgarten in his three-volume *Glaubenslehre* (1759–60).[95] We do not have sufficient information to verify the truth of his conjecture, but it is clear that Lessing found some philosophical difficulty with the idea of a "personal, extramundane divinity" that Jacobi espoused.[96] When we correlate this fact with Jacobi's admission that Lessing did not deny a personal God, we can infer that what he denied is perhaps not Christian theism as such but a heteronomous deity that remains above the world and tyrannically rules over it. Actually, this inference seems to go a long way toward accounting for the fact that Lessing, on reading Goethe's "Prometheus," said, "The orthodox concepts of the divinity are no longer for me; I cannot stand them."

In the final analysis, Lessing's words, "*Hen kai Pan*! I know naught else," can be taken as expressing his own *immanent* view of God and the world, a view that differs from the traditional Christian view. This immanent view of God and the world, however, must be clearly distinguished from that of Spinozism. For Lessing's God is not a substance possessing the two attributes of "thought" and "extension," as in Spinoza. Lessing's God is conceived, rather, as "a higher energy" (*eine höhere Kraft*)[97] in which the attributes of extension, movement, and idea are grounded. Lessing does agree with Spinoza, however, in his criticism of anthropomorphism. He finds fault with Jacobi's conception of God for the reason that it makes God conform to "our wretched way of acting in accordance with intentions" (*unsere elende Art, nach Absichten zu handeln*).[98] In his eyes, such a conception of God is mere anthropomorphism.

How, then, does Lessing understand God? One of the keys to answering this question is Jacobi's remark: "When Lessing wanted to imagine a *personal* divinity, he thought of it as the soul of the universe (*die Seele des Alls*), and he thought of the Whole as being analogous to an organic body."[99] Jacobi takes Lessing's words in the Spinozistic sense and concludes that "Lessing does not believe in a cause of things . . . distinct from the world," which is as much as to say, "Lessing is a Spinozist."[100] This interpretation, as pointed out above, is strained.

It is our contention that Lessing's ἕν καὶ πᾶν is to be understood not in terms of Spinozistic pantheism but in terms of a stream of thought which, though headed in "a direction that eventually leads to Spinoza,"[101] is clearly distinct from Spinozism. What we have in mind is spiritualism (*Spiritualismus*). This is "the stream of tradition which, since the sixteenth century, runs independently alongside Protestant ecclesiasticism and which is stamped more by individual thinkers than by the organization of sectarian groups."[102] Thinkers who belong to this tradition include such figures as Sebastian Franck, Paracelsus, Valentin Weigel, Jakob Boehme, and, in the eighteenth century in particular, Johann Konrad Dippel and Johann Christian Edelmann.

The relationship between Lessing's thought and the spiritualistic tradition was first proposed by Harald Schultze as a "working hypothesis."[103] This hypothesis was reinforced at many points by Wolfgang Gericke and is now on the way toward becoming a new theory.[104] Gericke, assuming a stream of intellectual history running from Nicholas of Cusa through the philosophers of the Italian Renaissance, the German philosophy of nature, and Leibniz to Lessing, calls this stream "the spiritualistic tradition" (*die spiritualistische Tradition*). His attempt to understand Lessing's thought by correlating it with this tradition is attractive and worthy of some consideration.[105] This is not to say that the whole of Lessing's thought is best understood from the point of view of the spiritualistic tradition. Lessing's thought is too pluralistic and compound to permit understanding from any single point of view or single source. But with particular regard to the matter of his ἕν καὶ πᾶν, if it does not signify the Spinozistic pantheism of "deus sive natura," we must look for a key to its interpretation in the spiritualistic tradition. According to Gericke, "Lessing's ἕν καὶ πᾶν has to be construed from the point of view of spiritualism, from the point of view, for example, of Boehme's conviction that God is 'all in all.' In distinction from Spinoza, however, [what Boehme] has in mind is not the identity of God with the universe but, rather, God's omnipresence and omnipotence."[106] We too think that Lessing's ἕν καὶ πᾶν is to be understood in this context.

But to interpret Lessing's ἕν καὶ πᾶν against the background of the spiritualistic tradition is to interpret it as a "panentheism," the doctrine that God includes all things in his own being as part, not the whole, of his being. Wilhelm Dilthey, at the close of his essay on the "Conception and Analysis of Man in the Fifteenth and Sixteenth Centuries" (in German), suggests an affinity between the thought and destiny of Sebastian Franck and Lessing.[107] It is conceivable, therefore, that the "religious, universalistic theism" (*der religiös universalistische Theismus*) or "refined panentheism" (*der geläuterte Panentheismus*) which Dilthey regards as Franck's worldview is also Lessing's own worldview. In fact, in his *Poetry and Lived Experience* (in German), Dilthey refers to Lessing's fragment "On the Reality of Things outside God" and affirms that Lessing's basic position, because it asserts that nothing is outside God but that "all things are real in God,"[108] is panentheism. Dilthey holds that "this panentheism of Lessing's is completely different from the doctrine that Jacobi ascribed to Spinoza. Lessing was not a Spinozist in Jacobi's sense.

Insofar as he was a Spinozist at all, he was so in his own—and in a more accurate and profound sense."[109]

It seems appropriate to conclude this section of our inquiry with a similar statement by Johannes Schneider:

> He [Lessing] thinks pantheistically: things are indeed in God, but are nevertheless distinct from God. . . . For Lessing, God is an imagining personality. In God the concept of things and the reality of things are one. God includes the reality but, as opposed to the case of Spinoza, does not completely dissolve in the reality. . . . The immanence of things in God is not alien to the Christian worldview, for it is directly given with the dogma of God's omnipresence. The only question is how that immanence should be understood.[110]

Lessing's View of God and the World

Our discussion has shown that Lessing's ἕν καὶ πᾶν signifies not a Spinozistic pantheism but a panentheism of spiritualistic stamp. But the question remains as to the substance of his panentheism. More specifically, the question at issue is that of how Lessing conceives "the immanence of the world in God" (*die Immanenz der Welt in Gott*).[111]

As indicated in the quotation from Schneider that closed the preceding section, the idea of panentheism, namely, that all things are in God, is not alien to Christianity. For example, Paul's words in Acts 17:28, "In him we live and move and have our being," have often been cited as one of the scriptural grounds for panentheism. If we ask, however, whether Lessing's ἕν καὶ πᾶν remains within the bounds of traditional Christian doctrine, we may find it impossible to deny that it oversteps these bounds. We propose, therefore, in concluding this inquiry, to take a close look at this issue.

Erich Schmidt, in his voluminous *Lessing: History of His Life and Writings* (in German), describes the second meeting between Lessing and Jacobi, this time at Gleim's summerhouse in Halberstadt. Toward the end of his description, he says, "On a concealed door of the cottage, which served as the guest book, Lessing wrote not only *dies in lite* (days in contention) but also his ἕν καὶ πᾶν."[112] Herder, who visited shortly after them, confirmed that Lessing had indeed written those epigrams on the door of the bower. To commemorate his visit, Herder wrote his own words between Jacobi's and Lessing's.[113] In a letter to Jacobi of 6 February 1784, he wrote:

> I finally snatch an hour to write you nothing other than εν και παν, which I myself found written by Lessing's hand in Gleim's summerhouse, but do not yet know how to explain. To explain, that is, in Lessing's spirit. For I could hardly think that you had such terrible metaphysical arguments with the latter-day Anacreon. . . . I would have [liked to] write my εν κ[αι] παν thereunder seven times, after I so unexpectedly found in Lessing a fellow-believer in my credo.[114]

Herder's letter is ample testimony to the authenticity of Lessing's ἕν καὶ πᾶν.

In any event, Lessing's ἕν καὶ πᾶν, disclosed by Jacobi to Mendelssohn in Berlin, soon spread to Herder and Goethe in Weimar, and to Hamann and

Kant in Königsberg, thus engaging all of them in the maelstrom of the pantheism controversy. But an important point that we should not overlook here, though usually unheeded, is that Lessing's ἕν καὶ πᾶν has a variant form, namely, ἕν ἐγὼ καὶ πάντα. It was again Erich Schmidt who first brought to light the existence of this second motto that originated with Lessing. In 1892, in the endnotes to the above-mentioned book, he said, "My friend Köster is in possession of a page from a family album, and has sent it to me by facsimile, on which is written [without accents] 'Εν εγω [unclear εχω] και παντα! Gotthold Ephraim Lessing. Hamburg 14 Oct. 1780'."[115] Later Franz Muncker, the editor of *Lessing's Complete Works* (in German), at last obtained the original. On a "coarse, yellow-white sheet of paper in crosswise octavo" were written "in a clear hand" the words "Εν εγω και παντα!   Gotthold Ephraim Lessing Hamburg   14 Oct. 1780."[116]

From this motto, as mentioned in the preceding chapter, Erwin Quapp draws the conclusion that the variant formula using εγω is the more authentic one, and he uses this formula as the exegetical principle for his interpretation of *The Education of the Human Race*. But his reliance on this formula involves a serious confusion. Quapp sets forth as Lessing's authentic formula, which he calls the "summerhouse formula" (*Gartenhausformel*), the words ἕν ἐγὼ καὶ πᾶν rather than the form verified as authentic by Schmidt and Muncker, namely, ἕν ἐγὼ καὶ πάντα. The cause of the confusion, in our view, is to be found in Alexander Altmann's essay "Lessing and Jacobi: The Conversations on Spinozism" (in German).[117] For in his description of the conversations between Lessing and Jacobi at Gleim's summerhouse, Altmann maintains that on the concealed door, Lessing wrote "ἕν ἐγὼ καὶ πᾶν."[118] Because Altmann is the author of a biography of Lessing's intimate friend Moses Mendelssohn, a biography so detailed and accurate that no one could compete with him, it is hardly conceivable that he would make a careless mistake in reporting on Lessing's epigram, which is so important, even decisive, for a proper interpretation of the Spinoza conversations between Lessing and Jacobi. But if the epigram that Lessing wrote is, as Altmann reports, the formula with ἐγώ in it, namely, ἕν ἐγὼ καὶ πᾶν, then a new question arises, namely, why is it that Herder, as an eyewitness, made no objection to the inaccuracy in Jacobi's report?

This confused situation is something like the one in Lessing's famous parable of the three rings. Which of the three Greek phrases is Lessing's authentic formula: εν και παν as Jacobi reports, εν εγω και παντα as Lessing's own handwritten epigram suggests, or εν εγω και παν as Altmann has newly proposed?

When we compare these three formulas, we see that the conspicuous differences are (1) whether the formula contains the word ἐγώ, and (2) whether the word meaning "all" is πᾶν or πάντα. If ἐγώ in the second and third formulas means Lessing himself, the existence of this ἐγώ would make a big difference in the meaning. The difference between the second and third formulas may seem to be trifling, since the only difference is that the word for "all" is singular in the one and plural in the other. In reality, however, there is a world of difference in meaning. For the singular form πᾶν includes ἐν (and therefore God) in itself; hence, a formula using πᾶν has strong pantheistic implications. The plural form πάντα, on the other hand, does not include ἐν (and therefore God) in itself, but means all things, or the universe, created by God; hence, a formula using πάντα carries theistic implications.

To the best of our knowledge, no Lessing scholar has perceived the existence of three different formulas for Lessing's ἕν καὶ πᾶν. Given this state of affairs in present-day Lessing studies, it is not easy to decide which of the three formulas is most authentic. In any event, however, it would be hasty and heedless to declare ἕν ἐγὼ καὶ πᾶν the proper formula and use it as the key to his theological thought, as Quapp did when he innocently placed his trust in Altmann's account. If one wishes to adopt a formula that includes ἐγώ instead of the commonly used ἕν καὶ πᾶν, then one ought to employ Lessing's handwritten formula, ἕν ἐγὼ καὶ πάντα, as Hermann Timm did. We consider ἕν ἐγὼ καὶ πάντα [I am One and All] as the formula most appropriate to Lessing's thought for two reasons.

First, judging from Jacobi's report on Lessing's Spinoza conversations, we see that special importance attaches to the word "I." For in the scene where Lessing first mentions ἕν καὶ πᾶν, this remark is immediately followed by the words, "*I* know naught else" (italics added). The next time he speaks of ἕν καὶ πᾶν, he says, "I came to talk with you about *my* ἕν καὶ πᾶν" (italics added). Second, though omitted from our summary in the second section of this chapter, Lessing developed some very interesting cabalistic speculations in his conversations with Jacobi, speculations which suggest that special importance is to be ascribed to the Lessingian self-reference, namely, the ἐγώ.

According to Jacobi, "Lessing once said with the trace of a smile that perhaps he himself was the Highest Being, present in the state of extreme contraction."[119] On another occasion, when they were at Gleim's summerhouse in Halberstadt, it suddenly began to rain. To Jacobi who was sitting beside him, Lessing then said, "You know, Jacobi, maybe it is *I* who am doing this [that is, causing it to rain]."[120] True, we do not know whether Lessing was serious or was just having fun with Jacobi when he made this statement. But when we take into consideration his idea of reincarnation in §100 of *The Education of the Human Race*, particularly his words, "Is not the whole of eternity mine?.," we find it difficult to treat Lessing's statement as a mere joke. Be that as it may, it is our opinion that on the basis of the considerations presented above, the formula most proper and authentic for Lessing's thought is the one that originated directly from Lessing himself, namely, ἕν ἐγὼ καὶ πάντα.

So far, we have characterized Lessing's view of God and the world as panentheism. But in view of this πάντα formula, we now assert that a better term, admittedly cumbersome, would be "pantaentheism." The reasons for this assertion are three. To begin with, the term "panentheism," originally coined from the two Greek words πᾶν and θεός, is in itself problematic from the Christian point of view. (From this point of view, the counterpart to the word θεός ought to be the word πάντα, not πᾶν.) In the second place, there are a great variety of panentheisms.[121] Third and most important, in Lessing πάντα and θέος, as suggested in his formula ἕν ἐγὼ καὶ πάντα, are mediated through ἐγώ. "Panentheism" is insufficient to express this mediation.[122]

For the reasons indicated above, our concluding proposal is to characterize Lessing's view of God and the world as "pantaentheism." This implies an interpretation of the world, in identifiably Christian and theistic terms, as God's self-replication. In any event, the formula "I am One and All" expressed by Lessing is replete with significant resonances. According to Hermann Timm, it is "one of the most difficult-to-satisfy programmatic formulas in European thought." It is a formula by which Lessing intends "to synthesize unity and plurality"—"the two greatest words we are capable of speaking"—through the medium of "I."[123] If Lessing's ἐγώ anticipates the Fichtean "*ich*," the *Grundwort* of the German *Subjektivitätsphilosophie*, then the formula ἕν ἐγὼ καὶ πάντα can be taken as a foretaste of the speculative philosophy of ensuing generations. It is possible, of course, to say that Timm's interpretation of Lessing's aphorism is "highly speculative" and "overly reflective,"[124] that he reads too much into it. But when we take into consideration both the pantheism controversy to which Lessing's alleged confession of ἕν καὶ πᾶν gave rise and the great German idealist philosophy that emerged by way of this event, it seems to us that Timm's interpretation includes much that is worth listening to.

Conclusion

The preceding chapters have drawn attention to several important aspects of Lessing's philosophy of religion in the course of its historical development. Though we have indicated the results, or at least some implications, of our observations in each chapter, it is appropriate, by way of conclusion, to undertake a general summary of our findings on Lessing's view of Christianity and reason and to discuss certain implications of his work for contemporary thinking.

Our observations have shown that Lessing is a thinker who stood at the turning point from the theological culture of "the Confessional Age"[1] to the eminently secular culture of modern times and that during this transition he rendered significant service to theology and philosophy. This does not mean, however, that he, like Voltaire and other French Enlightenment thinkers, turned his back on Christian tradition in favor of the emergent modern secular culture. His relationship with Christianity was dialectical. He was himself a child of the Enlightenment and deemed it the supreme end of his literary activity to make everyone think rationally about everything—including Christianity and religion. But he never sided either with the Enlightenment in its debunking of Christianity or with neology in its easy amalgamation of Christianity and modernity. While critical of both "the old religious system" and "the new-fashioned theology," he continued to hold the intellectual and cultural heritage of Christianity in the greatest respect. Having discerned the weaknesses of Christianity and its difficult situation in modern times, he sought to diagnose the main causes of the trouble so as to rehabilitate it for the modern age. Though not a theologian by profession, he engaged in theology with the utmost love and admiration for its subject matter throughout his life. In serious dialogue and inner battle with it, he developed his own sophisticated philosophy of religion. In this manner, he became the very first of the "non-theologians who propelled theology forward" and rendered notable service in the formation of modern Protestantism (*Neuprotestantismus*). There is thus good reason for regarding him as one of the founders of modern Protestantism.

As our inquiry has demonstrated, Christianity stood at the forefront of Lessing's concerns throughout his life. The Christianity he wished to preserve, however, was not institutional Christianity as such but its quintessence, or essential Christianity. He placed special importance on genuine Christian love. "Love thine enemy" is for him "one of the most important commandments of Christianity," the touchstone for whether one is truly Christian. What he calls the message of *The Testament of John*, "Little children, love one another" (*Kinderchen, liebt euch!*), is for him the *unum necessarium* of the Christian religion. "This alone, this alone, if it is done, is enough, is sufficient and adequate." Lessing's espousal of the idea of toleration as expressed in his early comedy *The Jews*, or in the dramatic masterpiece of his later years *Nathan the Wise*, is essentially the practical application of this genuine Christian love.

The reason Lessing is included among the founders of modern Protestantism is that he interpreted Luther's spirit, or the Reformation principle, in an utterly new, modern direction. As we have seen, he had recourse to Luther, especially to his spirit, in his theological battle with the Lutheran orthodox pastor Goeze. At that time he boldly asserted:

> The true Lutheran does not wish to be defended by Luther's writings but by Luther's spirit; and Luther's spirit absolutely requires that *no* man may be prevented from advancing in knowledge of the truth according to his own judgment.

This is a completely modern interpretation of Luther's doctrine of "justification by faith alone," a unique adaptation of this doctrine to the field of epistemology. One-sided though it may be in its subjectification of the Reformation principle, it is certain that Lessing hereby ushered in "a new concept of Protestantism." Protestantism appears here as "the religion of conscience and conviction, without dogmatic compulsion" (*die Religion des Gewissens und der Überzeugung ohne dogmatischen Zwang*).[2] The dogmatic, institutional religion of early Protestantism has thus been transformed into the subjective, individualistic religion of modern Protestantism.

The role Lessing played in the transformation of Protestantism is immensely significant. Yet his service to Protestant Christianity also involves a touch of irony. For the fragments controversy he ignited, particularly in his life-and-death struggle with Goeze, put an end to the period of Protestant Orthodoxy and brought about the final end of the lingering "Age of Religion."[3] To this extent, he gave impetus, however indirectly and unconsciously, to the arrival of a secular age.

To be sure, he did not endorse the French Enlightenment's out-and-out denial of religion. Instead, he held fast to religious piety despite his overwhelmingly positive view of life in this world. He also severely criticized the "Berlin freedom" of speech and thought under Frederick the Great as "the freedom to put so many silly and malicious remarks against religion on the market" (*die Freiheit, gegen die Religion so viel Sottisen zu Markte zu bringen*).[4] But the positive attitude toward this world that Lessing fostered turned, in later generations when the religious dimension was lost, into pure secularism. To this extent, his contribution to the history of Protestantism is actually Janus-faced.

Something similar is true of Lessing's relationship with the Enlightenment. His attitude toward this pan-European movement is indeed dialectical. He is correctly regarded as an Enlightenment thinker and indeed one of the most prominent promoters of the German Enlightenment. His friendship with Mendelssohn and Nicolai, two representatives of the Berlin Enlightenment, best illustrates this fact. But at the same time he far exceeded the Enlightenment. As our observations have shown, he attained a sublime position that transcended all the main trends of his age, trends that embraced not only orthodoxy and neology, but the overly rationalistic worldview of the Enlightenment as well. His last writings, including his Spinoza conversations with Jacobi, bear witness to this fact. The worldview contained in these writings foretells an emergent romanticism.

Our analysis of Lessingian reason confirms that Lessing went far beyond Enlightenment rationalism. The ideal of Lessingian reason expressed in *Nathan the Wise* and *The Education of the Human Race* is not the same as the ideal held by the rationalists of his time. We have shown that Nathan, contrary to the generally held view, is not an autonomous person of the modern type. For Nathan, the beginning of wisdom consists in what we, borrowing the concept from Troeltsch, call the "autotheonomous" structure of volition, a structure implied in his words, "I will! / If Thou wilt, then I will!" This is a structure of autonomy supported by theonomy, a duplex or multiplex structure of volition in which the human volition conforms to the divine volition that precedes and underlies it. Thus Nathan's reason is, first and foremost, "hearkening reason." It is not a self-centered reason that shuts itself up within itself. It signifies the ability to listen to what God commands. Accordingly, it can be designated as "believing reason" that opens itself to the transcendent. From a different angle, it is "boundary reason" that is fully aware of its own limitations. This is precisely what Strohschneider-Kohrs calls "reason as wisdom" (*Vernunft als Weisheit*). In any event, Nathan's reason is not mere autonomous reason in the modern sense. But if Nathan's reason is at the same time Lessing's, and if this "reason as wisdom" constitutes the essential core of Lessingian reason, it must be asserted that Lessing's ideal of human reason is not autonomous reason in the ordinary sense of the word but "autotheonomous" reason in the Troeltschian sense.

This finding from our analysis of the essential core of Lessingian reason leads to a suggestion as to how to understand Lessing's dialectical conception of the relationship between revelation and reason. A careful reading of the original German text of *The Education of the Human Race* made it clear that Lessing's thought by no means rules out the concept of transcendent revelation. On the contrary, the concept of revelation, in our view, continues to be valid for him throughout his life. Lessing conceives of the human race as finding fulfillment in a developmental process induced and propelled by divine revelation, and in this context he introduces the novel concept, or principle, of the development of human reason as a gradual appropriation of divine revelation. The notion of completely free self-development on the part of human reason is not to be found in Lessing. This holds true even if it is an easy step to move from this Lessingian principle to the conception of human history as the self-development and self-revelation of the human spirit.

But if this is the case, then we are compelled to reconsider Lessing's view of the goal of enlightenment. Lessing's contemporary Kant saw the goal of enlightenment in the attaining of moral autonomy. For Lessing, however, the goal is to attain the highest stage of "perfect illumination" and "purity of heart," the stage at which a person is "capable of loving virtue for its own sake alone" and "will do the right because it is right." This is, to be sure, a state in which moral autonomy will have been attained. But it would be insufficient to identify Lessing's goal as nothing but the attainment of autonomy. For the ideal of autonomy that Lessing envisioned is an autonomy backed by awareness of its own limitations, an autonomy buttressed by theonomy. That is to say, his ideal is a mature autonomy capable of confessing that absolute truth is for God alone. His famous dictum, "If God held all truth in his right hand and in his left everlasting striving after truth, so that I should always and everlastingly be mistaken, and said to me, 'Choose,' with humility I would pick the left hand and say, 'Father, grant me that. Absolute truth is for thee alone'" (or its concise version, "Let everyone tell what *seems* to him to be truth; and let *the truth itself* be entrusted to God!") attests the cogency of this view. If our interpretation is correct, it would be better to apply the term "autotheonomy" to this sort of autonomy. The ideal of Lessingian enlightenment can therefore be designated as the attainment of an "autotheonomy" in which "autonomy is at the same time theonomy." In order to attain such a goal, however, revealed truths must not remain unintelligible truths that are only to be believed. Instead, they must become truths of reason that are intrinsic to human reason. In this sense, "the development of revealed truths into truths of reason is absolutely necessary." And only when revealed truths thus become truths of reason can human reason find certitude and repose in God.

So far we have summarized the main points of our findings. Now that the contours of Lessing's thought are before us, we are in a position to comment on their implications for contemporary thinking. Our consideration of this matter must, however, be brief and merely suggestive because the task of developing a constructive, or systematic, work is a project that must be left to the future. Accordingly, we propose to limit ourselves here to suggesting certain elements in Lessing's thought that have the potential for becoming fundamental constituents in a postmodern theology.

To be viable for our time, a Christian theology must address the overwhelmingly difficult questions of the postmodern world. The fundamental challenge of postmodernity is said to be how the theologian can speak meaningfully of God's presence and action in the world. Despite the apparent loss of any meaningful discourse about God, theology, if it is to be a vital force in the contemporary world, must seek and discern a new revelation of the divine in the cultural crises of our time. According to Peter C. Hodgson, the cultural questions the theologian needs to attend to are three: the *emancipatory*, the *ecological*, and the *dialogical*.[5] The ongoing quests in the areas of emancipation, ecology, and dialogue must be incorporated into the reconstruction of theology for our time. It is no exaggeration to say that religious thought that does not refer to any of these human quests is disqualified as a candidate for supplying the constitutive elements of a viable postmodern theology. The question is whether Lessing's thought can pass this test.

As regards the *emancipatory* dimension of his thought, there is no room for question. Up to the present day Lessing has been admired as "a resolute enemy of anti-Semitism."[6] Quite apart from his dramatic masterpiece *Nathan the Wise*, the one-act play *The Jews*, written by the young Lessing, likewise attests the existence of the emancipatory dimension. Even if the vindication and emancipation of the Jewish people as such is not the author's real point in this comedy, the motif of emancipation is nevertheless present in his impeachment of the prejudice, hypocrisy, and intolerance against Jews prevalent in allegedly Christian society. Furthermore, the tragedy *Emilia Galotti*, written in 1772 on the occasion of the birthday celebration of the Duchess of Brunswick, has often been read as "an indictment of the feudal princes."[7] In any event, there is no doubt of the fact that Lessing was the foremost emancipator of "humanity in dark times."[8] And his thought will continue to inspire the emancipation of humanity.

The *dialogical* aspect of Lessing's thought needs no explanation. The modern quest for interreligious dialogue arises out of the awareness of a plurality of religious traditions. No matter what its goal may be, interreligious dialogue serves to expose idolatries and draw out convergent truths and practices. Through encounter with other religious traditions, one can attain a deeper understanding of one's own religious tradition and possibly improve and refine it. The eighteenth century is a period in which the problem of a plurality of religious traditions first came to the awareness of European intellectuals. Lessing was among the first European thinkers who paid serious attention to the problem of religious pluralism. The early work *Vindication of Hieronymus Cardanus* (1754) testifies to his keen awareness of this problem. Among his works, however, his best-known drama *Nathan the Wise*, not least its "parable of the three rings," has great potential for the furthering of dialogue. The parable of the three rings, when interpreted in the way we have suggested, supplies many insights for ongoing interreligious dialogue. From this parable one can learn an important lesson about the truth claim of a historical religion in the interim.

It is with regard to its *ecological* implication that Lessing's thought is most cryptic. The modern ecological quest arises out of sensitivity to the interrelatedness of life throughout the universe. This ecological sensitivity is closely related to a new scientific cosmology, which is not mechanical, atomistic, and substance-based but organic, interconnected, relational, and processual. From the perspective of this cosmology, everything in the entire cosmos, both living and nonliving, is viewed as intrinsically bound together in a very delicate web of interconnected systems. Our time requires, therefore, a theology that articulates God's presence in the dynamics of the cosmos. The question we need to pose in this connection is whether Lessing's thought contains any such ecological implication. Lessing, unlike Goethe, seems to have had little interest in nature. It is not easy to find any allusion to ecology in his entire corpus, or a work dedicated entirely to the topic of ecology. Nonetheless, an implicitly ecological concern is not completely lacking in his thought. Such a concern is to be found, we believe, in his idea of panentheism. Leaving aside the difficult question of how we should interpret his motto "*Hen kai Pan*," we consider it undeniable that Lessing held a panentheistic worldview akin to that of spiritualism. Jacobi reports that Lessing conceived the universe as "being analogous to an organic body" and the divinity as "the soul of the universe." If Jacobi's report is trustworthy, Lessing's God is "a higher energy" or a dynamic, cosmic power that draws all things together and into itself. Such a conception of God clearly has strong ecological implications.

To sum up, Lessing's thought passes the general test for postmodernity. It contains the potential needed for the constitutive elements of a viable theology in the postmodern age. But to acknowledge potentials is one thing, and to develop a viable theology or philosophy of religion quite another. To shape and organize Lessing's fragmentary, often contradictory thought into a systematic whole will be a task calling for fine distinctions and subtle reasoning. But this inquiry presents, we believe, a solid foundation for the systematic, or constructive, task that lies ahead.

Notes

Introduction

1. Immanuel Kant, *Kants Werke*, Akademie Textausgabe, vol. 8, *Abhandlungen nach 1781* (Berlin: Walter de Gruyter & Co., 1968), 35. The English is borrowed from Lewis White Beck's translation of Kant's *Foundations of the Metaphysics of Morals, and What is Enlightenment?* (Indianapolis and New York: Bobbs-Merrill, 1959), 85.

2. Wilhelm Dilthey, *Das Erlebnis und die Dichtung: Lessing-Goethe-Novalis-Hölderlin*, 16th ed. (Göttingen: Vandenhoeck & Ruprecht, 1985), 107.

3. Hannah Arendt, *Men in Dark Times* (New York: Harcourt, Brace & World, 1968), 8.

4. Cf. Benno von Wiese, "Dichtung und Geistesgeschichte des 18. Jahrhunderts," *Deutsche Vierteljahrschrift für Literaturwissenschaft und Geistesgeschichte* 12 (1934): 471.

5. Heinrich Heine, *Sämtliche Werke*, vol. 3, *Schriften zur Literatur und Politik 1* (Darmstadt: Wissenschaftliche Buchgesellschaft, 1992), 469.

6. Ibid., 472–73.

7. Johann Peter Eckermann, *Gespräche mit Goethe: In den letzten Jahren seines Lebens*, edited by Fritz Bergemann (Frankfurt am Main and Leipzig: Insel Verlag, 1992), 626. Goethe's remark that "Lessing sought to refuse the noble title of genius" apparently derives from Lessing's self-appraisal in his *Hamburg Dramaturgy*:

> I am neither actor nor poet.
> People do indeed sometimes pay their respects to me by way of recognizing me as a poet. But [they do so] only because they misunderstand me. . . . I do not feel within me the living spring that works its way up by its own strength, a spring that in its own strength shoots forth a rich, fresh, pure jet of water. I must squeeze everything out of myself by means of a force pump and pipes. I would be so poor, so cold, and so nearsighted if I had not learned, to some extent, to borrow from other people's treasure, to warm myself by other people's fire, and to strengthen my eyes with artificially contrived glasses. I have always, therefore, become ashamed or annoyed whenever I read or heard something deleterious to criticism. Criticism ought to suffocate genius. Yet I flatter myself that I was able to obtain from criticism something that came very close to genius. I am a cripple who cannot take delight in a

defamatory pamphlet that reviles crutches. (LM 10, 209–210; G 4, 694–95 [*Hamburgische Dramaturgie*, Stück 101–104]).

8. Of the various editions of Lessing's complete works, the 23-volume *Sämtliche Schriften* edited by Karl Lachmann and Franz Muncker and the 20-volume *Lessings Werke* edited by Julius Petersen and Waldemar von Olshausen have been held in high repute as standard critical editions. Some scholars, especially in what was formerly East Germany, prefer the 10-volume *Gesammelte Werke* edited by Paul Rilla because of its compactness and the novelty of its appended editorial comments. In recent times, however, an increasing number of scholars use the 8-volume *Werke* edited by Herbert G. Göpfert as their source for standard texts. But because this edition does not contain Lessing's letters, which are indispensable to research, those who use it as their text source have had to use Lachmann-Muncker's edition as well when referring to the letters. To overcome this inconvenience, the publication of a new 12-volume edition has been planned and is now being published under the title *Werke und Briefe in zwölf Bänden* (Frankfurt am Main: Deutscher Klassiker Verlag, 1985ff.).

9. The American Lessing Society, founded at Cincinnati University on 18 September 1966, developed, as its membership became worldwide, into an international academic organization called The Lessing Society (*Die internationale Lessing-Gesellschaft*). Its *Lessing Yearbook*, here abbreviated *LYB* and published by the society since 1969, is now one of the most important sources not only for the serious student of Lessing but also for every researcher engaging in study of the literary and intellectual history of eighteenth-century Germany.

10. With regard to the history of Lessing studies up to the 1970s, Karl S. Guthke's *Der Stand der Lessing-Forschung: Ein Bericht über die Literatur von 1932–1962* (Stuttgart: J. B. Metzlersche Verlagsbuchhandlung, 1965), and its sequel in his *Gotthold Ephraim Lessing*, 3d ed. (Stuttgart: J. B. Metzlersche Verlagsbuchhandlung, 1979), supply a superb overview. *Lessing: Epoche-Werke-Wirkung*, edited by Wilfried Barner et al. (Munich: Verlag C. H. Beck, 1975), and the *Internationale Bibliographie zur Geschichte der deutschen Literatur von den Anfängen bis zur Gegenwart*, part 1, *Von den Anfängen bis 1789* (Munich-Pullach and Berlin: Verlag Dokumentation, 1969), 963–86 are also useful.

As for the "Neuere Lessing-Studie" in the 1970s, see Arno Schilson, "Lessing und die Aufklärung: Notizen zur Forschung," *Theologie und Philosophie* 54 (1979): 379–405. Each issue of the *LYB* contains a number of valuable "review focus" articles and book reviews. For a general review of more recent Lessing studies during and since the 1980s, however, there is, to the best of my knowledge, no concise survey available as yet.

11. Dilthey, *Das Erlebnis und die Dichtung*, 19.

12. Guthke, *Der Stand der Lessing-Forschung*, 88.

13. Guthke, *Gotthold Ephraim Lessing*, 87.

14. LM 13, 109; G 8, 130 (*Axiomata*).

15. Only a few books have paid serious attention to Lessing. One can name, for example, Emanuel Hirsch, *Geschichte der neuern evangelischen Theologie*, 5 vols. (Gütersloh: C. Bertelsmann Verlag, 1949–54), Karl Barth, *Die protestantische Theologie im 19. Jahrhundert: Ihre Vorgeschichte und ihre Geschichte*, 5th ed. (Zurich: Theologischer Verlag, 1985), and Helmut Thielicke, *Glauben und Denken in der Neuzeit* (Tübingen: J. C. B. Mohr, 1983). Cf. W. Trillhaas, "Zur Wirkungsgeschichte Lessings in der evangelischen Theologie," in *Das Bild Lessings in der Geschichte* (*WSA*, vol. 9), edited by Herbert G. Göpfert (Heidelberg: Verlag Lambert Schneider, 1981), 57–67.

16. Wilhelm Windelband, *Die Geschichte der neueren Philosophie*, vol. 1 (Leipzig: Breitkopf and Härtel, 1878; reprint, Karben: Verlag Petra Wald, 1996), 525.

17. In his *Die Geschichte der neueren Philosophie*, Windelband assigns one chapter to a discussion of Lessing's philosophy (vol. 1, 524–34), but this is exceptional. Lewis White Beck's *Early German Philosophy: Kant and His Predecessors* (Cambridge, Massachusetts: Harvard University Press, 1969; reprint, Bristol: Thoemmes Press, 1996) also contains a chapter on Lessing. This seems to be partly because his delineation of the scope of the material to be considered is broad enough to include intellectual history. By contrast, it is seldom that ordinary books on the history of philosophy give more than a passing glance to Lessing. Maurice Dupuy, for example, assigns only a page or so to Lessing, despite his noteworthy comment that "Lessing seems to be the harbinger of both Kant's moral theory and Hegel's view of history" (Maurice Dupuy, *Doitsu Tetsugakushi* [History of German philosophy], translated by Yoshihiko Harada [Tokyo: Hakusuisha, 1995], 38–39).

18. With regard to the relationship between Lessing and Schleiermacher, see Carl Schwarz, *Gotthold Ephraim Lessing als Theologe* (Halle: C. E. M. Pfeffer, 1854), 4–5, 15, 22, 66–68. For the intellectual-historical connection between Lessing and Hegel, see Walter Kaufmann, *Hegel: Reinterpretation, Texts, and Commentary* (New York: Doubleday & Co., 1965), 67–70; Eckhard Heftrich, *Lessings Aufklärung* (Frankfurt am Main: Vittorio Klostermann, 1978), 34–35; Johannes von Lüpke, *Wege der Weisheit: Studien zu Lessings Theologiekritik* (Göttingen: Vandenhoeck & Ruprecht, 1989), 28–30. For the relationship between Lessing and Kierkegaard, see Richard Campbell, "Lessing's Problem and Kierkegaard's Answer," *Scottish Journal of Theology* 19 (1966): 35–54; Gordon E. Michalson, Jr., *Lessing's "Ugly Ditch": A Study of Theology and History* (University Park and London: Pennsylvania State University Press, 1985), especially chapters 3 and 4. In passing, it may be noted that Helmut Thielicke regards Lessing as "a precursor of Kierkegaard" (Helmut Thielicke, *Glauben und Denken in der Neuzeit*, 133. But a one-sided emphasis on this viewpoint will, as Thielicke's interpretation of Lessing shows, end up by distorting the actual Lessing. With regard to the relationship between Lessing and Troeltsch, further clarification is needed. Martin Haug, however, to take one example, suggests a significant relationship by regarding Troeltsch as "a reembodiment of further developed Lessingian reason" (Martin Haug, *Entwicklung und Offenbarung bei Lessing* [Gütersloh: C. Bertelsmann, 1928], 113). Hermann Diem discerns a continuation of the Lessingian problem in modern theological development culminating in Troeltsch (Hermann Diem, *Theologie als kirchliche Wissenschaft*, vol. 2, *Dogmatik: Ihr Weg zwischen Historismus und Existentialismus* [Munich: Chr. Kaiser Verlag, 1955], 13–14). Apart from these scholars, and from a completely different point of view, the present study will indicate the close connection between Lessing and Troeltsch with reference to the idea of "God's self-replication" (*die Selbstverdoppelung Gottes*). On this matter, see chapters 2 and 7.

19. Walter Nigg, *Das Ewige Reich: Geschichte einer Hoffnung*, 2d ed. (Zurich: Artemis Verlag, 1954), 215.

20. Regarding the analysis of Lessing's "ugly ditch," I have learned much from Gordon E. Michalson in his *Lessing's "Ugly Ditch."* To the best of my knowledge, Michalson's book is the finest theological work on this topic to date.

21. Frederick C. Beiser, *The Fate of Reason: German Philosophy from Kant to Fichte* (Cambridge, Massachusetts and London: Harvard University Press, 1987), 44.

22. Gottfried Fittbogen, *Die Religion Lessings* (Leipzig: Mayer & Müller, 1923; reprint, New York: Johnson Reprint Corporation, 1967), 310. On this point at least,

Ernst Cassirer is of a similar opinion. He says: "As in Lessing's dramas, such as *Minna von Barnhelm, Emilia Galotti,* and *Nathan the Wise,* not only are attempts made to attain a critical understanding, but also a new *form* of German literature ripens and grows to maturity; so Lessing has also become the founder and creator of a new form of Protestantism" (Ernst Cassirer, "Die Idee der Religion bei Lessing und Mendelssohn," in *Lessings »Nathan der Weise«* [Wege der Forschung, vol. 587], edited by Klaus Bohnen [Darmstadt: Wissenschaftliche Buchgesellschaft, 1984], 113).

23. Ernst Troeltsch, *Protestantisches Christentum und Kirche in der Neuzeit,* in *Die Kultur der Gegenwart,* edited by Paul Hinneberg, part 1/4, vol. 1, *Geschichte der christlichen Religion,* Mit Einleitung: Die israelitisch-jüdischen Religion, 2d ed. (Berlin and Leipzig: B. G. Teubner, 1909), 516.

24. Ernst Troeltsch, *Die Bedeutung des Protestantismus für die Entstehung der modernen Welt* (Munich and Berlin: R. Oldenbourg, 1911; reprint, Aalen: Otto Zeller, 1963), 98–99; *Protestantism and Progress: The Significance of Protestantism for the Rise of the Modern World* (Philadelphia: Fortress Press, 1986), 98.

25. Ernst Troeltsch, "Religionswissenschaft und Theologie des 18. Jahrhunderts," *Preussische Jahrbücher* 114 (1903): 30–36.

26. Ibid., 31.

27. Leopold Zscharnack, "Einleitung des Herausgebers," in Gotthold Ephraim Lessing's *Werke,* vol. 17 [of 25] (Hildesheim and New York: Georg Olms, 1970).

28. Leopold Zscharnack, "Einleitung des Herausgebers," 10–11.

29. LM 16, 475; G 7, 671 (*Bibliolatrie*). Besides comparing himself to a servant in the temple of Apollo, Lessing also considered himself the "beloved bastard of a noble, gracious lord" (*lieber Bastard eines großen, gnädigen Herrn*). This expression betrays something of his self-awareness. Cf. LM 18, 356 (Letter to Elise Reimarus of 28 November 1780); B 12, 361 (no. 1602).

30. Martin Haug, *Entwicklung und Offenbarung bei Lessing,* 7.

31. Guthke, *Der Stand der Lessing-Forschung,* 89.

32. Haug, *Entwicklung und Offenbarung bei Lessing,* 19.

33. To the best of my knowledge, the most exemplary study ever made (at least in English) on the intellectual and social situation of eighteenth-century Germany is W. H. Bruford's *Germany in the Eighteenth Century: The Social Background of the Literary Revival* (Cambridge: Cambridge University Press, 1935; reprint, 1952).

34. The case of Hermann Samuel Reimarus (1694–1768), who was a professor of Oriental languages at a Gymnasium in Hamburg and whose posthumous unpublished manuscripts Lessing brought to light under the title *Fragments from an Unnamed Author* (in German), best illustrates the religious situation in the Germany of Lessing's age. Reimarus never intended to publish the voluminous manuscripts into which he had poured his energy throughout his academic life. He showed his unpublished lifework to nobody but a few close friends and his two children. Otherwise he kept the work secret and never showed it to anybody, not even to his wife. It was only in 1972 that the two volumes of nearly 1600 pages appeared under the title *Apologie oder Schutzschrift für die vernünftigen Verehrer Gottes* (Frankfurt am Main: Insel Verlag).

Why did Reimarus keep his lifework secret? Why did he never wish to publish it during his lifetime? The reason seems to have been that he was afraid of the inquisition that might be instigated by "a clerical tyranny" (*eine geistliche Tyranney*). For in the Germany of his age, especially in Hamburg where Lutheran orthodoxy held sway over the entire town, the rumor that one was an "unbeliever" (*Unglaubige*), "free thinker" (*Freydenker*), "naturalist" (*Naturalisten*), or "mocker of religion" (*Religions-Spötter*), once disseminated, could be fatal to a person's citizenship and honor. Accusation by means of such a label sometimes led to arrest, imprisonment, or condemnation by the authorities. Thus mid-eighteenth-century Germany still retained some traces of medieval society where inquisition was a common practice. As far as Germany is concerned, it was only through and after Lessing's desperate battle against Goeze, nicknamed "the Inquisitor," that religious tolerance gained a firm footing.

35. Rationalistic theology in vogue in mid-eighteenth-century Germany is usually called *neology*, which Lessing pejoratively referred to as "our newfangled theology" (*unsere neumodische Theologie*). In his judgment, "our newfangled clergymen" (*unsere neumodischen Geistlichen*) were "far too little theologians and not nearly enough philosophers" (LM 18, 33 [Letter to Karl Lessing of 8 April 1773]; B 11/2, 540 [no. 906]).

According to Karl Aner's famous formulation, the transition from orthodoxy to rationalistic theology in the eighteenth century passed through three stages. The first phase was "rational orthodoxy" (*vernünftige oder rationale Orthodoxie*), or Wolffianism, which Aner characterized as V (*Vernunft*) + O (*Offenbarung*), or reason plus revelation. The second phase was "neology," which he characterized as $V + O^{begriff} - O^{inhalt}$, or reason plus the concept of revelation but minus revelatory content. The third phase was a full-fledged "rationalism," a rationalism that overcame the halfway character of neology by clearing away all supernatural elements. Aner characterized this phase as $V = O^{inhalt} - O^{begriff}$, or reason equals revelatory content minus the concept of revelation. See Karl Aner, *Die Theologie der Lessingzeit* (Halle: Max Niemeyer Verlag, 1929; reprint, Hildesheim: Georg Olms, 1964), 4.

36. Cf. Otto Mann, *Lessing: Sein und Leistung* (Berlin: Walter de Gruyter, 1965), 307.

37. Guthke, *Der Stand der Lessing-Forschung*, 89.

38. Haug, *Entwicklung und Offenbarung bei Lessing*, 21.

39. In his letter to Elise Reimarus, Lessing referred to Semler as "an impertinent goose of a professor" (*eine impertinente Professorengans*) (LM 18, 317 [Letter to Elise Reimarus of 14 May 1779]; B 12, 255 [no. 1472]). Semler was for him "a personal representative of the academic arrogance of the predominant theology" (Hermann Timm, *Gott und die Freiheit: Studien zur Religionsphilosophie der Goethezeit*, vol. 1, *Die Spinozarenaissance* [Frankfurt am Main: Vittorio Klostermann, 1974], 24).

40. In his preface to *The Education of the Human Race*, Lessing confessed that he stood on a higher plane that enabled him to see beyond the limits of the knowledge available to his contemporaries. Cf. LM 13, 415; G 8, 489 (*Die Erziehung des Menschengeschlechts*).

41. Cf. LM 13, 430; G 8, 504 (*Die Erziehung des Menschengeschlechts* §68): "And that is also of the greatest importance now. You who are cleverer than the rest, who wait fretting and impatient for the last page of the primer, take care! Take care that you do not let your weaker classmates notice what you are beginning to scent, or even see!"

42. LM 11, 69–70; G 7, 79–80 (*Berengarius Turonensis*).

43. LM 13, 353; G 8, 459 (*Ernst und Falk*, 2). The English translation is borrowed from Gotthold Ephraim Lessing, *Nathan the Wise, Minna von Barnhelm, and Other Plays and Writings*, The German Library, vol. 12, edited by Peter Demetz (New York: Continuum, 1995), 285.

44. According to Lessing, "the man who, threatened by dangers, becomes unfaithful to truth can nevertheless love truth very much, and truth forgives his unfaithfulness for the sake of his love. But he who thinks only of disposing of truth under sundry masks and cosmetics, such a man may well wish to be its matchmaker, but has never been its lover" (LM 11, 70; G 7, 80 [*Berengarius Turonensis*]).

Considering some of the tactics Lessing employed as unjustified, Fittbogen criticizes him severely. Nevertheless, a glance at the ecclesiastical-political situation in which Lessing found himself teaches us that Fittbogen's criticism is not necessarily justifiable. See Fittbogen, *Die Religion Lessings,* 79–83.

45. LM 18, 266 (Letter to Karl Lessing of 16 March 1778); B 12, 131 (no. 1351).

46. D, 587.

47. Ibid., 150–51; see also 216–17.

48. Ibid., 72.

49. LM 16, 473; G 7, 672 (*Bibliolatrie*).

50. Haug, *Entwicklung und Offenbarung bei Lessing,* 20.

51. Walter Jens and Hans Küng, *Dichtung und Religion: Pascal, Gryphius, Lessing, Hölderlin, Novalis, Kierkegaard, Dostojewski, Kafka* (Munich and Zurich: Piper, 1988), 90; cf. Carl Schwarz, *Gotthold Ephraim Lessing als Theologe,* 15.

52. Haug, *Entwicklung und Offenbarung bei Lessing,* 21.

53. Wolfgang Gericke, "Lessings theologische Gesamtauffassung," in *Sechs theologische Schriften Gotthold Ephraim Lessings,* edited by Wolfgang Gericke (Berlin: Evangelische Verlagsanstalt, 1985), 11.

54. Johann Melchior Goeze, the Hauptpastor, or Pastor Primarius, of Hamburg pastors, insisted that the logic used in theological argument and the logic employed in the theater were completely different. To him, the logic Lessing employed in theological argument was nothing but theatrical. Such logic, he insisted, could better be called "theater logic" (*Theaterlogik*).

Lessing's refutation of this accusation is worth citing at length:

> It does not matter how much we write, but how we think matters a lot. And yet you want to assert that a shaky, false meaning must necessarily lie in oblique words rich in imagery? that no one can think correctly and exactly except those who use the most proper, most common, and flattest expressions? that to seek to give cold, symbolic ideas some warmth and vividness from natural signs somehow does absolute harm to the truth?
>
> How ridiculous to ascribe the depth of a wound not to the sharp but to the shiny sword! How ridiculous it also is, therefore, to ascribe the superiority that the truth gives an adversary over us to the splendid style of the adversary! I know no splendid style that does not borrow its splendor more or less from the truth. Truth alone gives genuine splendor; even in mockery and farce it must lie underneath, at least by way of a foil.
>
> Let us speak of this, therefore, of the truth, not of the style. . . . Thought requires a steady, measured step, while dialogue demands leaps. Seldom is a high jumper a good, smooth dancer.
>
> But, Mr. Hauptpastor, this is my style, and my style is not my logic. . . . But, of course, my logic should also be what my style is: a theater logic (*eine Theaterlogik*). That is what you say. But say what you want! Good logic is always the same, whatever one may apply it to. Even the way of applying it is everywhere the same. . . . But who really doubts that Molière and Shakespeare would have written and delivered superb sermons if they had wanted to climb into a pulpit instead of into the theater? (LM 13, 149–51; G 8, 194–95 [*Anti-Goeze,* 2]).

55. Heinrich Scholz, "Einleitung," in *Hauptschriften,* lxix.

56. Hermann Timm, "Eine theologische Tragikomödie: Lessings Neuinszenierung der Geistesgeschichte," *Zeitschrift für Religions- und Geistesgeschichte* 34 (1982): 5.

57. Ibid.

58. Friedrich Loofs, *Lessings Stellung zum Christentum* (Halle: Waisenhauser, 1910), 24.

59. Schwarz, *Gotthold Ephraim Lessing als Theologe*, 12, 42.

60. Haug, *Entwicklung und Offenbarung bei Lessing*, 25; cf. ibid., 24.

61. Helmut Thielicke, *Offenbarung, Vernunft und Existenz: Studien zur Religionsphilosophie Lessings*, 4th ed. (Gütersloh: Gerd Mohn, 1957), 37, 40, 41, 54–55.

62. Haug, *Entwicklung und Offenbarung bei Lessing*, 17.

63. Thielicke, *Offenbarung, Vernunft und Existenz*, 54.

64. Henry E. Allison, *Lessing and the Enlightenment: His Philosophy of Religion and Its Relation to Eighteenth-Century Thought* (Ann Arbor: University of Michigan Press, 1966), 86.

65. LM 11, 479; G 7, 180–81 (*Leibniz von den ewigen Strafen*).

66. LM 11, 473; G 7, 183–84 (*Leibniz von den ewigen Strafen*).

67. Thielicke, *Offenbarung, Vernunft und Existenz*, 54–57.

1 Lessing and Christianity

1. Christopher Schrempf, *Lessing als Philosoph*, 2d ed. (Stuttgart: Fr. Frommanns Verlag, 1921), 18.

2. Karl S. Guthke, *Gotthold Ephraim Lessing*, 3d ed. (Stuttgart: J. B. Metzlersche Verlagsbuchhandlung, 1979), 19.

3. D, 14.

4. Ibid., 18.

5. Wilhelm Dilthey, *Das Erlebnis und die Dichtung: Lessing-Goethe-Novalis-Hölderlin*, 16th ed. (Göttingen: Vandenhoeck & Ruprecht, 1985), 64.

6. In his *Faust* (Part 1, the scene of Auerbach's Keller in Leipzig), Goethe, who like Lessing spent his student life in that city, depicted the Leipzig of that day. He had a man called Frosch speak as follows: "No doubt about it. Leipzig is a flower. It is a little Paris and educates its people" (2171–72). Johann Wolfgang von Goethe, *Goethe's Faust*, translated by Walter Kaufmann (New York: Doubleday, 1961), 216–17.

Judging from W. H. Bruford's dependable study of the social history of Germany in the eighteenth century, the Leipzig of Lessing's student days seems to have been not too far removed from that of Goethe's student days. See W. H. Bruford, *Germany in the Eighteenth Century: The Social Background of the Literary Revival* (Cambridge: Cambridge University Press, 1935; reprint, 1952), 182–84.

7. LM 17, 7–8 (Letter to Justina Salome Lessing of 20 January 1749); B 11/1, 15–16 (no. 11).

8. LM 17, 16 (Letter to Johann Gottfried Lessing of 28 April 1749); B 11/1, 24 (no. 7).

9. LM 17, 17–18 (Letter to Johann Gottfried Lessing of 30 May 1749); B 11/1, 26 (no. 21).

10. Ernst Cassirer, "Die Idee der Religion bei Lessing und Mendelssohn," in *Lessings >Nathan der Weise<*, Wege der Forschung, vol. 587, edited by Klaus Bohnen (Darmstadt: Wissenschaftliche Buchgesellschaft, 1984), 108.

11. LM 13, 415; G 8, 489 (*Vorbericht des Herausgebers*).

12. LM 1, 255; G 1, 169 (*Die Religion*).

13. Lessing's M.A. study was on the Spanish physician and philosopher Juan Huarte (c. 1530–1592). He translated Huarte's Spanish work into German under the title *Prüfung der Köpfe zu den Wissenschaften* (cf. LM 5, 4–8; G 8, 417–20) and was awarded a Master's degree in liberal arts (*der Magistertitel der freien Künste*).

14. Edwald von Kleist, a major in the Prussian army, was a talented poet. He and Lessing became close friends during Lessing's second period in Leipzig (1755–58). Unfortunately, shortly after they became acquainted, Kleist was killed in a battle during the Seven Years' War (1756–63). When Lessing wrote his famous comedy *Minna von Barnhelm* in 1767 (though according to Lachmann it had already been completed in 1763), he still had a vivid memory of his deceased friend and wanted to preserve it in his dramatic work. It is said, therefore, that Kleist was the real model for Major von Tellheim in *Minna von Barnhelm*.

15. D, 170–71.

16. This does not mean, however, that Lessing utterly neglected these minor thinkers. A couple of short refutations may be found among his literary remains. See LM 16, 405–407; G 7, 660–63 (*Gegen Friedrich Wilhelm Mascho*).

17. Erich Schmidt, ed., *Goezes Streitschriften gegen Lessing* (Stuttgart: G. J. Göschen'sche Verlagshandlung, 1893), 10.

18. Ibid., 105.

19. LM 18, 287 (Letter to Elise Reimarus of 6 September 1778); B 12, 193 (no. 1398).

20. LM 18, 285 (Letter to Karl Lessing of 11 August 1778); B 12, 186 (no. 1389).

21. LM 18, 319 (Letter to Friedrich Heinrich Jacobi of 18 May 1779); B 12, 156 (no. 1474).

22. LM 16, 444; G 2, 748 (*Vorrede und Abhandlungen zu Nathan dem Weisen*). Italics in original.

23. LM 16, 406; G 7, 661 (*Gegen Friedrich Wilhelm Mascho*). Cf. LM 13, 208; G 8, 304 (*Anti-Goeze*, 11).

24. LM 13, 142; G 8, 160 (*Anti-Goeze*, 1).

25. LM 12, 430; G 7, 459 (*Gegensätze des Herausgebers*).

26. LM 12, 430; G 7, 460 (*Gegensätze des Herausgebers*).

27. LM 18, 83 (Letter to Karl Lessing of 8 April 1773); B 11/2, 540 (no. 906).

28. LM 18, 101–102 (Letter to Karl Lessing of 2 February 1774); B 11/2, 614–15 (no. 957).

29. In a letter of 20 March 1777 to his brother Karl, in which he declared the theologians of orthodoxy "my obvious enemies," Lessing says: "I only prefer the old orthodox theology (at bottom, tolerant) to the new (at bottom, intolerant) because the former is in manifest conflict with human reason, whereas the latter might easily take one in. I conclude an agreement with my obvious enemies in order to be able to be the better on my guard against my secret adversaries." LM 18, 226–27 (Letter to Karl Lessing of 20 March 1777); B 12, 51–52 (no. 1257).

30. LM 11, 3; G 6, 407 (*Wie die Alten den Tod gebildet*).

31. LM 17, 17–18 (Letter to Johann Gottfried Lessing of 30 May 1749); B 11/2, 26 (no. 21).

32. LM 16, 16, 473; G 7, 668–69 (*Bibliolatrie*).

33. LM 16, 16, 476; G 7, 672 (*Bibliolatrie*).

34. LM 17, 364–65 (Letter to Moses Mendelssohn of 9 January 1771); B 11/2, 144–45 (no. 645).

35. Some scholars object to this interpretation. To begin with, no clarity at all has

been attained with regard to what book of Ferguson's is referred to in this letter. Danzel, Guhrauer, Dilthey, and Aner conjecture that Lessing here refers to Adam Ferguson's *Essay on the History of Civil Society* (1767), whereas Olshausen and Rilla claim that the book in question is Ferguson's *Institutes of Moral Philosophy* (1769). To date, nobody has offered a decisive answer to this question. As far as I can judge, however, Flajole's discussion seems to me the most instructive on this issue. See Edward S. Flajole, "Lessing's Retrieval of Lost Truths," *Publications of the Modern Language Association of America* 74 (1959): 52–66.

36. LM 13, 23–24; G 8, 32–33 (*Eine Duplik*).

37. LM 12, 428–29; G 8, 489. Dilthey has it that the "eminence" on which Lessing sets himself is "a lonely height, from which only general outlines of the world could be seen below." Dilthey, *Das Erlebnis und die Dichtung*, 92.

38. LM 12, 428–29; G 7, 457–59 (*Gegensätze des Herausgebers*). In the German original, the words here translated as "feels" (*fühlen*) and "experiences" (*erfahren*) appear in italics. Chadwick translates both German words as "feels." I have modified his translation at this point so as to come closer to Lessing's actual words. See *Lessing's Theological Writings*, translated by Henry Chadwick (Stanford: Stanford University Press, 1957).

39. Cf. LM 14, 157; G 3, 685 (*Gedanken über die Herrnhuter*); LM 5, 17; G 5, 44–45 (*Literaturbrief 1, 8. Brief*).

40. LM 14, 159; G 3, 687 (*Gedanken über die Herrnhuter*).

41. LM 14, 156; G 3, 683 (*Gedanken über die Herrnhuter*).

42. LM 14, 160; G 3, 688 (*Gedanken über die Herrnhuter*). Likewise, Lessing makes the following noteworthy statements through the mouth of Nathan: "[To] you alone I'll tell it./ To simple piety alone I'll tell it./ Since that alone can understand the deeds/ God-fearing man can force himself to do." (LM 3, 138; G 2, 316 [Nathan der Weise, 4/7]). It is important to notice that special importance attaches here to "simple piety" (*die fromme Einfalt*).

43. LM 13, 102; G 8, 125–26 (*Eine Parabel*).

44. LM 13, 143; G 8, 162 (*Anti-Goeze, 1*).

45. Erich Schmidt, ed., *Goezes Streitschriften gegen Lessing* (Stuttgart: G. J. Göschen'sche Verlagshandlung, 1893), 21.

46. LM 13, 128–29; G 8, 150 (*Axiomata*).

47. LM 12, 433; G 7, 463 (*Gegensätze des Herausgebers*). Here Lessing asserts that reason, if safeguarded by "the reality of revelation," is willing to surrender itself to faith. "Reason's surrender, to a certain extent, to the obedience of faith" (*eine gewisse Gefangennehmung der Vernunft under den Gehorsam des Glaubens*), according to Lessing, is simply based on "the essential concept of revelation" (*dem wesentlichen Begriffe einer Offenbarung*). This is also at the same time, says Lessing, reason's "confession of its limitations" (*das Bekenntnis ihrer Grenzen*).

2 The Religious Thought of the Young Lessing

1. A reprint edition was published by the Lessing Academy a few years ago. Cf. Theophil Lessing, *Die Religionum Tolerantia: Über die Duldung der Religionen*, edited and introduced by Günter Gawlick and Wolfgang Milde (Göttingen: Wallstein Verlag, 1991).

2. LM 1, 255; G 1, 169 (*Die Religion*).

3. LM 1, 255; G 1, 170 (*Die Religion*).

4. LM 1, 256; G 1, 170–71 (*Die Religion*).

5. Hans Leisegang, *Lessings Weltanschauung* (Leipzig: Felix Meiner, 1931), 27.

6. Johannes Schneider, *Lessings Stellung zur Theologie: Vor der Herausgabe der Wolfenbüttler Fragmente* (The Hague: Uitgeverij Excelsior, 1953), 57.

7. LM 1, 256; G 1, 171 (*Die Religion*).

8. Bernd Bothe, *Glauben und Erkennen: Studie zur Religionsphilosophie Lessings* (Meisenheim am Glan: Verlag Anton Hain, 1972), 15.

9. Leisegang, *Lessings Weltanschauung*, 55. For a criticism on this judgment of Leisegang's, see Schneider, *Lessings Stellung zur Theologie*, 237–38 n. 13.

10. Schneider, *Lessings Stellung zur Theologie*, 57.

11. Ibid., 58.

12. As to the reason the poem was left fragmentary, H. G. Göpfert conjectures that "the fragmentary character" of the poem "is ascribed to the young author's inability to cope intellectually with the major theme that he had taken on himself at a time of serious doubts." Herbert G. Göpfert, "Erläuterungen zu Band 1," in G 2, 614.

13. LM 14, 155; G 3, 683 (*Gedanken über die Herrnhuter*).

14. LM 14, 156; G 3, 684 (*Gedanken über die Herrnhuter*).

15. LM 14, 157; G 3, 685 (*Gedanken über die Herrnhuter*).

16. LM 14, 157; G 3, 685 (*Gedanken über die Herrnhuter*).

17. LM 14, 157; G 3, 685–86 (*Gedanken über die Herrnhuter*).

18. LM 14, 157–58; G 3, 686 (*Gedanken über die Herrnhuter*).

19. LM 14, 157; G 3, 686 (*Gedanken über die Herrnhuter*).

20. LM 14, 158; G 3, 687 (*Gedanken über die Herrnhuter*).

21. LM 14, 159; G 3, 687 (*Gedanken über die Herrnhuter*).

22. LM 14, 159; G 3, 687–88 (*Gedanken über die Herrnhuter*).

23. LM 14, 160; G 3, 688 (*Gedanken über die Herrnhuter*).

24. LM 4, 303–4; G 3, 54–55 (*Berlinische Privilegierte Zeitung*, 38. Stück, 30 March 1751).

25. The dramatic pieces he wrote earlier are *The Young Scholar* (*Der junge Gelehrte*, 1747), *Damon, or True Friendship* (*Damon, oder die wahre Freundschaft*, 1747), *The Misogynist* (*Der Misogyn*, 1748), and *The Old Maid* (*Die alte Jungfer*, 1749).

26. LM 5, 270; G 2, 645 (*Vorrede zum 3. Teil seiner Schriften*, Berlin 1754).

27. Julius W. Braun, ed., *Lessing im Urtheile seiner Zeitgenossen*, 2 vols. (Berlin: Verlag von Friedrich Stahn, 1884–93; reprint, Hildesheim: Georg Olms Verlagsbuchhandlung, 1969), vol. 1, 5.

28. LM 1, 378–79; G 1, 380–81 (*Die Juden*). The English translation, by Ingrid Walsøe-Engel, appears in Peter Demetz's edition of Gotthold Ephraim Lessing, *Nathan the Wise, Minna von Barnhelm, and Other Plays and Writings*, The German Library, vol. 12 (New York: Continuum, 1995), 141–42.

29. LM 1, 385–86; G 1, 388–89 (*Die Juden*). English translation borrowed from ibid., 147.

30. LM 1, 411; G 1, 414 (*Die Juden*). English translation borrowed from ibid., 166.

31. Hans Mayer, *Outsiders: A Study in Life and Letters*, translated by Denis M. Sweet (Cambridge, Massachusetts and London: MIT Press, 1982), 288.

32. The full text of Mayer's statement, in ibid., 290, is as follows:

> The dramatist could not [but] fail here with his properties taken from the world of the *Lustspiel*. The speculative proponent of the Enlightenment, Lessing, on the other hand, has at the same time accomplished an

astonishing task. By revealing against his will how little "the Jews" can be integrated into a communality with the other exceptions, he makes it evident that any endeavor on the part of the Enlightenment toward Jewish emancipation has got to distinguish between *general prejudice* against Jews, nourished by the sight of those who lived in the *real* ghetto, and the rigorous postulate of universal equality and the equality of rights of all men, including Jews.

33. Johann David Michaelis, "Rezension über *Die Juden*," in Horst Steinmetz, ed., *Lessing—Ein unpoetischer Dichter* (Frankfurt am Main: Athenäum Verlag, 1969), 49–50. The English translation is Denis M. Sweet's, borrowed from Mayer's *Outsiders*, 291–92.

34. According to Alexander Altmann, an authority in the field of Mendelssohn studies, it was the Jewish physician Aaron Salomon Gumpertz (1723–1770) who first introduced Mendelssohn to Lessing. It is said that these two young men of the same age first met in the early spring of 1754. See Alexander Altmann, *Moses Mendelssohn: A Biographical Study* (London: Routledge & Kegan Paul, 1973), 36.

35. LM 18, 356 (Letter to Elise Reimarus of 28 November 1780); B 12, 361 (no. 1602).

36. This phrase is currently taken to mean "From Moses [Maimonides] until Moses [Mendelssohn] no one arose with wisdom and understanding comparable to Moses." For more detailed information on this phrase, see Altmann, *Moses Mendelssohn*, 197, 758.

37. In a pithy statement Spicker suggests how important *The Christianity of Reason* is for understanding Lessing's philosophy of religion. "In truth, Lessing's central thoughts are contained in these few paragraphs. And essentially he never went beyond the line laid out in these paragraphs." Gideon Spicker, *Lessing's Weltanschauung* (Leipzig: Verlag von Georg Wigand, 1883), 7.

38. This moral proposition of Lessing's anticipates Kant's famous "fundamental law of pure practical reason": "Act in such a way that the maxim of your will can always be taken as a principle of universal law" (*handle so, daß die Maxime deines Willens jederzeit zugleich als Princip einer allgemeinen Gesetzgebung gelten könne*). Immanuel Kant, *Kants Werke*, Akademie Textausgabe, edited by the Königlich Preußischen Akademie, 9 vols. (Berlin: Walter de Gruyter & Co., 1968), vol. 5, *Kritik der praktischen Vernunft. Kritik der Urteilskraft*, 30.

39. Heinz Heimsoeth, *Die sechs großen Themen der abendländischen Metaphysik und der Ausgang des Mittelalters*, 8th ed. (Darmstadt: Wissenschaftliche Buchgesellschaft, 1987), 40.

40. Wolfgang Gericke, "Lessings theologische Gesamtauffassung," in *Sechs theologische Schriften Gotthold Ephraim Lessings*, introduced and annotated by Wolfgang Gericke (Berlin: Evangelische Verlagsanstalt, 1985), 9–62, esp. 14–15.

41. Leisegang, *Lessings Weltanschauung*, 63–64.

42. For persuasive discussions on this point, see Leisegang, *Lessings Weltanschauung*, 59–65 and Johannes Schneider, *Lessings Stellung zur Theologie*, 112–13.

43. Ernst Troeltsch, *Glaubenslehre*, edited by Gertrud von le Fort (Munich and Leipzig: Verlag von Duncker & Humblot, 1925), 220 (emphasis omitted).

44. Wataru Mizugaki first posed the subject of "God's self-replication" as a topic worthy of serious consideration. He presents a very instructive discussion of "God's self-replication," giving special attention to Hosea, Eckhart, Boethius, and Troeltsch—though he makes no mention of Lessing. His conclusion with regard to Troeltsch is as

follows: "Troeltsch reached the profound conception of God's love as 'God's taking suffering into himself' (*die Selbstunterziehung Gottes unter die Leiden*). But he was unable to develop it into a clear-cut dogmatic conception, remaining content to speak of devotion and piety." Wataru Mizugaki, "Kami no Jiko Nijūka ni tsuite" (On God's self-replication), in *Naze Kirisutokyō ka* (Why Christianity?), edited by Yasuo Furuya (Tokyo: Sōbunsha, 1993), 144–45.

45. Troeltsch, *Glaubenslehre*, 176.

46. To understand how Lessing thought of the relationship between God and the world, we should take into consideration a fragment written during his Breslau years, namely, "On the Reality of Things outside God" (*Über die Wirklichkeit der Dinge außer Gott*, 1763). Scholars unanimously affirm that the position Lessing takes in this fragment is that of "panentheism." See, inter alia, Spicker, *Lessing's Weltanschauung*, 167; Th. C. van Stockum, *Spinoza-Jacobi-Lessing* (Groningen: P. Noordhoff, 1916), 64; Wilhelm Dilthey, *Das Erlebnis und die Dichtung: Lessing-Goethe-Novalis-Hölderlin*, 16th ed. (Göttingen: Vandenhoeck & Ruprecht, 1985), 116; Hans Leisegang, *Lessings Weltanschauung*, 63–65; Johannes Schneider, *Lessings Stellung zur Theologie*, 146–47; and Henry E. Allison, *Lessing and the Enlightenment: His Philosophy of Religion and Its Relation to Eighteenth-Century Thought* (Ann Arbor: University of Michigan Press, 1966), 69.

47. In a letter to his friend Moses Mendelssohn of 1 May 1774, Lessing, referring to his earlier metaphysical speculation in *The Christianity of Reason*, says, "I still remember well my former idea on this very subject. And I also remember very well what you said in response to my assertions at that time, and that I, for that reason, discontinued thinking seriously about this subject for myself." LM 18, 110 (Letter to Moses Mendelssohn of 1 May 1774); B 11/2, 643 (no. 970).

48. In §73 of *The Education of the Human Race* (in German) Lessing speaks not of "God's self-replication" (*Selbstverdoppelung Gottes*) but of "a similar replication in God" (*eine ähnliche Verdoppelung in Gott*) analogous to "a true double of myself" (*eine wahre Verdoppelung meiner Selbst*). But it is self-evident that Lessing's phrase denotes "God's self-replication." See Heinrich Scholz, "Einleitung," in *Die Hauptschriften zum Pantheismusstreit zwischen Jacobi und Mendelssohn* (Berlin: Verlag von Reuther & Reichard, 1916), lxx n. 1; Helmut Thielicke, *Offenbarung, Vernunft und Existenz: Studien zur Religionsphilosophie Lessings*, 4th ed. (Gütersloh: Gerd Mohn, 1957), 49, 50 n. 72; Hermann Timm, *Gott und die Freiheit: Studien zur Religionsphilosophie der Goethezeit*, vol. 1, *Die Spinozarenaissance* (Frankfurt am Main: Vittorio Klostermann, 1974), 122; Alexander Altmann, "Lessing und Jacobi: Das Gespräch über den Spinozismus," in *LYB* 3 (1971): 56–57.

49. In any event, Jacobi's assertion that "Lessing was a Spinozist" must be shaken to its foundations if one takes seriously Lessing's idea of "God's self-replication." For §73 of *The Education of the Human Race* undoubtedly presents the idea of God's self-replication, which cannot hold good on Spinozist premises. Jacobi mistakenly refers to §73 for clear evidence of Lessing's Spinozism, interpreting the paragraph in terms of *natura naturans* (or to use Jacobi's term, *natura naturanti*) and *natura naturata*. Cf. Friedrich Heinrich Jacobi, WW 4/1, 86–88; *Hauptschriften*, 99–101.

50. Leisegang, *Lessings Weltanschauung*, 104–107.

3 The Controversy between Lessing and Goeze

1. The Herzog-August-Bibliothek is a historic library where Leibniz once served as director. Cf. Eric John Aiton, *Leibniz: A Biography* (Bristol and Boston: Adam Hilger Ltd., 1985), chap. 7.

2. The Reimarus manuscripts, part of which Lessing had published as *Fragments from an Unnamed Author*, were first published in their entirety in 1972. Cf. Hermann Samuel Reimarus, *Apologie oder Schutzschrift für die vernünftigen Verehrer Gottes*, edited by Gerhard Alexander, 2 vols. (Frankfurt am Main: Insel Verlag, 1972).

3. For the life and thought of Goeze, the following writings are of some help: Heimo Reinitzer, ed., *Johann Melchior Goeze, 1717–1786. Abhandlungen und Vorträge*, Vestigia Bibliae, no. 8 (Hamburg: Friedrich Wittig Verlag, 1986); Heimo Reinitzer and Walter Sparn, eds., *Verspätete Orthodoxie: Über D. Johann Melchior Goeze*, Wolfenbütteler Forschungen, vol. 45 (Wiesbaden: Otto Harrassowitz, 1989); and Gerhard Freund, *Theologie im Widerspruch: Die Lessing-Goeze-Kontroverse* (Stuttgart-Berlin-Cologne: Verlag W. Kohlhammer, 1989).

4. LM 18, 287 (Letter to Elise Reimarus of 6 September 1778); B 12, 193 (no. 1398).

5. B 9, 753.

6. LM 15, 259–60; G 5, 732–33 (*Collectanea*).

7. Goeze was one of the most avid collectors of various versions of the Bible. His collection, handed down to the present, attests to his extraordinary collecting mania. Cf. Heimo Reinitzer, ed., *Johann Melchior Goeze, 1717–1786*. Lessing himself acknowledges Goeze's thoroughgoing knowledge of German versions of the Bible, saying, "So it might be rather difficult, for example, to prove that my unnamed author had as broad and fundamental a knowledge of all the Low German Bibles as the Hauptpastor has. Even the various versions of Luther's translation of the Bible itself can hardly have been so thoroughly well-known to him as they are to the Hauptpastor, who has made the extraordinary discovery that he can come within a hair of telling the extent to which the orthodox faith of the deceased matches up with each version" (LM 13, 195; G 8, 292 [*Anti-Goeze*, 9]).

8. B 9, 777. The Bahrdt mentioned here, incidentally, is Karl Friedrich Bahrdt (1741–1792).

9. With regard to this affair, Goeze, in *Lessing's Weaknesses* (in German), wrote as follows:

> So I wrote to Mr. Lessing. With my letter I enclosed a sheet on which I had entered various unmistakable differentia of the copy in my hands, with references to page numbers and columns. I requested him to compare these differentia with the copy in the ducal library and, if they agreed, as I surely believed they would, simply to write at the bottom of the sheet the word "Concordat," to sign his name, and send it straight back to me. I held the greatest hope that my request would be fulfilled, all the more because I had had the pleasure of making his acquaintance in person during his stay here in Hamburg. During that time, he did me the honor of visiting me several times, and I spent some truly pleasurable hours in his company. . . . But my hope was in vain. No answer was forthcoming. (Erich Schmidt, ed., *Goezes Streitschriften gegen Lessing*, 94)

10. Ibid., 189.

11. See Th. W. Danzel and G. E. Guhrauer, *Gotthold Ephraim Lessing: Sein Leben und seine Werke*, 2d ed., vol. 2 [of 2] (Berlin: Verlag von Theodor Hofmann, 1881), 434–35.

12. Cf. Franklin Kopitzsch, "Politische Orthodoxie: Johann Melchior Goeze 1717–1786," in *Profile des neuzeitlichen Protestantismus*, edited by Friedrich Wilhelm Graf, vol. 1, *Aufklärung-Idealismus-Vormärz* (Gütersloh: Gerd Mohn, 1990), 72–79; Bernhard Lohse, "Johann Melchior Goeze als Theologe des 18. Jahrhunderts," in Reinitzer, ed., *Johann Melchior Goeze, 1717–1786*, 43.

13. Lessing made friends with the silk dealer Engelbert König (1728–1769) and his family during his Hamburg period (1767–70). Engelbert, however, died an unexpected death on a business trip to Venice in December 1769. He is said to have asked Lessing, who accompanied him halfway on his trip, to take care of his wife and children if the worst should happen to him. After Engelbert's death, Lessing therefore lent a helping hand to the young widow. In the course of time, love grew between them, and they were engaged in September 1771. But Lessing continued to be poor even after obtaining his post at the ducal library. And it took Eva a considerable time to liquidate her deceased husband's business. As a result, they had to wait over five years from the time of their engagement until they could marry.

14. The first half of Goeze's *Something Preliminary against Court Councillor Lessing's Direct and Indirect Malevolent Attacks on Our Most Holy Religion, and on Its Single Foundation, the Bible* (in German) was published on 17 December 1777. The second half was published on 30 January 1778. For Lessing, who had just lost his new-born baby and had been attending his dying wife day and night, Goeze's *Something Preliminary*, sent by his friend Eschenburg, must have been galling. In a reply to Eschenburg, he makes the ironical remark, "Thank you for sending me Goeze's treatise. These materials are now truly the only ones that can distract me" (LM 18, 261 [Letter to Johann Joachim Eschenburg of 7 January 1778]; B 12, 119 [no. 1336]).

15. Schmidt, ed., *Goezes Streitschriften gegen Lessing*, 13.

16. LM 12, 428–29; G 7, 458 (*Gegensätze des Herausgebers*).

17. Schmidt, ed., *Goezes Streitschriften gegen Lessing*, 13.

18. Ibid., 14.

19. Ibid., 15.

20. Ibid. To illustrate his own assertion, Goeze sets forth an example that is altogether characteristic of his argumentative style. "We want to call the will of the Lord, in accordance with which subjects should comport themselves, the *rule for the country.* But the book in which the Lord has his regulations drawn up may be called the *constitution for the country.* Now if a subject, in order to deprive the latter of its high reputation, were to raise an objection to it and argue to the judge that 'the constitution for the country is not the rule for the country, so objections to the former are not objections to the latter,' would such a counterargument have the power to justify him?" (Ibid., 15–16).

21. Ibid., 16.

22. Ibid.

23. Ibid., 17–18.

24. Ibid., 18.

25. Ibid., 18–19.

26. Ibid., 20.

27. Ibid., 21.

28. Ibid.

29. Ibid., 23.

30. Cf. LM 13, 93–96; G 8, 118–120 (*Eine Parabel*).

31. LM 12, 428; G 7, 458 (*Gegensätze des Herausgebers*). See the remark appended to note 36 in chapter 1.

32. Albert Schweitzer, in his *The Quest of the Historical Jesus*, refers to an apologue by Johann S. Semler in which this neological theologian ridiculously compared the editor of the *Fragments from an Unnamed Author* to a madman arrested on a charge of arson. See Albert Schweitzer, *Geschichte der Leben-Jesu-Forschung*, vol. 1 (Hamburg: Siebenstern Taschenbuch Verlag, 1972), 58. What Schweitzer referred to is the *Anhang zur Beantwortung der Fragmenten des Ungenanten* (Halle, 1779, pp. 10–15), published as an appendix to Semler's refutation of the *Fragments from an Unnamed Author* (B 9, 1346–50). It has been shown, however, that this apologue was written not by Semler himself but by a professor of medicine, physics, and mathematics at Halle, Johann Peter Eberhard.

Lessing, though somewhat doubtful as to whether Semler was the author of this piece (cf. LM 16, 492; G 7, 681 [*Sogenannte Briefe an verschiedene Gottesgelehrten*]), seems to have been bitterly resentful of the author who had disparagingly compared the editor of the fragments to a madman, who "is not a criminal, only a little weak in the head" and would have had him sent to the "madhouse" (*Tollhaus*). He intended, therefore, to write a refutation of this piece, but his polemic was left incomplete and therefore unpublished (cf. G 7, 663; B 9, 719 [*Gegen Johann Salomo Semler*]).

33. LM 13, 96; G 8, 120 (*Eine Parabel*).

34. LM 13, 96; G 8, 120 (*Eine Parabel*).

35. LM 13, 96–97; G 8, 120–21 (*Eine Parabel*).

36. Schmidt, ed., *Goezes Streitschriften gegen Lessing*, 24.

37. LM 13, 97; G 8, 121 (*Eine Parabel*).

38. LM 13, 98; G 8, 122 (*Eine Parabel*).

39. LM 13, 98; G 8, 122 (*Eine Parabel*).

40. LM 13, 99; G 8, 123 (*Eine Parabel*).

41. LM 13, 101; G 8, 125 (*Eine Parabel*).

42. LM 13, 101; G 8, 125 (*Eine Parabel*).

43. LM 13, 102; G 8, 125–26 (*Eine Parabel*).

44. LM 13, 103; G 8, 127 (*Eine Parabel*). Italics in original.

45. Henry Chadwick, "Introduction," in *Lessing's Theological Writings* (Stanford: Stanford University Press, 1957), 24.

46. LM 13, 142; G 8, 160 (*Anti-Goeze*, 1).

47. LM 13, 142; G 8, 160 (*Anti-Goeze*, 1).

48. LM 13, 142; G 8, 161 (*Anti-Goeze*, 1).

49. LM 13, 143; G 8, 162 (*Anti-Goeze*, 1).

50. LM 13, 155; G 8, 219 (*Anti-Goeze*, 3).

51. LM 13, 156–57; G 8, 220 (*Anti-Goeze*, 3).

52. LM 13, 164; G 8, 227 (*Anti-Goeze*, 4).

53. LM 13, 164; G 8, 227 (*Anti-Goeze*, 4).

54. LM 13, 169; G 8, 232 (*Anti-Goeze*, 5).

55. LM 13, 175; G 8, 238 (*Anti-Goeze*, 6).

56. Schmidt, ed., *Goezes Streitschriften gegen Lessing*, 3: "I understand the publishing of the fragments that he organized, and the advocacy of the author that he took on himself, in terms of his *indirect* attack on our religion and on the Holy Scripture."

57. LM 13, 181; G 8, 244 (*Anti-Goeze*, 7).

58. LM 13, 182; G 8, 245 (*Anti-Goeze*, 7).

59. LM 13, 183; G 8, 246 (*Anti-Goeze, 7*).

60. LM 13, 183; G 8, 246 (*Anti-Goeze, 7*).

61. LM 13, 186; G 8, 249 (*Anti-Goeze, 7*).

62. LM 13, 158; G 8, 222 (*Anti-Goeze, 3*).

63. LM 13, 172; G 8, 235 (*Anti-Goeze, 5*).

64. LM 13, 196; G 8, 293 (*Anti-Goeze, 9*).

65. LM 13, 207; G 8, 303 (*Anti-Goeze, 11*).

66. LM 13, 209–10; G 8, 305 (*Anti-Goeze, 11*).

67. Albrecht Schöne, "In Sachen des Ungenannten: Lessing contra Goeze," in *Text + Kritik* 26/27 (1975): 3.

68. LM 12, 430; G 7, 460 (*Gegensätze des Herausgebers*).

69. LM 13, 142; G 8, 160 (*Anti-Goeze, 1*).

70. See Lothar Steiger, "Die 'gymnastische' Wahrheitsfrage: Lessing und Goeze," *Evangelische Theologie* 43 (1983): 430–45.

71. William Boehart, *Politik und Religion: Studien zum Fragmentenstreit (Reimarus, Goeze, Lessing)* (Schwarzenbek: Verlag Dr. Rüdiger Martienss, 1988), 200.

72. Hermann Timm, "Eine theologische Tragikomödie: Lessings Neuinszenierung der Geistesgeschichte," *Zeitschrift für Religions- und Geistesgeschichte* 34 (1982): 5.

73. It is for this reason that Goeze has been ridiculed as a representative of "political orthodoxy" (*politische Orthodoxie*). See Franklin Kopitzsch, "Politische Orthodoxie: Johann Melchior Goeze 1717–1786." Cf. also Schmidt, ed., *Goezes Streitschriften gegen Lessing*, 24 and B 9, 754, 789–91.

74. LM 13, 128; G 8, 150 (*Axiomata*); cf. Freund, *Theologie im Widerspruch*, 157–220.

4 Lessing's "Ugly Broad Ditch"

1. Gordon E. Michalson, Jr., *Lessing's "Ugly Ditch": A Study of Theology and History* (University Park and London: Pennsylvania State University Press, 1985), 2.

2. Ernst Troeltsch, "Glaube: 4. Glaube und Geschichte," in *RGG*, vol. 2 [1910], cols. 1447–56.

3. LM 13, 7; G 8, 13 (*Beweis des Geistes und der Kraft*).

4. LM 13, 5; G 8, 11–12 (*Beweis des Geistes und der Kraft*).

5. *Lessing's Theological Writings*, translated by Henry Chadwick (Stanford: Stanford University Press, 1957).

6. Henry Chadwick, "Introduction," in *Lessing's Theological Writings*, 31.

7. Ibid., 32. On the relationship between Lessing and Coleridge, see Samuel Taylor Coleridge, *Confessions of an Inquiring Spirit*, edited by H. StJ. Hart (Stanford: Stanford University Press, 1957), 17–33.

8. Michalson, *Lessing's "Ugly Ditch*," 27.

9. Johann Daniel Schumann, *Über die Evidenz der Beweise für die Wahrheit der christlichen Religion* (Hanover: Verlag der Schmidtschen Buchhandlung, 1778).

10. Origène, *Contre Celse*, Tome 1, 1, 2, *Sources Chrétiennes* 132 (Paris: Les Editions du Cerf, 1967). The English translation below is cited from Origen, *Contra Celsum*, translated by Henry Chadwick (Cambridge: Cambridge University Press, 1980), 8:

> Moreover, we have to say this, that the gospel has a proof which is peculiar to itself, and which is more divine than a Greek proof based on dialectical argument. This more divine demonstration the apostle calls a

"demonstration of the Spirit and of power"—of spirit because of the prophecies and especially those which refer to Christ, which are capable of convincing anyone who reads them; of power because of the prodigious miracles which may be proved to have happened by this argument among many others, that traces of them still remain among those who live according to the will of the Logos.

11. LM 13, 3; G 8, 9 (*Beweis des Geistes und der Kraft*).

12. LM 13, 3–4; G 8, 9–10 (*Beweis des Geistes und der Kraft*).

13. LM 13, 4; G 8, 10 (*Beweis des Geistes und der Kraft*).

14. LM 13, 4; G 8, 10 (*Beweis des Geistes und der Kraft*).

15. LM 13, 5; G 8, 11 (*Beweis des Geistes und der Kraft*).

16. LM 13, 6; G 8, 12 (*Beweis des Geistes und der Kraft*).

17. LM 13, 31–32; G 8, 41 (*Eine Duplik*).

18. LM 13, 6; G 8, 12–13 (*Beweis des Geistes und der Kraft*).

19. LM 13, 7; G 8, 13 (*Beweis des Geistes und der Kraft*).

20. LM 13, 7; G 8, 13 (*Beweis des Geistes und der Kraft*).

21. Michalson, *Lessing's "Ugly Ditch,"* 27.

22. Gottfried Wilhelm Leibniz, *Philosophische Schriften*, vol. 1, *Kleine Schriften zur Metaphysik*, edited and translated by Hans Heinz Holz (Darmstadt: Wissenschaftliche Buchgesellschaft, 1985), 452–53.

23. Gottfried Wilhelm Leibniz, *Philosophische Schriften*, vol. 3/1, *Neu Abhandlungen über den menschlichen Verstand*, edited and translated by Wolf von Engelhardt and Hans Heinz Holz (Darmstadt: Wissenschaftliche Buchgesellschaft, 1985), 16–17.

24. Spinoza, *Opera*, edited by Carl Gebhardt, vol. 3 [of 5], *Tractatus Theologico-Politicus / Adnotationes ad Tractatum Theologico-Politicum / Tractatus Politicus* (Heidelberg: Carl Wintersuniversitätsbuchhandlung, 1972), 61–62.

25. Michalson, *Lessing's "Ugly Ditch,"* 14.

26. Rudolf Bultmann's advocacy of "demythologization" (*Entmythologisierung*) is understandable in this context. It is essentially a hermeneutical attempt to bridge the gap between the gospel message and present-day believers.

27. Sören Kierkegaard, *Gesammelte Werke*, edited by Emanuel Hirsch, Hayo Gerdes, and Hand Martin Junghaus, vol. 16 [of 31], *Abschließende unwissenschaftliche Nachschrift zu den Philosophischen Brocken*, part 1 (Gütersloh: Gerd Mohn, 1982), 70–71.

28. Ibid., 57. The English translation is borrowed from Søren Kierkegaard, *Concluding Unscientific Postscript*, translated by David F. Swenson and Walter Lowrie (Princeton: Princeton University Press, 1941), 61.

29. Hermann Diem, *Theologie als kirchliche Wissenschaft*, vol. 2, *Dogmatik: Ihr Weg zwischen Historismus und Existentialismus* (Munich: Chr. Kaiser Verlag, 1955), 13–23; Richard Campbell, "Lessing's Problem and Kierkegaard's Answer," *Scottish Journal of Theology* 19 (1966): 35–54; Michalson, *Lessing's "Ugly Ditch,"* especially chapter 4.

30. LM 13, 7–8; G 8, 13–14 (*Beweis des Geistes und der Kraft*).

31. It may be helpful to add a word of clarification about what Lessing intended by the word "autonomy." Only insofar as he wished to rule out "false heteronomy" did he advocate the "autonomy of reason." In this, he differed greatly from ordinary Enlightenment thinkers who held to the sheer autonomy of reason. As will be shown in chapters 5 and 6, Lessing's position is ultimately that of "autotheonomy" (*Autotheonomie*), in which "autonomy" and "theonomy" are inseparably united.

32. LM 13, 143; G 8, 162 (*Anti-Goeze*, 1).

33. LM 12, 429; G 7, 458–59 (*Gegensätze des Herausgebers*).

34. Cf. LM 13, 157; G 8, 220 (*Anti-Goeze*, 3).

35. Harald Schultze mentions Thomas Münzer's "inner word" (*das innere Wort*) and Gottfried Arnold's "inward Christianity" (*das inwendige Christentum*) as forerunners of Lessing's concept of "inner truth." He thus suggests a definite relationship between Lessing and "the spiritualistic tradition." See Harald Schultze, "Lessings Auseinandersetzung mit Theologen und Deisten um die 'innere Wahrheit'," in *Lessing in heutiger Sicht*, edited by Edward P. Harris and Richard E. Schade (Bremen and Wolfenbüttel: Jacobi Verlag, 1977), 181. He also points out that Sigmund Jakob Baumgarten, who had studied under Christian Wolff and taught theology to both Semler and Goeze, had already used the concept of inner truth in his dogmatics and defined it as "*dispositio rei ad finem suum*" (182).

On the other hand, Wolfgang Gericke, though following Schultze in his emphasis on the spiritualistic background of Lessing's philosophy of religion, opposes the attempt to derive Lessing's concept of inner truth from the spiritualistic tradition. In his view, Lessing's concept of inner truth does not originate in spiritualism but is worked out by Lessing himself in connection with John Toland's *Christianity Not Mysterious* (1696). See Wolfgang Gericke, "Lessings theologische Gesamtauffassung," in his *Sechs theologische Schriften Gotthold Ephraim Lessings* (Berlin: Evangelische Verlagsanstalt, 1985), 51.

36. Erich Schmidt, ed., *Goezes Streitschriften gegen Lessing* (Stuttgart: G. J. Göschen'sche Verlagshandlung, 1893), 21–22.

37. LM 13, 128–29; G 8, 150 (*Axiomata*).

38. LM 13, 95; G 8, 119 (*Eine Parabel*).

39. LM 12, 428; G 7, 458 (*Gegensätze des Herausgebers*).

40. H. Richard Niebuhr, *The Meaning of Revelation* (New York: Macmillan Publishing Co., 1941; paperback ed., 1960), 44.

41. For Niebuhr's distinction between inner and outer history, see Van A. Harvey, *The Historian and the Believer: The Morality of Historical Knowledge and Christian Belief* (Philadelphia: Westminster Press, 1966), 234–42.

42. From the above consideration it will be clear that Lessing's assertion of the inner truth of religion has some analogy to the Tillichean "knowledge of participation."

43. LM 13, 8; G 8, 14 (*Beweis des Geistes und der Kraft*).

44. LM 13, 12; G 8, 15 (*Das Testament Johannis*).

45. This anecdote is taken from Jerome's *Commentaria in Epistolam ad Galatas*, 3, 6, which has to do with Gal. 6:10. See Eusebius Hieronymus, *Opera Omnia*, in the *Patrologiæ cursus completus. Series Latina*, edited by J.-P. Migne (Paris: Vrayet, 1845–46), vol. 26, 433. In order to support his own assertion, Lessing appended to his tract an excerpt from the Latin text. Cf. LM 13, 17; G 8, 20 (*Das Testament Johannis*).

46. Jerome's original Latin is "Filioli diligite alterutrum."

47. Lessing's knowledge of patristics is remarkable. In citing the opening words of the Fourth Gospel, he is referring to an episode recorded in Augustine's *De Civitate Dei*, 10, 29, 2. According to this episode, a certain Platonist once said that the opening words of John's gospel deserve to be inscribed in letters of gold in the most prominent places in all churches. Cf. LM 13, 15; G 8, 18 (*Das Testament Johannis*).

48. LM 16, 390; G 7, 635 (*Hypothese über die Evangelisten*, §63).

49. LM 13, 16; G 8, 19 (*Das Testament Johannis*).

50. Wolfhart Pannenberg, *Ethik und Ekklesiologie* (Göttingen: Vandenhoeck & Ruprecht, 1977), 71.

51. LM 17, 17–18 (Letter to Johann Gottfried Lessing of 30 May 1749); B 11/1, 26 (no. 21).

52. LM 3, 94–95; G 2, 280 (*Nathan der Weise*, 3/7). The English translation is borrowed from Lessing's *Nathan the Wise: A Dramatic Poem in Five Acts*, translated by Bayard Quincy Morgan (New York: Frederick Ungar Publishing Co., 1955).

53. This is a translation of the Latin epigraph of *The Testament of John*, cited from the prologue to Jerome's *Commentaria in Epistolam ad Ephesios*.

54. Cf. Phillip Vielhauer, *Geschichte der urchristlichen Literatur*, 4th ed. (Berlin: Walter de Gruyter & Co., 1975), 501–502; Leonhard Goppelt, *Theologie des Neuen Testaments*, 3d ed. (Göttingen: Vandenhoeck & Ruprecht, 1978), 510.

55. Closely related to the issue of the connection between Lessing's emphasis on *The Testament of John* and his appeal to the "new, eternal Gospel" in the book of Revelation is the question, of major importance to intellectual history, of what influence Lessing's rediscovery of *The Testament of John* exerted on the resurgence of "Johannine Christianity" in Franz von Baader, Fichte, Hegel, Schelling, and others in the nineteenth century. We are not yet ready to discuss this question, but it is certainly an important theme that is bound to call for discussion in future. See Ernst Benz, *Evolution and Christian Hope: Man's Concept of the Future, from the Early Fathers to Teilhard de Chardin* (Garden City, New York: Doubleday & Co., 1968), 46; cf. Marjorie Reeves and Warwick Gould, *Joachim of Fiore and the Myth of the Eternal Evangel in the Nineteenth Century* (Oxford: Clarendon Press, 1987), 2, 53, 57, 60, 62–65 passim.

In this context it is important to take note of Hermann Timm's suggestion of a close relationship between Lessing's emphasis on "Johannine Christianity" and the idealist philosophy of the post-Lessing generations. He says, "Lessing's 'eternal gospel' has made the fundamental connection between an ontological and economic Trinity, between a metaphysical concept of God and an eschatological concept of history into a theme that inspired the next generation." Hermann Timm, *Gott und die Freiheit: Studien zur Religionsphilosophie der Goethezeit*, vol. 1, *Die Spinozarenaissance* (Frankfurt am Main: Vittorio Klostermann, 1974), 16; cf. 8–10, 97, 101–102.

56. LM 13, 8; G 8, 14 (*Beweis des Geistes und der Kraft*).

57. In Lessing's proposition, the exact words are these: "If no historical truth can be demonstrated, then nothing can be demonstrated by means of historical truths (*historische Wahrheiten*). That is, accidental truths of history (*Geschichtswahrheiten*) can never become the proof for necessary truths of reason" LM 13, 5; G 8, 11–12 (*Beweis des Geistes und der Kraft*).

58. In addition to these two expressions, Lessing also speaks of "historically proven truths" (*historisch erwiesene Wahrheiten*) (LM 13, 5; G 8, 11). This term may be interchangeable with "historical truths" (*historische Wahrheiten*), but is it also interchangeable with "truths of history" (*Geschichtswahrheiten*)? Hardly! True, there was no clear-cut distinction between *Historie* and *Geschichte* until the beginning of the twentieth century, but we cannot fail to observe that Lessing's argument, when seen in the light of twentieth-century thought, involves a lack of conceptual clarity at this point.

59. Arno Schilson, *Geschichte im Horizont der Vorsehung: G. E. Lessings Beitrag zu einer Theologie der Geschichte* (Mainz: Matthias-Grünewald-Verlag, 1974), 124.

60. Helmut Thielicke, *Offenbarung, Vernunft und Existenz: Studien zur Religionsphilosophie Lessings*, 4th ed. (Gütersloh: Gerd Mohn, 1957), 70.

61. LM 13, 432; G 8, 506 (*Die Erziehung des Menschengeschlechts*, §76). For my interpretation of this proposition, see chapter 6.

62. Karl Barth, *Die protestantische Theologie im 19. Jahrhundert: Ihre Vorge-*

schichte und ihre Geschichte, 5th ed. (Zurich: Theologischer Verlag, 1985), 224.

63. Ibid., 226.

64. Ibid.

65. Ibid., 235–36.

66. Karl Barth, "Das Problem Lessings und das Problem des Petrus," *Evangelische Theologie*, Sonderheft: Ernst Wolf zum 50. Geburtstag (Munich: Chr. Kaiser Verlag, 1952), 4–17. This treatise is now incorporated into his magnum opus, *Die kirchliche Dogmatik* , vol. 4/1 (Zurich: Theologischer Verlag, 1953), 312–23.

67. Barth, "Das Problem Lessings und das Problem der Petrus," 10.

68. Ibid., 12.

69. Ibid., 11–12.

70. Ibid., 13–15.

71. Wolfgang Trillhaas is of the same opinion. Though he praises Barth for selecting Lessing as a topic for discussion in *Protestant Theology in the Nineteenth Century*, he nevertheless criticizes Barth in these words: "But this 'vindication' of Lessing will please nobody. For in the end Barth dresses him up as a witness, if a secret witness, to what he himself thinks." See Wolfgang Trillhaas, "Zur Wirkungsgeschichte Lessings in der evangelischen Theologie," in *WSA*, vol. 9, *Das Bild Lessings in der Geschichte*, edited by Herbert G. Göpfert (Heidelberg: Verlag Lambert Schneider, 1981), 61.

72. See Michalson, *Lessing's "Ugly Ditch,"* Introduction and chapter 1.

5 Nathan the Wise *and Lessing's "Ideal of Humanity"*

1. Friedrich Schlegel, "Über Lessing," in *Gotthold Ephraim Lessing*, Wege der Forschung, vol. 211, edited by Gerhard and Sibylle Bauer (Darmstadt: Wissenschaftliche Buchgesellschaft, 1968), 34.

2. Wilhelm Dilthey, *Das Erlebnis und die Dichtung: Lessing-Goethe-Novalis-Hölderlin*, 16th ed. (Göttingen: Vandenhoeck & Ruprecht, 1985), 90.

3. Ibid., 90–91.

4. Ernst Troeltsch, "Der deutsche Idealismus," in *Gesammelte Schriften*, vol. 4, *Aufsätze zur Geistesgeschichte und Religionssoziologie*, edited by Hans Baron (Tübingen: J. C. B. Mohr, 1925; reprint, Aalen: Scientia Verlag, 1966), 550, 552.

5. LM 21, 224 (Letter from Duke Karl of Brunswick of 17 August 1778); B 12, 187 (no. 1390).

6. LM 18, 285–86 (Letter to Karl Lessing of 11 August 1778); B 12, 186 (no. 1389).

7. LM 21, 225 (Letter from Karl Lessing of 18 August 1778); B 12, 188 (no. 1392).

8. LM 21, 226 (Letter from Karl Lessing of 25 August 1778); B 12, 189 (no. 1393).

9. LM 21, 215 (Letter from Karl Lessing of July 1778); B 12, 165 (no. 1369).

10. LM 21, 226 (Letter from Karl Lessing of 25 August 1778); B 12, 189 (no. 1393).

11. LM 18, 289–90 (Letter to Karl Lessing of 20 October 1778); B 12, 200 (no. 1405).

12. LM 18, 287 (Letter to Elise Reimarus of 6 September 1778); B 12, 193 (no. 1398).

13. In a letter of 7 November 1778 to his brother Karl, Lessing says: "My *Nathan*, as Professors Schmid and Eschenburg can attest, is a piece for which, as early as three years ago, shortly after my return from a trip [to Italy], I wanted to complete a fair

copy and have it printed. I have now sought it out again only because it suddenly occurred to me that by making just a few small changes in the plan, I can from a different angle make a flank attack on the enemy. I am now finished with these changes, and the work is as ready as any of my pieces has ever been when I began sending it to the press. All the same, I want to revise and polish it further until Christmas. By Christmastime I want to start writing out the entire manuscript in a final copy and have it printed little by little so that I can appear with it at the Easter fair without fail. I do not want to appear with it any earlier; for you will remember that in my Christmas announcement I asked to be informed in advance as to the number of subscribers." LM 18, 191 (Letter to Karl Lessing of 7 November 1778); B 12, 207 (no. 1410).

14. LM 18, 323 (Letter to Tobias Philipp Freiherrn von Gebler of 13 August 1779); B 12, 270 (no. 1492).

15. LM 18, 319 (Letter to Friedrich Heinrich Jacobi of 18 May 1779); B 12, 256 (no. 1474).

16. LM 16, 444 (*Vorrede und Abhandlungen zu Nathan dem Weisen*); cf. G 2, 748.

17. From early on, attempts have been made to see Nathan the Wise as "a noble, Mendelssohnian character" (*ein edler Mendelssohnischer Charakter*). Cf. LM 21, 261 (Letter from Elise Reimarus of 3 June 1779). Some scholars, however, oppose such a view. For example, G. E. Guhrauer asserts that "Nathan—this is Lessing himself—is not, as people always say, his Jewish friend Mendelssohn." Th. W. Danzel and G. E. Guhrauer, *Gotthold Ephraim Lessing: Sein Leben und seine Werke*, 2d ed., vol. 2 [of 2] (Berlin: Verlag von Theodor Hofmann, 1881), 465–66. In Guhrauer's view, "Nathan is almost an idealistic figure, anything but a copy" of Moses Mendelssohn or anyone else (465).

18. A biography of Saladin has recently been published in Japanese. The comparison between Lessing's dramatic depiction in *Nathan the Wise* and the historian's objective description based on historical sources is very instructive. See Tsugitaka Satō, *Isuramu no "Eiyū" Saradin: Jūjigun to Tatakatta Otoko* (Saladin the hero of Islam: A man who fought against the crusades) (Tokyo: Kōdansha, 1996).

19. See Danzel and Guhrauer, *Gotthold Ephraim Lessing*, vol. 2, 465–66.

20. Gottfried Fittbogen, *Die Religion Lessings* (Leipzig: Mayer & Müller, 1923; reprint, New York: Johnson Reprint Corporation, 1967), 161.

21. H. A. Korff, *Geist der Goethezeit: Versuch einer ideellen Entwicklung der klassisch-romantischen Literaturgeschichte*, part 2, *Klassik*, 2d ed. (Leipzig: Koehler & Amelang, 1955), 147. Korff holds that it was through *Nathan the Wise* that Lessing freed himself completely of the Enlightenment and stepped into "the sphere of classicism" (*die klassische Sphäre*) (154).

22. Dilthey, *Das Erlebnis und die Dichtung*, 98.

23. Ibid., 94.

24. An important difference from Boccaccio's work is that in the original novel, the ring is described merely as an "exceptionally beautiful and priceless" ring, whereas in Lessing's parable, the ring has, in addition to such attributes, "the magic power that he who [wears] it, / Trusting its strength, [is] loved of God and men" (LM 3, 90; G 2, 276 [*Nathan der Weise*, 3/7]). As a result, Lessing's parable, because it amalgamates human subjective elements with objective truth, impels us to ceaseless striving and praxis, while Boccaccio's suggests that the truth claims of historical religions are hard to ascertain, thus leading to religious relativism or indifference.

Cesare Cases's suggestion that "Protestantism and the Enlightenment stand between Boccaccio and Lessing" must be asserted in a more fundamental sense than he seems to imply (Cesare Cases, "Lessings >*Nathan der Weise*<," in Klaus Bohnen, ed., *Lessings* >*Nathan der Weise*< [Darmstadt: Wissenschaftliche Buchgesellschaft, 1984], 333). For the novel idea that Lessing has introduced into Boccaccio's original parable of the three rings is nothing other than the main idea of modern Protestantism, namely, that the truth is validated through inwardness and praxis. We have already learned that Lessing takes "Luther's spirit" as signifying that "no man may be prevented from advancing in the knowledge of truth according to his own judgment." We have also learned of his famous dictum, "The worth of a man does not consist in the truth he possesses, or thinks he possesses, but in the pains he has taken to attain that truth. . . . Absolute truth is for thee [that is, for God] alone." Lessing's parable of the three rings has to be construed against the background of these words. Only when we read it against the background of his theological, or religious-philosophical, thought can we really understand how significantly the central thought of "the founder of modern Protestantism" is expressed in this parable.

25. LM 3, 90–95; G 2, 276–80 (*Nathan der Weise*, 3/7). Most English translations for *Nathan der Weise* are borrowed from the slightly abridged version published in Lessing's *Nathan the Wise, Minna von Barnhelm, and Other Plays and Writings*, translated by Bayard Quincy Morgan (New York: Continuum Publishing Co., 1991). A few citations, however, have been borrowed from the unabridged version published under the title *Nathan the Wise: A Dramatic Poem in Five Acts*, translated by Bayard Quincy Morgan (New York: Frederick Ungar Publishing Co., 1955). Citations from the latter are identified in the notes.

26. Stuart Atkins, "The Parable of the Rings in Lessing's *Nathan der Weise*," *Germanic Review* 26 (1951): 259.

27. Ibid., 259.

28. LM 3, 87–88; G 2, 273–74 (*Nathan der Weise*, 3/5).

29. LM 3, 88; G 2, 274 (*Nathan der Weise*, 3/5).

30. LM 3, 88–89; G 2, 274–75 (*Nathan der Weise*, 3/6).

31. LM 3, 92; G 2, 278 (*Nathan der Weise*, 3/7).

32. LM 3, 92; G 2, 278 (*Nathan der Weise*, 3/7).

33. LM 3, 92–93; G 2, 278 (*Nathan der Weise*, 3/7).

34. LM 13, 5; G 8, 12 (*Beweis des Geistes und der Kraft*).

35. This seems to have some connection with the fact that in the fragments controversy, Lessing consistently emphasizes the "inner truth of a religion."

36. Cf. Benno von Wiese, *Lessing: Dichtung, Aesthetik, Philosophie* (Leipzig: Verlag Quelle & Meyer, 1931), 66–67; Fittbogen, *Die Religion Lessings*, 163.

37. Wiese, *Lessing*, 67.

38. LM 3, 54; G 2, 247 (*Nathan der Weise*, 2/3).

39. Wiese, *Lessing*, 70.

40. LM 3, 61; G 2, 252 (*Nathan der Weise*, 2/5).

41. LM 3, 63; G 2, 253 (*Nathan der Weise*, 2/5).

42. Cf. Wiese, *Lessing*, 67.

43. LM 3, 123; G 2, 304 (*Nathan der Weise*, 4/4); *Nathan the Wise: A Dramatic Poem in Five Acts*, translated by Bayard Quincy Morgan (New York: Frederick Ungar Publishing Co., 1955), p. 103.

44. LM 3, 99; G 2, 283 (*Nathan der Weise*, 3/8).

45. The templar compares Rachel to "The artist's [creation], who in that abandoned block / Thought out the form divine which he portrayed." LM 3, 148; G 2, 324 (*Nathan der Weise*, 5/3).

46. Cf. Fittbogen, *Die Religion Lessings*, 160–61.

47. LM 3, 75; G 2, 263 (*Nathan der Weise*, 3/1).

48. LM 3, 117; G 2, 299 (*Nathan der Weise*, 4/2).

49. LM 3, 140; G 2, 317–18 (*Nathan der Weise*, 4/7); *Nathan the Wise: A Dramatic Poem in Five Acts*, translated by Bayard Quincy Morgan (New York: Frederick Ungar Publishing Co., 1955), p. 119.

50. Fittbogen, *Die Religion Lessings*, 161.

51. Wiese, *Lessing*, 75.

52. Ibid., 76.

53. Ibid., 70–77.

54. Ibid., 77.

55. Nathan's adoptive daughter Rachel's words are instructive: "Yes, I do. My father loves, you see, too little / That cold book-learning, which impresses on / The mind just lifeless symbols" (LM 3, 161; G 2, 334–35 [*Nathan der Weise*, 5/6]; *Nathan the Wise: A Dramatic Poem in Five Acts* [New York: Frederick Ungar, 1955, p. 137]). Nathan's wisdom is undoubtedly the opposite of such "cold book-learning." In another place, Lessing makes an observation that seems apropos in this connection: "The wealth of other people's experience obtained from books is called erudition. One's own experience is wisdom. The smallest chapter of the latter is worth more than millions of the former" (LM 16, 535; G 5, 788 [*Selbstbetrachtung und Einfälle*]).

56. LM 3, 86–87; G 2, 272–73 (*Nathan der Weise*, 3/5).

57. LM 3, 138; G 2, 316 (*Nathan der Weise*, 4/7).

58. LM 3, 139; G 2, 316–17 (*Nathan der Weise*, 4/7).

59. LM 3, 139; G 2, 317 (*Nathan der Weise*, 4/7).

60. That the calamities which befell Nathan and his family should remind us of Job's hardships is quite natural. A comparison of Job and Nathan the Wise is therefore a worthy topic of investigation. For such a comparison, see Ingrid Strohschneider-Kohrs, *Vernunft als Weisheit: Studien zum späten Lessing* (Tübingen: Max Niemeyer Verlag, 1991).

61. LM 3, 163; G 2, 336 (*Nathan der Weise*, 5/6).

62. "Autotheonomy" (*Autotheonomie*) is a term borrowed from Ernst Troeltsch. As he puts it, "*Christian autonomy is at the same time theonomy*" (italics in original). He coined the term "autotheonomy" to make this point clear. See Ernst Troeltsch, *Glaubenslehre*, edited by Gertrud von le Fort (Munich and Leipzig: Verlag von Duncker & Humblot, 1925), 201–202.

In this connection, Troeltsch elsewhere expresses the remarkable view that "autonomy and theonomy are not opposites if the divine origin of moral law is traced back not to externally revealed, statutory law, but to the compulsion of moral reason itself"; "theonomy is only an emphasizing of the religious presuppositions contained in the idea of autonomy itself." See his "Praktische christliche Ethik: Diktate zur Vorlesung im Wintersemester 1911/12. Aus dem Nachlaß Gertrud le Forts herausgegeben von Elenore von la Chevallerie und Friedrich Wilhelm Graf," in *Mitteilungen der Ernst-Troeltsch-Gesellschaft*, vol. 6 (Augsburg, 1991), 143.

63. In these words one may discern the idea of *Deus operans operari*, an idea traceable to Philippians 2:13: "θεὸς γάρ ἐστιν ὁ ἐνεργῶν ἐν ὑμῖν καὶ τὸ θέλειν καὶ τὸ ἐνεργεῖν ὑπὲρ τῆς εὐδοχίας" (RSV: "for God is at work in you, both to will and to work for his good pleasure"). For more discussion of this idea, see Wataru Mizugaki, *Shūkyō teki Tankyū no Mondai* (The problem of religious quest) (Tokyo: Sōbunsha, 1984), chapter 10.

At any rate, the words "I will! / If Thou wilt, then I will!" (*Ich will! / Willst du nur, daß ich will!*) strike me as highly significant. Günter Rohrmoser likewise calls attention to this point. He says:

> The organ with which Nathan carries out his hearkening to God is
> reason, and no appeal is made to the historical figure of Founder,
> Redeemer, or Savior. What is heard is, in a word, acceptance of one's
> fate as divine providence. This occurs in the remarkable statement, "I
> will! / If Thou wilt, then I will!" His turning to God bears, therefore, the
> character of personal address. But God is not addressed on behalf of
> anyone or anything. Instead, Nathan subjects himself to God with the
> humble request that his sacrifice may be found acceptable. Nathan's self-
> negation as unconditional yielding of the self to God may be taken as
> Lessing's real opinion as to what constitutes the problem of religions.

See Günter Rohrmoser, "Aufklärung und Offenbarungsglaube (Lessing-Kant)," in
Emanzipation und Freiheit (Munich: Wilhelm Goldmann Verlag, 1970), 50; cf. Arno
Schilson, *Lessings Christentum* (Göttingen: Vandenhoeck & Ruprecht, 1980), 39–40.

64. Johannes von Lüpke, *Wege der Weisheit: Studien zu Lessings Theologiekritik*
(Göttingen: Vandenhoeck & Ruprecht, 1989), 123.

65. Otto Mann, *Lessing: Sein und Leistung* (Berlin: Walter de Gruyter, 1965),
319.

66. Cf. Hans Michael Baumgartner, "Wandlungen des Vernunftbegriffs in der
Geschichte des europäischen Denkens," in *Grenzfragen*, vol. 16, *Rationalität: Ihre
Entwicklung und ihre Grenzen* (Freiburg & Munich, 1989), 167–203.

67. See Strohschneider-Kohrs, *Vernunft als Weisheit*.

68. Lüpke, *Wege der Weisheit*, 123.

69. John van den Hengel seems to be right, therefore, when he maintains that "for
him reason has limits" ("Reason and Revelation in Lessing's Enlightenment," *Église et
Théologie* 17 [1986]: 192). Indeed, Lessing himself suggests "the limits of reason"
when he says that reason is ready to submit itself to revelation so long as it is guaran-
teed by "the reality of revelation." LM 12, 433; G 7, 463 (*Gegensätze des Herausgebers*).

70. Lüpke, *Wege der Weisheit*, 69.

71. LM 18, 358 (Letter to Elise Reimarus of 28 November 1780); B 12, 360–61
(no. 1602).

72. It is very significant, therefore, that in the epigraph to *The Testament of John*
Lessing cited Jerome's words, "qui in pectus Domini recubuit et de purissimo fonte
hausit rivulum doctrinarum." Cf. LM 13, 9; G 8, 15 (*Das Testament Johannis*).

6 Lessing's Basic Thought in The Education of the Human Race

1. Johann Gottfried Herder, "Gotthold Ephraim Lessing. Geb. 1729, gest. 1781,"
in Horst Steinmetz, ed., *Lessing—Ein unpoetischer Dichter* (Frankfurt am Main:
Athenäum Verlag, 1969), 133.

2. Helmut Thielicke, *Offenbarung, Vernunft und Existenz: Studien zur Religionsphilosophie Lessings*, 4th ed. (Gütersloh: Gerd Mohn, 1957), 57.

3. Paul Tillich, *Gesammelte Werke*, vol. 12, *Begegnungen* (Stuttgart: Evangelisches Verlagswerk, 1971), 99.

4. This does not mean, however, that all of Lessing's final convictions pertaining
to theology and philosophy of religion are expressly manifested in this work. For in
Ernst and Falk (1778–80) he says through the mouth of Falk that there are "truths

which are better left unsaid" and that "the wise man *cannot* say what is better left unsaid" (LM 13, 353; G 8, 459 [*Ernst und Falk*, 2]).

5. Carl Schwarz, *Gotthold Ephraim Lessing als Theologe* (Halle: C. E. M. Pfeffer, 1854), 79.

6. Wilhelm Lütgert, *Die Religion des deutschen Idealismus und ihre Ende*, vol. 1, *Die religiöse Krise des deutschen Idealismus* (Gütersloh: Gerd Mohn, 1923; reprint, Hildesheim: Georg Olms, 1967), 154. Mandelbaum, by defining Lessing's position in the history of philosophy as "an intermediate position" between the Enlightenment and romanticism, suggests that Lessing was overstepping the horizon of the Enlightenment and coming close to the spirit of romanticism. But it is difficult to say that Mandelbaum has recognized Lessing's significance as a pioneer of German idealism as well as of romanticism. See Maurice Mandelbaum, *History, Man, and Reason: A Study in Nineteenth-Century Thought* (Baltimore and London: Johns Hopkins University Press, 1971), 384.

7. See introduction.

8. Martin Haug, *Entwicklung und Offenbarung bei Lessing* (Gütersloh: C. Bertelsmann, 1928), 32.

9. Ibid., p. 31.

10. Ibid., p. 35.

11. LM 12, 446; G 7, 476 (*Gegensätze des Herausgebers*).

12. LM 12, 368; G 7, 398 (*Aus den Papieren des Ungenannten*, 4); cf. Hermann Samuel Reimarus, *Apologie oder Schutzschrift für die vernünftigen Verehrer Gottes*, edited by Gerhard Alexander, 2 vols. (Frankfurt am Main: Insel Verlag, 1972), vol. 1, 770–71.

13. Cf. LM 12, 443–46; G 7, 472–76 (*Gegensätze des Herausgebers*).

14. LM 12, 447; G 7, 489 (*Gegensätze des Herausgebers*).

15. Cf. Martha Waller, *Lessings Erziehung des Menschengeschlechts: Interpretation und Darstellung ihres rationalen und irrationalen Gehaltes* (Berlin: Verlag Dr. Emil Ebering, 1935), 4–5.

16. Other forms of division are possible, to be sure. For example, Erwin Quapp, from a very different point of view, divides the book into four parts:

A. Main Theses (§§1–3)
B. Education of the Human Race at the First, Old Testament Stage (§§4–53)
C. Education of the Human Race at the Second, New Testament Stage (§§54–81)
D. The Final Stage of the Education of the Human Race (§§82–100)

See Erwin Quapp, *Lessings Theologie statt Jacobis Spinozismus* (Bern: Peter Lang, 1992), 33. Quapp's main concern, however, is not with the division as such but with demonstrating that what he calls the *Gartenhausformel*, namely, "ἕν ἐγὼ καὶ πᾶν," is "the systematic clue to Lessing's theology." He seeks to prove that this "ἕν ἐγὼ καὶ πᾶν," not the allegedly Spinozistic "ἕν καὶ πᾶν," is the formula most essential to understanding Lessing's theology or philosophy of religion. For this purpose, he attempts to provide a systematic, unified interpretation of *The Education of the Human Race* from this point of view. Though his assertion is fresh and exciting, it strikes me as a bit too bold and too forced. Furthermore, it involves a fatal mistake. For more detail on this point, see our discussion in the next chapter.

17. With respect to their connection with Lessing's discussions in the main body of *The Education of the Human Race*, there is controversy as to how this Latin statement should be translated. Paul Rilla, for example, translates it as "All dies ist aus denselben

Gründen in gewisser Hinsicht wahr, aus denen es in gewisser Hinsicht falsch ist" (R 8, 590). Helmut Göbel's translation is almost the same: "Dieses alles ist aus denselben Gründen in gewisser Hinsicht wahr, aus denen es in gewisser Hinsicht falsch ist" (G 8, 709; G 7, 854). By contrast, Eckhard Heftrich, dealing with this issue under the heading "Augustinus contra Augustinum," maintains that the statement should be translated thus: "Dies alles ist von einem bestimmten Gesichtspunkt aus je nachdem ebenso wahr wie falsch" (Eckhard Heftrich, *Lessings Aufklärung* [Frankfurt am Main: Vittorio Klostermann, 1978], 43). Erwin Quapp is critical even of this rendering and proposes yet another way to translate it, insisting that the translation should be in the form of indirect narration so as to show clearly where truth lies: "Dies alles seien von dorther in gewissem wahr, von woher sie in gewissem unwahr sind" (Quapp, *Lessings Theologie statt Jacobis Spinozismus*, 43). The English translator of Augustine's *Soliloquies*, in *A Select Library of the Nicene and Post-Nicene Fathers*, vol. 7 (edited by Philip Schaff [Grand Rapids, Michigan: Wm. B. Eerdmans Publishing Co., 1986]), renders the sentence as follows: "that all these things are in certain aspects true, by this very thing that they are in certain aspects false."

18. Heftrich, *Lessings Aufklärung*, 42.

19. Ibid., 42.

20. Augustine, *Soliloquies*, in *A Select Library of the Nicene and Post-Nicene Fathers*, vol. 7, 553.

21. Heftrich, *Lessings Aufklärung*, 45.

22. Willi Oelmüller, *Die unbefriedigte Aufklärung: Beiträge zu einer Theorie der Moderne von Lessing, Kant und Hegel* (Frankfurt am Main: Suhrkamp, 1979), 78.

23. Ibid.

24. Thielicke, *Offenbarung, Vernunft und Existenz*, 58. According to Thielicke, such a "point of view" is implied by the term "quibusdam" (see p. 58 n. 12).

25. Thielicke pays special attention to the problem of *Standort*. He repeatedly emphasizes that Lessing stood in the midst of an ongoing process that was still open to the future (Thielicke, *Offenbarung, Vernunft und Existenz*, 26 n. 60, 45, 46, 77, 78, 113). As the title of Wilm Pelters's book shows, he too attaches special importance to this point. See Wilm Pelters, *Lessings Standort: Sinndeutung der Geschichte als Kern seines Denkens* (Heidelberg: Lothar Stiehm Verlag, 1972).

26. LM 13, 415; G 8, 489 (*Die Erziehung des Menschengeschlechts*). All English translations from *The Education of the Human Race* are from *Lessing's Theological Writings*, translated by Henry Chadwick (Stanford: Stanford University Press, 1957).

27. This posturing has given rise to the conjecture that the real author of *The Education of the Human Race* was someone other than Lessing. In fact, there was a time when Albrecht Thaer was plausibly alleged to have been the real author. But Heinrich Schneider's solid study has dispelled all doubts about Lessing's authorship. See Heinrich Schneider, "Lessings letzte Prosaschrift," in his *Lessing: Zwölf biographische Studien* (Munich: Leo Lehnen Verlag, 1951), 222–30.

28. We consider it most likely that when Lessing made public *The Education of the Human Race*, he deliberately chose to publish it anonymously. Consequently, we agree with Timm when he asserts that "the anonymity is intended" (*die Anonymität ist gewollt*). Hermann Timm, *Gott und die Freiheit: Studien zur Religionsphilosophie der Goethezeit*, vol. 1, *Die Spinozarenaissance* (Frankfurt am Main: Vittorio Klostermann, 1974), 134.

29. LM 18, 269 (Letter to Johann Albert Reimarus of 6 April 1778); B 12, 143 (no. 1358).

30. Quapp, *Lessings Theologie statt Jacobis Spinozismus*, 61.

31. Thielicke points out that "waiting" (*Warten*) is a term of special importance to Lessing. See his *Offenbarung, Vernunft und Existenz*, 23, 24, 55.

32. That special importance attaches to this metaphor of "a soft evening glow" may be inferred from *Ernst and Falk: Conversations for the Freemasons* (in German), a work closely related to the subject taken up in *The Education of the Human Race*. The conversations between Ernst, the pursuer of truth, and Falk, the spiritually awakened, center on the essence of freemasonry. The conversations begin with a scene in which Falk is "enjoying the refreshing morning" (G 8, 452) and end with a scene in which "the sun is going down" (G 8, 488). It is significant that the evening scene, when the natural sun is sinking, is also a time when Ernst's eyes are opened to the truth and "another sun" is rising in his heart (G 8, 452).

33. In an earlier fragment called *On the Origin of Revealed Religion* (in German), which presumably dates from his Breslau period (1763–64), Lessing asserts that "all positive and revealed religions are equally true and equally false" (LM 14, 313; G 7, 283). It is evident that the words of Augustine cited in the epigraph already lie behind this assertion. Given this early date, we may safely suppose that the consciousness of "historical ambivalence" came to Lessing much earlier than the time of the writing of *The Education of the Human Race*.

34. Karlmann Beyschlag, *Grundriß der Dogmengeschichte*, vol. 1, *Gott und Welt* (Darmstadt: Wissenschaftliche Buchgesellschaft, 1988), 201 n. 19. Beyschlag is the editor of the third volume of *Lessings Werke* (Frankfurt am Main: Insel Verlag, 1972), for which Kurt Wölfel is the general editor. Beyschlag's editorial essay, appended to volume 3, is very instructive (W 3, 593–617).

35. See, e.g., Gal. 4:1–9; Col. 2:17; Heb. 1:1, 8:4 passim.

36. For example, *The Epistle to Diognetus*, chapters 8–9; Irenaeus, *Adversus Haereses*, book 4; Tertullian, *Adversus Marcionem*, book 4; Clement of Alexandria, *Paedagogos*, book 1, chapter 6ff.; *Stromateis*, book 1, chapter 5 and book 2, chapter 18. As for Origen, some scholars maintain that in his works there is no discussion of the idea of the education of the human race. His main work Περὶ Ἀρχῶν, however, translated into Latin as *De Principiis*, does contain some expressions that suggest familiarity with this idea. As the respected Origen scholar Jean Daniélou puts it, "It might be said that being a *didaskalos* himself, Origen regarded his God as a *Didaskalos* too, as a Master in charge of the education of children, and looked on God's universe as a vast *didaskaleion* in which every single thing contributed to the education of the free human beings at school there" (Jean Daniélou, *Origen*, translated by Walter Mitchell [New York: Sheed and Ward, 1955], 276).

37. Hans W. Liepmann, *Lessing und die mittelalterliche Philosophie* (Stuttgart: W. Kohlhammer, 1931), 128; cf. Erich Schmidt, *Lessing: Geschichte seines Lebens und seiner Schriften*, 4th ed., vol. 2 (Berlin: Weidmannsche Buchhandlung, 1923; reprint, Hildesheim: Georg Olms Verlag, 1983), 433–34.

38. R. Piepmeier, "Erziehung des Menschengeschlechts," in *Historisches Wörterbuch der Philosophie*, vol. 2, edited by Joachim Ritter (Darmstadt: Wissenschaftliche Buchgesellschaft, 1972), 735–36.

39. See G. Hornig, "Akkommodation," in *Historisches Wörterbuch der Philosophie*, edited by Joachim Ritter (Darmstadt: Wissenschaftliche Buchgesellschaft, 1971), vol. 1, 125–26.

40. Lessing's concept of progressive revelation throws its shadow over Troeltsch. See Ernst Troeltsch, *Glaubenslehre*, edited by Gertrud von le Fort (Munich and Leipzig: Verlag von Duncker & Humblot, 1925), §3. Benjamin A. Reist's *Processive Revelation* (Louisville: Westminster/John Knox Press, 1992) may be regarded as an attempt to

develop the Troeltschian concept of revelation in the direction of process theology. In this case, however, there is no longer any contact with, or relation to, Lessing.

41. LM 12, 432; G 7, 462 (*Gegensätze des Herausgebers*).

42. Karl Aner, *Die Theologie der Lessingzeit* (Halle: Max Niemeyer Verlag, 1929; reprint, Hildesheim: Georg Olms, 1964), 356.

43. To name a few among many, Th. C. van Stockum, *Spinoza-Jacobi-Lessing* (Groningen: P. Noordhoff, 1916), 80; Carl Stange, "Lessings Erziehung des Menschengeschlechts," *Zeitschrift für systematische Theologie* 1 (1923): 153–67; Martin Haug, *Entwicklung und Offenbarung bei Lessing*, 64–65, 79–80, 106, 107–8 passim; Israel S. Stamm, "Lessing and Religion," *Germanic Review* 43 (1968): 239–57; Pelters, *Lessings Standort*, 47. For a concise overview of this issue, see Karl S. Guthke, *Gotthold Ephraim Lessing*, 3d ed. (Stuttgart: J. B. Metzlersche Verlagsbuchhandlung, 1979), 87–89.

44. Thielicke, *Offenbarung, Vernunft und Existenz*, 59, 60, 66, 71, etc.; Otto Mann, *Lessing: Sein und Leistung* (Berlin: Walter de Gruyter, 1965), 305–6.

45. The clue to answering this question seems implied in the word "mystery" (*Geheimnis*) that appears immediately before this sentence. There Lessing says, "the word mystery signified, in the first age of Christianity, something quite different from what it means now." As Göbel points out, Lessing apparently relies for this assertion on John Toland's *Christianity Not Mysterious* (London, 1696; reprint, *Christianity Not Mysterious* [New York: Garland, 1978]; German translation, *Christentum ohne Geheimnis*, translated by W. Lunde, edited by Leopold Zscharnack [Giessen: Töpelmann, 1908]). For, according to Toland, the mystery of the gospel was originally manifest. It is called a mystery only because it was once covered with a veil. But since, in the gospel, the veil has been removed, mystery is no longer mysterious. Thus revelation, once revealed, is never mysterious or incomprehensible.

If we understand the word "mystery" in the sense Toland understood it, revealed truths cannot be incomprehensible but must be manifest to human understanding. This makes it understandable that Lessing, immediately after expounding the meaning of the word "mystery," speaks of "the development of revealed truths into truths of reason."

46. Marjorie Reeves and Warwick Gould, *Joachim of Fiore and the Myth of the Eternal Evangel in the Nineteenth Century* (Oxford: Clarendon Press, 1987), chapter 3.

47. Some scholars point to Johann Mosheim's 4-volume *Institutionum Historiae Christianae Compendium* (Helmsted: Weygand, 1752) as one of the primary sources for Lessing's knowledge of Joachim of Fiore (cf. Reeves and Gould, *Joachim of Fiore and the Myth of the Eternal Evangel*, 60), while others allude to older sources (cf. Heinz Bluhm, "Ist Lessings Auffassung des 'Ewigen Evangeliums' neu?" in *Aquila: Chestnut Hill Studies in Modern Languages and Literatures* 1 [1969]: 9–11). Bluhm's essay, incidentally, because it contains an interesting analysis of Lessing's "new, eternal gospel," is highly instructive and very worth reading for everyone interested in this topic.

48. Bluhm, "Ist Lessings Auffassung des 'Ewigen Evangeliums' neu?" 25. According to Bluhm, a high assessment should attach to Lessing's giving an ethical definition to the eternal gospel, for there is no such definition in Joachim of Fiore. One can therefore speak of something new in Lessing's concept to this extent. But, Bluhm contends, what Lessing set forth as a higher morality had actually been taught by Tauler, Johann Geiler (1445–1510), and especially Luther. Bluhm asserts, therefore, that any idea of absolute novelty in Lessing's concept is out of the question. He may be right. But latent in this relativizing of Lessing's novelty is his overestimation of Luther's ideas. He seems

to me to lay undue stress on Luther's importance for any discussion of the new, eternal gospel, so much so that he fails to do justice to Lessing.

49. Christoph Schrempf, *Lessing als Philosoph*, 2d ed. (Stuttgart: Fr. Frommanns Verlag, 1921), 172. According to Schrempf, "the day of this [new] covenant has not only been proclaimed but also has already begun in the New Testament" (172). His discussion, incidentally, whether intentionally or not, replaces "a new, eternal gospel" (*ein neues ewiges Evangelium*) with "a new, eternal covenant" (*ein neuer ewiger Bund*).

50. As indicated above, Thielicke pays special attention to Lessing's attitude of "waiting." According to him, Lessing's waiting attitude is to be ascribed not only to his thoughtfulness as a pedagogue but also, and more essentially, to his awareness of the interim in history. "This 'waiting' of the advanced interpreter of history would be incomparably comprehensible if what reason waited for here was not itself but the complete development of *something that confronts us*, something the administration of which would not (or *as yet* would not) be entrusted to the autonomy of reason" (Thielicke, *Offenbarung, Vernunft und Existenz*, 23).

51. Falk's words reflect Lessing's attitude very well: "A Freemason calmly awaits the rising of the sun and lets the candles burn as long as they want or can. Putting candles out and, when they are out, finally recognizing that the stumps have got to be lit again and that new ones may even have to be set up, that's nothing for a Freemason" (LM 13, 400–401; G 8, 480 [*Ernst und Falk*, 5]).

52. Lessing's "faith in providence" (*Vorsehungs-Glaube*) should clearly be distinguished from the ordinary "belief in providence" (*Vorsehungsglaube*) that prevailed in eighteenth-century Germany. For details on this distinction, the book to see is Arno Schilson, *Lessings Christentum* (Göttingen: Vandenhoeck & Ruprecht, 1980).

53. When referring to God's providence, Lessing prefers to use the term *Vorsicht* rather than the term *Vorsehung*. His faith in providence, moreover, finds simple expression in his personal letters. For example: "What is yet to come, I leave to providence. I can hardly believe that a man could be more indifferent to the future than I am" (LM 17, 41 [Letter to Johann David Michaelis of 16 October 1754]); "Reason orders me to submit myself to providence in everything" (LM 17, 247 [Letter to Heinrich Wilhelm von Gerstenberg of 25 February 1768]); "And leave all the rest calmly to providence" (LM 17, 409 [Letter to Eva König of 20 November 1771]).

In one of his literary criticisms set forth in epistolary form, Lessing speaks of "that wise providence which knows how to use even the error of its tools" (LM 5, 54; G 3, 280 [*Briefe*]). Moreover, *Minna von Barnhelm* and *Emilia Galotti*, not to mention *Nathan der Weise*, can be classified under the heading "providence drama" because providence plays an important role in the unfolding of these stories.

54. LM 3, 140; G 2, 317 (*Nathan der Weise*, 4/7). These words, composed immediately after the tragic death of his wife Eva and of his newborn baby Traugott, should be taken as expressing Lessing's own personal feeling.

55. It may be of some use to remember the last sentence of the "Editor's Preface": "Is God to have part in everything except our mistakes?"

56. Tillich, *Gesammelte Werke*, vol. 12, 107ff. The discussion that follows owes much to Tillich's penetrating interpretation.

In his study of metempsychosis in East and West, Moore asserts that Lessing's idea of reincarnation is a corollary of the idea of the education of the human race. According to Moore, the latter idea demands that every individual person should travel along the same path by which the human race reaches perfection. See George Foot Moore, *Metempsychosis* (Cambridge: Harvard University Press, 1914), 57–58.

57. According to Paul Althaus, the idea of transmigration of souls (*Seelenwan-*

derung) "does not express an experience, but is speculation from certain motives, essentially from moralistic thinking." It is true that "a truly moral world order seems to demand the transmigration of souls," but this kind of moralistic thinking "does not accord with Christian thinking." Consequently, the doctrine of transmigration of souls has no place in Christian theology. See Paul Althaus, "Seelenwanderung. 2. Dogmatisch," in *RGG*, 3d ed. (Tübingen: J. C. B. Mohr, 1961).

58. Ernst Benz admits that "the theme of reincarnation does not belong to that of Christian theology." Nevertheless, pointing out the fact that the idea of reincarnation has appeared again and again in the history of Western Christian thought, he emphasizes the importance of reconsidering this idea. See Ernst Benz, "Die Reinkarnationslehre in Dichtung und Philosophie der deutschen Klassik und Romantik," *Zeitschrift für Religions- und Geistesgeschichte* 9 (1957): 150–75.

59. Tillich, *Gesammelte Werke*, vol. 12, 108–109.

60. Ibid., 111.

61. Ibid.

62. Benz, "Die Reinkarnationslehre," 153.

63. Alexander Altmann indicates that there are roughly two different kinds of thought in Lessing's idea of reincarnation. One is the idea of "transmigration of souls" (metempsychosis, *Seelenwanderung*) in the literal sense, according to which "souls transmigrate through various human bodies." The other can be called *Metaschematismus*, or "metamorphosis," because it stresses the developmental "transformation" (*Umgestaltung*) of human souls. According to this latter idea, humans develop into higher beings both physically and psychically. It is hard to determine, says Altmann, which is more authentic in Lessing. Moreover, neither goes beyond the confines of hypothesis. Consequently Altmann names the former "hypothesis a" and the latter "hypothesis b." For the details of his instructive analysis, see Alexander Altmann, *Die trostvolle Aufklärung: Studien zur Metaphysik und politischen Theorie Moses Mendelssohns* (Stuttgart-Bad Cannstatt: Friedrich Frommann Verlag, 1982), 109–34.

64. LM 18, 269 (Letter to Johann Albert Reimarus of 6 April 1778); B 12, 144 (no. 1358).

65. Cf. Johannes Hoffmeister, ed., *Wörterbuch der philosophischen Begriffe*, 2d ed. (Hamburg: Felix Meiner, 1955), s.v. "Dialektik," 163–64.

66. LM 18, 269 (Letter to Johann Albert Reimarus of 6 April 1778); B 12, 144 (no. 1358).

67. LM 13, 24; G 8, 33 (*Eine Duplik*).

68. Lütgert, *Die Religion des deutschen Idealismus und ihre Ende*, vol. 1, 155.

69. Wilhelm Windelband, *Die Geschichte der neueren Philosophie*, vol. 1 [of 2], *Von der Renaissance bis Kant* (Leipzig: Breitkopf and Härtel, 1878; reprint, Karben: Verlag Petra Wald, 1996), 532.

70. Johannes von Lüpke, *Wege der Weisheit: Studien zu Lessings Theologiekritik* (Göttingen: Vandenhoeck & Ruprecht, 1989), 171.

71. Hermann Timm, *Gott und die Freiheit*, 77.

72. Arno Schilson, *Geschichte im Horizont der Vorsehung: G. E. Lessings Beitrag zu einer Theologie der Geschichte* (Mainz: Matthias-Grünewald-Verlag, 1974), 124.

73. On the concept of "autotheonomy," see our discussion in chapter 5, including note 62.

7 Lessing's "Spinozism"

1. Kant's influence was comparatively limited even after the publication of the *Critique of Pure Reason*. Only after Karl Leonhard Reinhold published his *Briefe über die kantische Philosophie* in the autumn of 1786 and explained the significance of Kant's philosophy to a wider circle of readers did the situation radically change. It was from that time that Kant's philosophy became famous.

2. Hermann Timm, *Gott und die Freiheit: Studien zur Religionsphilosophie der Goethezeit*, vol. 1, *Die Spinozarenaissance* (Frankfurt am Main: Vittorio Klostermann, 1974), 6.

3. For an account of the reception of Spinoza's philosophy in Germany, see David Bell, *Spinoza in Germany from 1670 to the Age of Goethe* (Leeds: University of London, 1984). This book provides a good survey of how Spinoza was received in Germany from the late seventeenth century to the early nineteenth century. Bell acknowledges the importance of the pantheism controversy for the Spinoza renaissance, but asserts that both Mendelssohn and Jacobi held biased views of Spinoza and that consequently the controversy did little to deepen true understanding of Spinoza (ix, 71, 75–76, 84–85).

4. *Die Hauptschriften zum Pantheismusstreit zwischen Jacobi und Mendelssohn* (hereafter cited as *Hauptschriften*), edited by Heinrich Scholz (Berlin: Verlag von Reuther & Reichard, 1916), 88; *WW* 4/1–2, 68.

5. Hegel, for example, speaks of Spinoza as follows: "Spinoza is the key point of modern philosophy: either Spinozism or no philosophy." G. W. F. Hegel, *Werke in 20 Bänden*, vol. 20, *Vorlesungen über die Geschichte der Philosophie 3* (Frankfurt am Main: Suhrkamp Verlag, 1983), 163–64. Schleiermacher also offers a tribute of praise: "Offer with me reverently a tribute to the manes of the holy, rejected Spinoza. The high World-Spirit pervaded him; the Infinite was his beginning and his end; the Universe was his only and his everlasting love. In holy innocence and in deep humility he beheld himself mirrored in the eternal world, and perceived how he also was its most worthy mirror. He was full of religion, full of the Holy Spirit." Friedrich Schleiermacher, *On Religion: Speeches to Its Cultured Despisers*, translated by John Oman (New York: Harper & Row, 1958), 40.

6. Frederick C. Beiser, *The Fate of Reason: German Philosophy from Kant to Fichte* (Cambridge, Massachusetts and London: Harvard University Press, 1987), 44. This book of Beiser's, in chapter 2, contains a superb description and analysis of "Jacobi and the Pantheism Controversy." It is particularly instructive for understanding "its underlying philosophical dimension" (48).

7. Ibid., 48.

8. Gérard Vallée, "Introduction," in *The Spinoza Conversations between Lessing and Jacobi: Text with Excerpts from the Ensuing Controversy* (hereafter referred to as *The Spinoza Conversations*), translated by G. Vallée, J. B. Lawson, and C. G. Chapple (Lanham, New York and London: University Press of America, 1988), 2. This book, incidentally, is a partial translation of the *Hauptschriften*.

9. All the important documents relating to this controversy, including valuable testimonies by contemporaries, are now collected in the *Hauptschriften*. In what follows, all English translations cited from this book are borrowed, wherever available, from *The Spinoza Conversations*.

10. Beiser, *The Fate of Reason*, 47. According to Beiser's perceptive and incisive analysis, "the biographical issue of Lessing's Spinozism" is "an outer shell," "the exegetical question of the proper interpretation of Spinoza" is "an inner layer," and "the

problem of the authority of reason" is "a hidden inner core" of the pantheism controversy (47).

11. Heinrich Scholz, "Einleitung," in *Hauptschriften*, xi (emphases omitted).

12. For the whole story of the pantheism controversy, see the thoroughgoing analysis in Hermann Timm's significant work, *Gott und die Freiheit: Studien zur Religionsphilosophie der Goethezeit*, vol. 1, *Die Spinozarenaissance*. On the Spinoza controversy between Mendelssohn and Jacobi, see Kurt Christ, *Jacobi und Mendelssohn: Eine Analyse des Spinozastreits* (Würzburg: Königshausen & Neumann, 1988).

13. Vallée, "Introduction," *The Spinoza Conversations*, 2.

14. G. E. Lessing, *Theologischer Nachlaß*, edited by K. G. Lessing (Berlin: C. F. Voß und Sohn, 1784); *Theatralischer Nachlaß*, edited by K. G. Lessing (Berlin: C. F. Voß und Sohn, 1784–86); *Gotthold Ephraim Lessings Leben, nebst seinem noch übrigen literarischen Nachlasse* (Berlin: Vossische Buchhandlung, 1793–95). Regrettably, however, none of these works were available for my use.

15. Beiser, *The Fate of Reason*, 73.

16. *Hauptschriften*, 298; JubA 3, 2: 190–91; *The Spinoza Conversations*, 132.

17. Moses Mendelssohn's letter of 20 February 1781 to Karl Wilhelm Ferdinand, Duke of Brunswick, in JubA 13: 5; cf. his letter of 18 May 1781 to J. G. Herder, in JubA 13: 18–19.

18. Heinrich Friedrich Jacobi's letter to Elise Reimarus of 21 July 1783, quoted in *Hauptschriften*, 67; *The Spinoza Conversations*, 79 n.

19. Bell's *Spinoza in Germany from 1670 to the Age of Goethe* provides a trustworthy overview of how Spinoza had been treated up to that time. In addition, the following statement by Philolaus in Herder's *God: Some Conversations* well illustrates how ordinary people regarded Spinoza and his philosophy in the 1770s and 1780s:

> No, I have not read him [i.e., Spinoza]. And who would want to read every obscure book a madman might write? But I have heard from many who have read him, that he was an atheist and pantheist, a teacher of blind necessity, an enemy of revelation, a mocker of religion, and withal, a destroyer of the state and of all civil society. In short, he was an enemy of the human race, and as such he died. He therefore deserves the hatred and aversion of all friends of humanity and of true philosophers.

Johann Gottfried Herder, *Werke*, vol. 2 [of 3], *Herder und Anthropologie der Aufklärung*, edited by Wolfgang Pross (Darmstadt: Wissenschaftliche Buchgesellschaft, 1987), 737. The English translation is borrowed from Johann Gottfried Herder, *God: Some Conversations*, translated by Frederick H. Burkhardt (New York: Hafner Publishing Company, 1949), 76.

20. Letter of 4 August 1783 from Elise Reimarus to Moses Mendelssohn, in JubA 13: 120–23.

21. *Hauptschriften*, 293; JubA 3, 2: 186; *The Spinoza Conversations*, 128.

22. Letter of 16 August 1783 from Moses Mendelssohn to Elise Reimarus, in JubA 13: 123–25; cf. *Hauptschriften*, 103–104; *The Spinoza Conversations*, 103–104.

23. *Hauptschriften*, 70. Until his death Mendelssohn never ruled out the possibility that Lessing's alleged "Spinozistic confession" had been a joke (*Schäkerey*). See *Hauptschriften*, 118, 304; JubA 3, 2: 195, 205.

24. *Hauptschriften*, 72–105; JubA 13: 135–53.

25. *Hauptschriften*, 296; JubA 3, 2: 189; *The Spinoza Conversations*, 131.

26. *Hauptschriften*, 297; JubA 3, 2: 190; *The Spinoza Conversations*, 131.

27. *Hauptschriften*, 105; JubA 13: 157; *The Spinoza Conversations*, 105.

28. *Hauptschriften*, 301, 298; JubA 3, 2: 193, 191; *The Spinoza Conversations*, 134, 132.

29. As will be shown in the third section of this chapter, Jacobi and Spinozism, there are convincing reasons for believing that Jacobi made use of Lessing to damage Mendelssohn and thus to discredit the reputation of the Berlin *Aufklärer* he represented. This circle of Enlightenment adherents consisted of Engel, Nicolai, Eberhard, Spalding, Zöllner, Biester, and others. See Beiser, *The Fate of Reason*, 75–77; Bell, *Spinoza in Germany*, 84–85; Vallée, "Introduction," *The Spinoza Conversations*, 3 n. 6.

30. Beiser, *The Fate of Reason*, 62. Some scholars are of the opinion that Jacobi had not only laid a trap for Mendelssohn but had also set a similar trap for Lessing himself. See, e.g., Erwin Quapp, *Lessings Theologie statt Jacobis Spinozismus* (Bern: Peter Lang, 1992), 12.

31. The conversations between Lessing and Jacobi are recorded in *Hauptschriften*, 76–91; WW 4/1–2, 53–79; JubA 13: 137–47.

32. Johann Wolfgang Goethe, *Werke* (Hamburg edition in 14 vols.), edited by Erich Trunz, vol. 1, *Gedichte und Epen 1* (Munich: Verlag C. H. Beck, 1993), 44–46. The English translation, by Michael Hamburger, is borrowed from *Goethe's Collected Works*, vol. 1, *Selected Poems*, edited by Christopher Middleton (Boston: Suhrkamp/Insel, 1983), 27, 29, 31.

33. *Hauptschriften*, 76–77; *The Spinoza Conversations*, 85–86. With regard to the *Hauptschriften*, it should be noted that a bracketed remark beginning with an equal sign [= . . .] represents an explanation inserted by the *Hauptschriften* editor, Heinrich Scholz.

34. *Hauptschriften*, 77–79; *The Spinoza Conversations*, 86–87.

35. *Hauptschriften*, 80–81; *The Spinoza Conversations*, 88–89.

36. *Hauptschriften*, 83; *The Spinoza Conversations*, 90.

37. *Hauptschriften*, 88; *The Spinoza Conversations*, 93.

38. *Hauptschriften*, 88; *The Spinoza Conversations*, 94.

39. *Hauptschriften*, 88; *The Spinoza Conversations*, 94.

40. *Hauptschriften*, 89–90; *The Spinoza Conversations*, 94–95.

41. *Hauptschriften*, 90; *The Spinoza Conversations*, 95–96.

42. *Hauptschriften*, 91; *The Spinoza Conversations*, 96.

43. *Hauptschriften*, lx–lxii. According to Scholz, it was on Thursday, 6 July 1780, that Lessing confessed to his "Spinozism" (lxi).

44. Beiser, *The Fate of Reason*, 75.

45. Ibid., 75–76.

46. Ibid., 76.

47. Ibid.

48. Ibid., 77.

49. Quapp, for example, takes Jacobi's ostensibly innocent surprise on hearing that Lessing was a Spinozist as a manifestation of the "trap" he had set for him. See Quapp, *Lessings Theologie statt Jacobis Spinozismus*, 12.

50. Beiser, *The Fate of Reason*, 77.

51. Vallée, "Introduction," *The Spinoza Conversations*, 33.

52. *Hauptschriften*, 138; WW 4/1–2, 165; *The Spinoza Conversations*, 117.

53. *Hauptschriften*, 88; WW 4/1–2, 69; *The Spinoza Conversations*, 93.

54. Scholz, "Einleitung," *Hauptschriften*, xix; cf. *The Spinoza Conversations*, 28. Jacobi's six basic theses on Spinozism, incidentally, are the following:

1. Spinozism is atheism.
2. Cabbalistic *philosophy*, as *philosophy*, is but an *undeveloped* Spinozism, or a version thereof, *confused anew*.
3. The Leibniz-Wolffian philosophy is not less fatalistic than the Spinozist philosophy and inevitably leads the persistent scholar back to its principles.
4. All ways of demonstration end in fatalism.
5. We can demonstrate only similarities (*agreements, conditionally necessary truths*, progressing in identical statements). Every proof presupposes something already proven, the first principle of which is *revelation*.
6. The prime element of all human knowledge and action is faith.

Hauptschriften, 173–80; *WW* 4/1–2, 216–33; *The Spinoza Conversations*, 123.

55. *Hauptschriften*, 89; *WW* 4/1–2, 70; *The Spinoza Conversations*, 94.

56. Jacobi: "But my credo is not to be found in Spinoza. *I believe in an intelligent personal first cause of the world.*" *Hauptschriften*, 80; *WW* 4/1–2, 58–59; *The Spinoza Conversations*, 88.

57. Scholz, "Einleitung," *Hauptschriften*, xix.

58. *Hauptschriften*, 175; *WW* 4/1–2, 218.

59. With regard to Jacobi's philosophy, Klaus Hammacher's *Die Philosophie Friedrich Heinrich Jacobis* (Munich: Wilhelm Fink Verlag, 1969) is a good overall study. *Friedrich Heinrich Jacobi: Philosoph und Literat der Goethezeit* (Frankfurt am Main: Vittorio Klostermann, 1971), edited by Klaus Hammacher, is the report of an international conference held in Düsseldorf in commemoration of the 150th anniversary of his death; it too is useful for understanding Jacobi, both as a person and in terms of the nature of his work. As for Jacobi's relationship to modern Protestant thought, a book by Brian A. Gerrish, *Continuing the Reformation: Essays on Modern Religious Thought* (Chicago: University of Chicago Press, 1993), contains an excellent analysis of "Faith and Existence in Jacobi's Philosophy" (79–108). With regard to the problem of his understanding of Spinozism, see Alexander Altmann, "Lessing und Jacobi: Das Gespräch über den Spinozismus," in *LYB* 3 (1971): 25–70, especially 28–40.

60. Altmann, "Lessing und Jacobi," 27.

61. Bell, *Spinoza in Germany*, 84–85.

62. *Hauptschriften*, 293; *The Spinoza Conversations*, 129.

63. Mendelssohn coped with the issue of Jacobi's charge against Lessing while presupposing the authenticity of Jacobi's report in principle. Many Lessing scholars, including Heinrich Scholz, likewise consider Jacobi's account to be trustworthy overall. Cf. Scholz, "Einleitung," *Hauptschriften*, lxiii; Vallée, "Introduction," *The Spinoza Conversations*, 18.

Today, however, some scholars raise serious objections to this point. For example, Alexander Altmann emphasizes that interpretation of the philosophical conversations between Lessing and Jacobi requires scrupulous care because Jacobi's account is "a mesh of various things not easy to disentangle." Cf. Altmann, "Lessing und Jacobi," *LYB* 3 (1971): 27; see also Quapp, *Lessings Theologie statt Jacobis Spinozismus*, 17–18, 235–39.

64. JubA 3, 2: 104–37. Mendelssohn's strategy was clever, but in reality, it backfired. Jacobi, driven by his suspicion that Mendelssohn might misuse the information he had confided to him *sub rosa* about Lessing's "Spinozistic" confession, resorted to publishing the content of his conversations with Lessing so as to avoid having his thunder stolen by the Jewish philosopher. To make matters worse, Jacobi even put into

print private letters from Elise Reimarus and Mendelssohn without their permission.

65. *Hauptschriften*, 25; JubA 3, 2: 121.

66. The title of chapter 14 of *Morning Hours* (in German) is "Continued Dispute with the Pantheists: Approximation to, and the Point of Unification with Them—the Harmlessness of Refined Pantheism—Compatibility with Religion and Morality insofar as they are Practical."

Mendelssohn uses, incidentally, two different terms for refined pantheism: *der geläuterte Pantheismus* and *der verfeinerte Pantheismus*. From my perspective, however, there is no difference in meaning. He also speaks of "refined Spinozism" (*der geläuterte Spinozismus*). See *Hauptschriften*, 15, 28, 29, 30, 43, 295; JubA 3, 2: 114, 123, 125, 133, 136, 188.

67. On this point we are in agreement with Vallée when he says, "The concept of 'refined pantheism' remains artificial throughout and betrays an intention of exculpating Lessing from the charge of atheism. The concept would have received clearer contours had Mendelssohn been able to make it overlap with the less defensive concept of panentheism to express the immanence of the world in God" (*The Spinoza Conversations*, 36).

68. *Hauptschriften*, 43; JubA 3, 2: 136; *The Spinoza Conversations*, 77.

69. *Hauptschriften*, 39; JubA 3, 2: 133; *The Spinoza Conversations*, 73.

70. For details of the circumstances in which doubts engendered doubts on both sides, see Beiser, *The Fate of Reason*, 68–75.

71. A reviewer of Mendelssohn's posthumous work wrote that Mendelssohn "became a victim of his friendship with Lessing and died as a martyr defending the suppressed prerogatives of reason against fanaticism and superstition.—Lavater's importunity dealt his life the first blow. Jacobi completed the work." Quoted in Alexander Altmann, *Moses Mendelssohn: A Biographical Study* (London: Routledge & Kegan Paul, 1973), 745.

72. *Hauptschriften*, 302; JubA 3, 2: 194; *The Spinoza Conversations*, 135.

73. *Hauptschriften*, 303; JubA 3, 2: 194; *The Spinoza Conversations*, 135.

74. *Hauptschriften*, 310; JubA 3, 2: 207; *The Spinoza Conversations*, 140.

75. *Hauptschriften*, 118; cf. *Hauptschriften*, 304; JubA 3, 2: 195.

76. As is well known, this question, whether Lessing's "confession" of Spinozism was perhaps a joke that he was playing on Jacobi, having seen through him, has one of its sources in LM 18, 166 (Letter to Karl Lessing of 16 March 1778); B 12, 131 (no. 1351). Though many scholars, including Friedrich Loofs and Helmut Thielicke, have attempted to solve this problem, as yet no satisfactory answer has been attained. See Loofs, *Lessings Stellung zum Christentum* (Halle: Waisenhauser, 1910) and Thielicke, *Offenbarung, Vernunft und Existenz: Studien zur Religionsphilosophie Lessings*, 4th ed. (Gütersloh: Gerd Mohn, 1957).

77. Scholz, "Einleitung," *Hauptschriften*, lxix.

78. The book resulting from the international conference held on the 150th anniversary of Jacobi's death bears the subtitle *Philosoph und Literat der Goethezeit*. See Hammacher, ed., *Friedrich Heinrich Jacobi*.

79. Scholz, "Einleitung," *Hauptschriften*, lix; cf. 97, 293 passim.

80. According to Goethe scholars, this poem was presumably composed in the autumn of 1773 in connection with the drama "Prometheus," the plot of which Goethe was working on at that time. At first Goethe held back from publishing the poem, but it caught the attention of Jacobi, who happened to visit him. Borrowing the unpublished manuscript, Jacobi showed it to Lessing without Goethe's permission. When the dispute with Mendelssohn flared up over Lessing's "Spinozistic" confession,

Jacobi published Goethe's poem as one of the appendices to his *Concerning the Doctrine of Spinoza in Letters to Moses Mendelssohn* (1785)—again without the author's permission. It was only in 1789 that Goethe himself published the poem.

81. Vallée is of the same opinion. He says, "Lessing did not have Spinoza in mind when he read Goethe's poem, but rather the point of view of the ancient tragedy of Aeschylus." Vallée, "Introduction," *The Spinoza Conversations*, 23.

82. Johann Wolfgang von Goethe, *Werke* (Hamburg edition in 14 vols.), edited by Erich Trunz, vol. 10, *Autobiographische Schriften 2* (Munich: Verlag C. H. Beck, 1993–94), 48–49. The English translation, by Robert R. Heitner, appears in Goethe, *Goethe's Collected Works*, vol. 4, *From My Life: Poetry and Truth*, parts 1 to 3, edited by Thomas P. Saine and Jeffrey L. Sammons (New York: Suhrkamp, 1987), 469–70.

83. Cf. Erich Trunz, "Anmerkungen," in Johann Wolfgang von Goethe, *Werke*, vol. 1, *Gedichte und Epen 1*, 484–85.

84. Goethe, *Werke*, vol. 10, *Autobiographische Schriften 2*, 47–48; Goethe, *Goethe's Collected Works*, vol. 4, *From My Life: Poetry and Truth*, 468–69.

85. Goethe, *Werke*, vol. 10, *Autobiographische Schriften 2*, 49; Goethe, *Goethe's Collected Works*, vol. 4, *From My Life: Poetry and Truth*, 470.

86. H. A. Korff, *Geist der Goethezeit: Versuch einer ideellen Entwicklung der klassisch-romantischen Literaturgeschichte*, 2d ed., part 1 (Leipzig: Koehler & Amelang, 1955), 273.

87. Ibid., 275.

88. Ibid.; cf. Goethe, *Werke*, vol. 10, *Autobiographische Schriften 2*, 177.

89. See Korff, *Geist der Goethezeit*, 274–78.

90. Wilhelm Windelband, *Die Geschichte der neueren Philosophie*, vol. 1 [of 2] (Leipzig: Breitkopf and Härtel, 1878; reprint, Karben: Verlag Petra Wald, 1996), 525.

91. Herder is perhaps right when he speaks of Lessing through the mouth of Philolaus: "He was not made to be an 'ist,' whatever letters may be prefixed to that ending." Herder, *Werke*, vol. 2, 791; *God: Some Conversations*, 135. Arendt too emphasizes Lessing's *"Selbstdenken—*independent thinking." Hannah Arendt, *Men in Dark Times* (New York: Harcourt, Brace & World, 1968), 8–11.

92. *Hauptschriften*, 78; WW 4/1–2, 56. It is characteristic of Lessing to use the term "spirit" when inquiring about the essence of things. He speaks, for example, of the "spirit of the Bible" (*Geist der Bibel*) (LM 12, 115; G 8, 136), of the "spirit of Christianity" (*Geist des Christentums*) (LM 13, 164; G 8, 227), of "Luther's spirit" (*Luthers Geist*) (LM 13, 143; G8, 162), of Reimarus's "spirit" (LM 12, 255; G 7, 314), etc.

93. *Hauptschriften*, 80. These words of Lessing can be found only in the first edition (1785) and the second (1789). For some reason they have been deleted in the third and final edition (1819).

94. *Hauptschriften*, 92–93; WW 4/1–2, 75–76; *The Spinoza Conversations*, 97 [italics removed]. Jacobi's full statement is: "When Lessing wanted to imagine a *personal* divinity, he thought of it as the soul of the universe, and he thought of the Whole as being analogous to an organic body."

95. Reinhard Schwarz, "Lessings 'Spinozismus'," *Zeitschrift für Theologie und Kirche* 65 (1968): 271–90, esp. 274ff.

96. See *Hauptschriften*, 83–84; WW 4/1–2, 63; *The Spinoza Conversations*, 90.

97. *Hauptschriften*, 82; WW 4/1–2, 61.

98. See *Hauptschriften*, 83; WW 4/1–2, 62; *The Spinoza Conversations*, 90.

99. See note 83 above.

100. *Hauptschriften*, 102; *WW* 4/1–2, 90; *The Spinoza Conversations*, 103.

101. Siegfried Wollgast, *Der deutsche Pantheismus im 16. Jahrhundert: Sebastian Franck und seine Wirkungen auf die Entwicklung der pantheistischen Philosophie in Deutschland* (Berlin: VEB Deutscher Verlag der Wissenschaften, 1972), 158.

102. Harald Schultze, *Lessings Toleranzbegriff: Eine theologische Studie* (Göttingen: Vandenhoeck & Ruprecht, 1969), 111. Schultze's definition of spiritualism is not improper, to be sure. (Cf. "Spiritualisten, religiöse," *RGG*, 3d ed., vol. 6, cols. 255–57). But it should also be observed, as George H. Williams indicates, that spiritualism in general can further be divided into three prominent types: "revolutionary spiritualists" (such as the *Schwärmer* Luther castigated, and Thomas Münzer), "evangelical spiritualists" (such as Caspar Schwenckfeld and Gabriel Ascherham), and "rational spiritualists" (such as Paracelsus, Valentin Weigel, and Sebastian Franck). See George H. Williams, "Introduction," in *Spiritual and Anabaptist Writers*, edited by G. H. Williams and A. M. Mergal (Philadelphia: Westminster Press, 1957), esp. 31–35.

103. According to Schultze, it was his teacher at Jena, Gerhard Glege, who first suggested to him "the productive working hypothesis that Lessing may well be understood from the heritage of spiritualism." Schultze, *Lessings Toleranzbegriff*, 7.

104. Wolfgang Gericke, "Lessings theologische Gesamtauffassung," in *Sechs theologische Schriften Gotthold Ephraim Lessings*, introduced and annotated by Wolfgang Gericke (Berlin: Evangelische Verlagsanstalt, 1985), 14–35.

105. See Gericke, "Lessings theologische Gesamtauffassung," 14–15.

106. Gericke, "Lessings theologische Gesamtauffassung," 34. In a subsequent book, Gericke no longer describes the conviction of God's omnipresence and omnipotence in the world as Boehme's, but clearly presents it as Lessing's own conviction. Cf. Wolfgang Gericke, *Theologie und Kirche im Zeitalter der Aufklärung*, Kirchengeschichte in Einzeldarstellungen, vol. 3/2 (Berlin: Evangelische Verlags-anstalt, 1989), 126.

107. Wilhelm Dilthey, *Gesammelte Schriften*, vol. 2, *Weltanschauung und Analyse des Menschen seit Renaissance und Reformation*, 5th ed. (Stuttgart: B. G. Teubner Verlagsgesellschaft, 1957), 89.

108. LM 14, 292; G 8, 515 (*Über die Wirklichkeit der Dinge*).

109. Dilthey, *Das Erlebnis und die Dichtung: Lessing-Goethe-Novalis-Hölderlin*, 16th ed. (Göttingen: Vandenhoeck & Ruprecht, 1985), 116.

110. Johannes Schneider, *Lessings Stellung zur Theologie: Vor der Herausgabe der Wolfenbüttler Fragmente* (The Hague: Uitgeverij Excelsior, 1953), 147.

111. U. Dierse and W. Schröder, "Panentheismus," in *Historisches Wörterbuch der Philosophie*, vol. 7, col. 48 (Darmstadt: Wissenschaftliche Buchgesellschaft, 1989). According to this article, the term *Panentheismus* was coined by Karl Christian Friedrich Krause in 1825 in order to correct the fundamental errors of *Pantheismus*. The primary object of this term is to maintain simultaneously both "the immanence of the world in God" and "the transcendence of God over the world."

112. Erich Schmidt, *Lessing: Geschichte seines Lebens und seiner Schriften*, 4th ed., vol. 2 [of 2] (Berlin: Weidmannsche Buchhandlung, 1923; reprint, Hildesheim: Georg Olms Verlag, 1983), 560.

113. Cf. Johann Gottfried Herder, *Briefe*, edited by Wilhelm Dobbek and Günter Arnold, vol. 4, *Oktober 1776–August 1783* (Weimar: Hermann Bohlaus Nachfolger, 1986), 274–75.

114. Johann Gottfried Herder, *Briefe*, edited by Wilhelm Dobbek and Günter Arnold, vol. 5, *September 1783–August 1788* (Weimar: Hermann Bohlaus Nachfolger, 1986), 27. In this letter the words "εν κ[αι] παν" appear without accents.

115. Schmidt, *Lessing*, vol. 2, 596.

116. LM 22, ix.

117. Alexander Altmann, "Lessing und Jacobi: Das Gespräch über den Spinozismus," *LYB* 3, 25–70.

118. Ibid., 41.

119. *Hauptschriften*, 92; *WW* 4/1–2, 74; *The Spinoza Conversations*, 96. The doctrine of "zimzum" that goes back to Isaak Luria is no doubt latent in and underlies Lessing's words. According to this doctrine, God, before creating the world, had been contracted into himself, had retreated into himself. For a detailed account of zimzum teaching, see chapter 7 of Gershom Scholem, *Major Trends in Jewish Mysticism*, 6th ed. (New York: Schocken Publishing, 1972). Akira Kogishi's *Risan suru Yudayajin* (Jews in dispersal) (Tokyo: Iwanami, 1997) is a thrilling and instructive essay on modern Jewish intellectual and cultural history written from the viewpoint of the doctrine of zimzum.

120. *Hauptschriften*, 95; *WW* 4/1–2, 79; *The Spinoza Conversations*, 98.

121. Charles Hartshorne, for example, raises five questions: (1) Is God eternal? (2) Is he temporal? (3) Is he conscious? (4) Does he know the world? (5) Does he include the world? Affirmative answers to the questions he signifies by the following letters: E (Eternal—in some [or if T is omitted, in all] aspects of his reality devoid of change, whether as birth, death, increase, or decrease), T (Temporal—in some [or if E is omitted, in all] aspects capable of change, at least in the form of increase of some kind), C (Conscious, self-aware), K (Knowing the world or universe, omniscient), and W (World-inclusive, having all things as constituents). He then defines "panentheism" (or to use yet another of his terms, "surrelativism") as a position that asserts all five factors together: ETCKW. According to Hartshorne, Plato, Sri Jiva, Schelling, Fechner, Whitehead, Iqbal, Radhakrishnan, and others represent this position. See Charles Hartshorne and William L. Reese, *Philosophers Speak of God* (Chicago and London: University of Chicago Press, 1953), 16–17.

But the fact that such a great variety of thinkers of different religious backgrounds are jumbled together into a single pot suggests that his term "panentheism" is merely a general, all-inclusive concept. Further differentiation must therefore be made among the thinkers so categorized. Otherwise, our argument on panentheism would lack clarity and precision.

122. Strictly speaking, Lessing's formula ἕν ἐγὼ καὶ πάντα is itself insufficient from the Christian point of view. For to be sufficiently Christian, the counterpart of πάντα is not the neutral form ἕν but the masculine form εἷς. With regard to this point, I have learned much from the personal instruction of Professor Wataru Mizugaki. In any event, Lessing's ἕν ἐγὼ καὶ πάντα suggests both an interesting connection and an interesting difference between him and Christian thought. To attain greater clarity about this issue, however, calls for a much deeper study of the intellectual-historical background of Lessing's ἐγώ and its religious-philosophical implications.

123. Timm, *Gott und die Freiheit*, 15.

124. Arno Schilson, "Lessing und die Aufklärung," *Theologie und Philosophie* 54 (1979): 400, 401.

8 Conclusion

1. Ernst Troeltsch, *Die Bedeutung des Protestantismus für die Entstehung der modernen Welt* (Munich and Berlin: R. Oldenbourg, 1911; reprint, Aalen: Otto Zeller, 1963), 46.

2. Ibid., 97.

3. For the concept of the "Age of Religion" and its meaning, see Franklin L. Baumer, *Main Currents of Western Thought* (New Haven and London: Yale University Press, 1978).

4. LM 17, 298 (Letter to Friedrich Nicolai of 25 August 1769); B 11/1, 622 (no. 501).

5. The discussion that follows owes much to the insights of Peter C. Hodgson in his *Winds of the Spirit: A Constructive Christian Theology* (Louisville, Kentucky: Westminster John Knox Press, 1994).

6. Peter Demetz, "Introduction" to *Nathan the Wise, Minna von Barnhelm, and Other Plays and Writings*. The German Library, vol. 12, edited by Peter Demetz with a foreword by Hannah Arendt (New York: Continuum, 1995), xxvi.

7. Ibid., xxiv.

8. See Hannah Arendt, *Men in Dark Times* (New York: Harcourt, Brace & World, 1968).

Bibliography

I. *Lessing's Works*

A. *Lessing's Complete Works*

Werke und Briefe in zwölf Bänden. Edited by Wilfried Barner in collaboration with Klaus Bohnen, Gunter E. Grimm, Helmuth Kiesel, Arno Schilson, Jürgen Stenzel and Conrad Wiedemann. 12 vols. Frankfurt am Main: Deutscher Klassiker Verlag, 1985ff.

Werke. Edited by Herbert G. Göpfert in collaboration with Karl Eibl, Helmut Göbel, Karl S. Guthke, Gerd Hillen, Albert von Schirnding and Jöorg Schönert. 8 vols. Munich: Carl Hanser Verlag, 1970–79.

Sämtliche Schriften. Edited by Karl Lachmann and Franz Muncker. 3d, newly revised and enlarged edition. 23 vols. Stuttgart (vols. 12ff.), Leipzig (vols. 22f., Berlin & Leipzig, 1886–1924; reprint, Berlin: Walter de Gruyter & Co., 1968.

Gesammelte Werke. Edited by Paul Rilla. 10 vols. Berlin, 1954–58; 2d ed., Berlin & Weimar: Aufbau-Verlag, 1968.

Lessings Werke. Edited by Kurt Wölfel. 3 vols. Frankfurt am Main: Insel Verlag, 1972.

B. *English Translations*

Lessing's Theological Writings. Selections in translation with an introductory essay by Henry Chadwick. Stanford: Stanford University Press, 1957.

Nathan the Wise: A Dramatic Poem in Five Acts. Translated with an introduction by Bayard Quincy Morgan. New York: Frederick Ungar Publishing Co., 1955.

Nathan the Wise, Minna von Barnhelm, and Other Plays and Writings. The German Library, vol. 12. Edited by Peter Demetz with a foreword by Hannah Arendt. New York: Continuum, 1995.

II. *Other Primary Sources*

Augustine. *Soliloquies.* In *A Select Library of the Nicene and Post-Nicene Fathers.* Vol. 7. Edited by Philip Schaff. Grand Rapids, Michigan: Wm. B. Eerdmans Publishing Co., 1986.

Eckermann, Johann Peter. *Gespräche mit Goethe: In den letzten Jahren seines Lebens.* Edited by Fritz Bergemann. Frankfurt am Main and Leipzig: Insel Verlag, 1992.

Goethe, Johann Wolfgang von. *Werke.* Hamburg edition in 14 vols. Edited by Erich Trunz. Munich: Verlag C. H. Beck, 1993–94.

———. *Goethes Briefe und Briefe an Goethe.* Hamburg edition in 6 vols. Edited by Karl Robert Mandelkow. Munich: Verlag C. H. Beck, 1988.

———. *Goethe's Collected Works.* Vol. 1, *Selected Poems.* Translated by Michael Hamburger, David Luke, Christopher Middleton, John Fredrick Nims, and Vernon Watkins. Edited by Christopher Middleton. New York: Suhrkamp, 1983.

———. *Goethe's Collected Works.* Vol. 4, *From My Life: Poetry and Truth.* Parts 1–3. Translated by Robert R. Heitner. Edited by Thomas P. Saine and Jeffrey L. Sammons. New York: Suhrkamp, 1987.

———. *Goethe's Faust.* Translated with an introduction by Walter Kaufmann. New York: Doubleday, 1961.

Hegel, Georg Wilhelm Friedrich. *Werke in 20 Bänden.* 20 vols. Frankfurt am Main: Suhrkamp Verlag, 1983.

———. *Vorlesungen: Ausgewählte Nachschriften und Manuskripte.* Vols. 3–5, *Vorlesungen über die Philosophie der Religion.* Edited by Walter Jaeschke. Hamburg: Felix Meiner Verlag, 1983–85.

Heine, Heinrich. *Sämtliche Werke.* Vol. 3, *Schriften zur Literatur und Politik 1.* Darmstadt: Wissenschaftliche Buchgesellschaft, 1992.

Herder, Johann Gottfried. *Werke.* 3 vols. Edited by Wolfgang Pross. Darmstadt: Wissenschaftliche Buchgesellschaft, 1987ff.

———. *Briefe: Gesamtausgabe.* 10 vols. Edited by Wilhelm Dobbek and Günter Arnold. Weimar: Hermann Bohlaus Nachfolger, 1977–86.

———. *God: Some Conversations.* Translated by Frederick H. Burkhardt. New York: Hafner Publishing Company, 1949.

———. "Gotthold Ephraim Lessing. Geb. 1729, gest. 1781." In Horst Steinmetz, ed., *Lessing—Ein unpoetischer Dichter.* Dokumente aus drei Jahrhunderten zur Wirkungsgeschichte Lessings in Deutschland. Frankfurt am Main: Athenäum Verlag, 1969.

Hieronymus, Eusebius. *Opera Omnia.* In *Patrologiæ cursus completus. Series Latina,* edited by J.-P. Migne. Vols. 22–30. Paris: Vrayet, 1845–46.

Jacobi, Friedrich Heinrich. *Werke.* 6 vols. Edited by Friedrich Roth and Friedrich Köppen. Leipzig: Gerhàrd Fleischer, 1812–25; reprint, Darmstadt: Wissenschaftliche Buchgesellschaft, 1976.

———. *Friedrich Heinrich Jacobi's auserlesener Briefwechsel.* 2 vols. Leipzig: Gerhard Fleischer, 1825–27; reprint, Bern: Herbert Lang, 1970.

———. *The Main Philosophical Writings and the Novel Allwill.* Translated with an introductory study, notes, and bibliography by George di Giovanni. Montreal and Kingston: McGill-Queen's University Press, 1994.

Kant, Immanuel. *Kants Werke.* Akademie Textausgabe. 9 vols. Edited by Königlich Preußischen Akademie. Berlin: Walter de Gruyter & Co., 1968.

———. *Foundations of the Metaphysics of Morals, and What Is Enlightenment?* Translated and edited by Lewis White Beck. Indianapolis: Bobbs-Merrill, 1959.

Kierkegaard, Søren. *Concluding Unscientific Postscript.* Translated by David F. Swenson and Walter Lowrie. Princeton: Princeton University Press, 1941.

Kierkegaard, Sören. *Gesammelte Werke.* 31 vols. Edited by Emanuel Hirsch, Hayo Gerdes, and Hand Martin Junghaus. Gütersloh: Gerd Mohn, 1979–86.

Leibniz, Gottfried Wilhelm. *Philosophische Schriften.* 5 vols. Edited and translated by Hans Heinz Holz, Herbert Herring, Wolf von Engelhardt and Werner Wiater. Darmstadt: Wissenschaftliche Buchgesellschaft, 1985–89.

Lessing, Theophil. *Die Religionum Tolerantia: Über die Duldung der Religionen.* Edited and introduced by Günter Gawlick and Wolfgang Milde. Göttingen: Wallstein Verlag, 1991.

Mendelssohn, Moses. *Gesammelte Schriften.* Jubilee edition. Edited by I. Elbogen, J. Guttmann, E. Mittwoch, A. Altmann et al. Vol. 3, 2, *Schriften zur Philosophie und Ästhetik.* Edited by Leo Strauss. Stuttgart-Bad Cannstatt: Friedrich Frommann Verlag, 1974.

————. *Gesammelte Schriften.* Jubilee edition. Edited by I. Elbogen, J. Guttmann, E. Mittwoch, A. Altmann et al. Vol. 13, *Briefwechsel 3.* Edited by Alexander Altmann. Stuttgart-Bad Cannstatt: Friedrich Frommann Verlag, 1977.

————. *Philosophical Writings.* Translated and edited by Daniel O. Dahlstrom. Cambridge: Cambridge University Press, 1997.

Reimarus, Hermann Samuel. *Apologie oder Schutzschrift für die vernünftigen Verehrer Gottes.* Edited by Gerhard Alexander. 2 vols. Frankfurt am Main: Insel Verlag, 1972.

Schleiermacher, Friedrich. *On Religion: Speeches to Its Cultured Despisers.* Translated by John Oman with an introduction by Rudolf Otto. New York: Harper & Row, 1958.

Schmidt, Erich, ed. *Goezes Streitschriften gegen Lessing.* Stuttgart: G. J. Göschen'sche Verlagshandlung, 1893.

Schumann, Johann Daniel. *Über die Evidenz der Beweise für die Wahrheit der christlichen Religion.* Hanover: Verlag der Schmidtschen Buchhandlung, 1778.

Spinoza, Baruch de. *Opera.* 5 vols. Edited by Carl Gebhardt. Heidelberg: Carl Wintersuniversitätsbuchhandlung, 1972.

III. *Lessing: Documents, Proceedings, and Yearbooks*

Aufklärung nach Lessing. Beiträge zur gemeinsamen Tagung der Lessing Society und des Lessing-Museums Kamenz aus Anlaß seines 60-jährigen Bestehens. Edited by Wolfgang Albrecht, Dieter Fratzke and Richard E. Schade. Kamenz: Lessing-Museum Kamenz, 1992.

Bauer, Gerhard and Sibylle, eds. *Gotthold Ephraim Lessing.* Wege der Forschung, vol. 211. Darmstadt: Wissenschaftliche Buchgesellschaft, 1968.

Das Bild Lessings in der Geschichte. Wolfenbütteler Studien zur Aufklärung, vol. 9. Edited by Herbert G. Göpfert. Heidelberg: Verlag Lambert Schneider, 1981.

Bohnen, Klaus, ed. *Lessings >Nathan der Weise<.* Wege der Forschung, vol. 587. Darmstadt: Wissenschaftliche Buchgesellschaft, 1984.

Braun, Julius W., ed. *Lessing im Urtheile seiner Zeitgenossen.* 2 vols. Berlin: Verlag von Friedrich Stahn, 1884–93; reprint, Hildesheim: Georg Olms Verlagsbuchhandlung, 1969.

Daunicht, Richard, ed. *Lessing im Gespräch: Berichte und Urteile von Freunden und Zeitgenossen.* Munich: Wilhelm Fink Verlag, 1971.

Harris, Edward P. and Richard E. Schade, eds. *Lessing in heutiger Sicht.* Beiträge zur Internationalen Lessing-Konferenz Cincinnati, Ohio, 1976. Bremen and Wolfenbüttel: Jacobi Verlag, 1977.

Hillen, Gerd. *Lessing Chronik: Daten zu Leben und Werk.* Munich: Carl Hanser Verlag, 1979.

Humanität und Dialog: Lessing und Mendelssohn in neuer Sicht. Beiträge zum Internationalen Lessing-Mendelssohn-Symposium anläßlich des 250. Geburtstages von Lessing und Mendelssohn, veranstaltet im November 1979 in Los Angeles, Kalifornien. Beiheft zum Lessing Yearbook. Edited by E. Bahr, E. P. Harris and L. G. Lyon. Detroit: Wayne State University Press, 1982.

Internationale Bibliographie zur Geschichte der deutschen Literatur von den Anfängen bis zur Gegenwart. Part 1, *Von den Anfängen bis 1789*, 963–83. Munich-Pullach and Berlin: Verlag Dokumentation, 1969.

Lessing-Bibliographie. Edited by Siegfried Seifert. Berlin: Aufbau-Verlag, 1973.

Lessing-Bibliographie 1973–1985. Edited by Doris Kuhles. Berlin: Aufbau-Verlag, 1988.

Lessing: Epoche-Werke-Wirkung. Arbeitsbuch für den literaturgeschichtlichen Unterricht. Edited by Wilfried Barner, Gunter Grimm, Helmuth Kiesel and Martin Kramer. Munich: Verlag C. H. Beck, 1975.

Lessing und die Zeit der Aufklärung. Vorträge gehalten auf der Tagung der Joachim Jungius-Gesellschaft der Wissenschaften Hamburg am 10. u. 11. 10. 1967. Göttingen: Vandenhoeck & Ruprecht, 1968.

Lessing und der Kreis seiner Freunde. Wolfenbütteler Studien zur Aufklärung, vol. 8. Edited by Günter Schulz. Heidelberg: Verlag Lambert Schneider, 1985.

Lessing und die Toleranz. Beiträge der vierten Internationalen Konferenz der Lessing Society in Hamburg vom 27.–29. 6. 1985. Sonderband zum Lessing Yearbook. Edited by P. Freimark, F. Kopitzsch and H. Sleesarev. Detroit and Munich: Wayne State University Press, 1986.

Lessing Yearbook. Edited by der Lessing Society. Vols. 1–11, Munich: Max Hueber Verlag, 1969–79; vols. 12–28, Detroit: Wayne State University Press, 1980–96; vol. 29, Göttingen: Wallstein Verlag, 1997.

Nation und Gelehrtenrepublik: Lessing im europäischen Zusammenhang. Beiträge zur Internationalen Tagung der Lessing Society in der Werner-Reimers-Stiftung Bad Homburg v. d. H. 11. bis 13. 7. 1983. Sonderband zum *Lessing Yearbook*. Edited by W. Barner and A. M. Reh. Detroit: Wayne State University Press, 1984.

Steinmetz, Horst, ed. *Lessing—Ein unpoetischer Dichter.* Dokumente aus drei Jahrhunderten zur Wirkungesgeschichte Lessings in Deutschland. Frankfurt am Main: Athenäum Verlag, 1969.

Streitkultur: Strategien des Überzeugens im Werk Lessings. Referate der Internationalen Lessing-Tagung der Albert-Ludwigs-Universität Freiburg und der Lessing Society an der University of Cincinnati, Ohio/USA, vom 22. bis 24. Mai 1991 in Freiburg im Breisgau. Edited by Wolfram Mauser und Günter Saße. Tübingen: Max Niemeyer Verlag, 1993.

Vanhelleputte, Michel, ed. *G. E. Lessing und die Freiheit des Denkens.* Tijdschrift voor de Studie van de Verlichting en van het Vrije Denken, vol. 10. Brussel: Vrije Universiteit Brussel, 1982.

Wölfel, Kurt, ed. *Lessings Leben und Werk in Daten und Bildern.* Frankfurt am Main: Insel Verlag, 1967.

IV. *Lessing: Secondary Sources*

Allison, Henry E. *Lessing and the Enlightenment: His Philosophy of Religion and Its Relation to Eighteenth-Century Thought.* Ann Arbor: University of Michigan Press, 1966.

Altenhofer, Norbert. "Gotthold Ephraim Lessing." In *Deutsche Dichter: Leben und Werk deutschsprachiger Autoren vom Mittelalter bis zur Gegenwart.* Edited by Gunter E. Grimm and Frank Rainer Max, 160–75. Darmstadt: Wissenschaftliche Buchgesellschaft, 1995.

Althaus, Horst. "Vom 'toten Hunde' Spinoza und Lessings 'Atheismus'." *Studia Germanica Gandensia* 14 (1973): 161–81.

Altmann, Alexander. *Moses Mendelssohn: A Biographical Study.* London: Routledge & Kegan Paul, 1973.

————. "Lessing und Jacobi: Das Gespräch über den Spinozismus." In *LYB* 3: 25–70. Munich: Max Niemeyer Verlag, 1971.

————. *Die trostvolle Aufklärung: Studien zur Metaphysik und politischen Theorie Moses Mendelssohns.* Stuttgart-Bad Cannstatt: Friedrich Frommann Verlag, 1982.

Amberg, Ernst-Heinz. "Lessings Gottesanschauung in heutiger Sicht." *Theologische Literaturzeitung* 106 (1981): 466–72.

Aner, Karl. *Die Theologie der Lessingzeit.* Halle: Max Niemeyer Verlag, 1929; reprint, Hildesheim: Georg Olms, 1964.

Arx, Arthur von. *Lessing und die geschichtliche Welt.* Frauenfeld/Leipzig: Huber & Co. Aktiengesellschaft, 1964.

Atkins, Stuart. "The Parable of the Rings in Lessing's *Nathan der Weise.*" *Germanic Review* 26 (1951): 259–67.

Barth, Karl. *Die kirchliche Dogmatik.* Vol. 4/1. Zurich: Theologischer Verlag, 1953.

————. *Die protestantische Theologie im 19. Jahrhundert: Ihre Vorgeschichte und ihre Geschichte.* 5th ed. Zurich: Theologischer Verlag, 1985.

————. "Das Problem Lessings und das Problem des Petrus." *Evangelische Theologie.* Sonderheft: Ernst Wolf zum 50. Geburtstag, 4–17. Munich: Chr. Kaiser Verlag, 1952.

Batley, Edward M. *Catalyst of Enlightenment, Gotthold Ephraim Lessing: Productive Criticism of Eighteenth-Century Germany.* Bern: Peter Lang, 1990.

Beck, Lewis White. *Early German Philosophy: Kant and His Predecessors.* Cambridge, Massachusetts: Harvard University Press, 1969; reprint, Bristol: Thoemmes Press, 1996.

Beiser, Frederick C. *The Fate of Reason: German Philosophy from Kant to Fichte.* Cambridge, Massachusetts and London: Harvard University Press, 1987.

Bell, David. *Spinoza in Germany from 1670 to the Age of Goethe.* Leeds: University of London, 1984.

Benz, Ernst. "Die Reinkarnationslehre in Dichtung und Philosophie der deutschen Klassik und Romantik." *Zeitschrift für Religions- und Geistesgeschichte* 9 (1957): 150–75.

Beyschlag, Karlmann. "Einführung in Lessings theologisch-philosophische Schriften." In *Lessings Werke.* Edited by Kurt Wölfel. Vol. 3, *Antiquarische Schriften: Theologische und philosophische Schriften,* 593–617. Frankfurt am Main: Insel Verlag, 1969.

Bluhm, Heinz. "Ist Lessings Auffassung des 'Ewigen Evangeliums' neu?" *Aquila: Chestnut Hill Studies in Modern Languages and Literatures* 1 (1969): 8–25.

Boehart, William. *Politik und Religion: Studien zum Fragmentenstreit (Reimarus, Goeze, Lessing).* Schwarzenbek: Verlag Dr. Rüdiger Martienss, 1988.

Bohnen, Klaus. *Geist und Buchstabe: Zum Prinzip des kritischen Verfahrens in Lessings literar-ästhetischen und theologischen Schriften.* Cologne and Vienna: Böhlau Verlag, 1974.

Bollacher, Martin. *Lessing: Vernunft und Geschichte.* Tübingen: Max Niemeyer Verlag, 1978.

Bothe, Bernd. *Glauben und Erkennen: Studie zur Religionsphilosophie Lessings.* Meisenheim am Glan: Verlag Anton Hain, 1972.

Campbell, Richard. "Lessing's Problem and Kierkegaard's Answer." *Scottish Journal of Theology* 19 (1966): 35–54.

Cassirer, Ernst. "Die Idee der Religion bei Lessing und Mendelssohn." In *Lessings >Nathan der Weise<*. Wege der Forschung, vol. 587. Edited by Klaus Bohnen, 94–115. Darmstadt: Wissenschaftliche Buchgesellschaft, 1984.

Chadwick, Henry. "Introduction." In *Lessing's Theological Writings*. Selected and translated by Henry Chadwick. Stanford: Stanford University Press, 1957.

Christ, Kurt. *Jacobi und Mendelssohn: Eine Analyse des Spinozastreits*. Würzburg: Königshausen & Neumann, 1988.

Coleridge, Samuel Taylor. *Confessions of an Inquiring Spirit*. Edited by H. StJ. Hart. Stanford: Stanford University Press, 1957.

Danzel, Th. W. and G. E. Guhrauer. *Gotthold Ephraim Lessing: Sein Leben und seine Werke*. 2d ed. 2 vols. Berlin: Verlag von Theodor Hofmann, 1881.

Dilthey, Wilhelm. *Das Erlebnis und die Dichtung: Lessing-Goethe-Novalis-Hölderlin*. 16th ed. Göttingen: Vandenhoeck & Ruprecht, 1985.

Drews, Wolfgang. *Gotthold Ephraim Lessing*. Hamburg: Rowohlt Taschenbuch Verlag, 1962.

Durzak, Manfred. *Zu Gotthold Ephraim Lessing: Poesie im bürgerlichen Zeitalter*. Stuttgart: Ernst Klett Verlag, 1984.

Eichholz, Georg. *Die Geschichte als theologisches Problem bei Lessing*. Gotha: Schmidt & Thelow, 1937.

Fischer, Kuno. *G. E. Lessing als Reformator der deutschen Literatur*. 2d ed. Stuttgart and Berlin: I. G. Cotta'sche Buchhandlung, 1904.

Fittbogen, Gottfried. *Die Religion Lessings*. Leipzig: Mayer & Müller, 1923; reprint, New York: Johnson Reprint Corporation, 1967.

Flajole, Edward S. "Lessing's Attitude in the Lavater-Mendelssohn Controversy." *Publications of the Modern Language Association of America* 73 (1958): 201–214.

———. "Lessing's Retrieval of Lost Truths." *Publications of the Modern Language Association of America* 74 (1959): 52–66.

Freund, Gerhard. *Theologie im Widerspruch: Die Lessing-Goeze-Kontroverse*. Stuttgart-Berlin-Cologne: Verlag W. Kohlhammer, 1989.

Garland, Henry Burnand. *Lessing: The Founder of Modern German Literature*. Cambridge: Bowes & Bowes, 1949.

Gericke, Wolfgang. "Lessings theologische Gesamtauffassung." In *Sechs theologische Schriften Gotthold Ephraim Lessings*, 9–62. Introduced and annotated by Wolfgang Gericke. Berlin: Evangelische Verlagsanstalt, 1985.

———. *Theologie und Kirche im Zeitalter der Aufklärung*. Kirchengeschichte in Einzeldarstellungen, vol. 3/2. Berlin: Evangelische Verlagsanstalt, 1989.

Göpfert, Herbert G. "Erläuterungen zu Band 1." In Gotthold Ephraim Lessing, *Werke*. Edited by Herbert G. Göpfert. Vol. 2 [of 8]. Munich: Carl Hanser Verlag, 1970–79.

Graß, Hans. "Lessing als Theologe." *Luther* 50 (1979): 102–116.

Guthke, Karl S. *Der Stand der Lessing-Forschung: Ein Bericht über die Literatur von 1932–1962*. Stuttgart: J. B. Metzlersche Verlagsbuchhandlung, 1965.

———. *Gotthold Ephraim Lessing*. 3d ed. Stuttgart: J. B. Metzlersche Verlagsbuchhandlung, 1979.

Harth, Dietrich. *Gotthold Ephraim Lessing, oder die Paradoxien der Selbsterkenntnis*. Munich: Verlag C. H. Beck, 1993.

Haug, Martin. *Entwicklung und Offenbarung bei Lessing*. Gütersloh: C. Bertelsmann, 1928.

———. "Lessing, Gotthold Ephraim." In *RGG*, 2d ed. Tübingen: J. C. B. Mohr, 1929. Vol. 3, cols. 1592–94.

Heftrich, Eckhard. *Lessings Aufklärung*. Frankfurt am Main: Vittorio Klostermann, 1978.

Heller, Peter. *Dialectics and Nihilism: Essays on Lessing, Nietzsche, Mann and Kafka*. Amherst, Massachusetts: University of Massachusetts Press, 1966.

Hengel, John van den. "Reason and Revelation in Lessing's Enlightenment." *Église et Théologie* 17 (1986): 171–94.

Hermann, Rudolf. "Zu Lessings religions-philosophischer und theologischer Problematik." *Zeitschrift für systematische Theologie* 22 (1953): 127–48.

Höhle, Thomas, ed. *Lessing und Spinoza*. Halle (Saale): Martin-Luther-Universität Halle-Wittenberg, 1982.

Jens, Walter and Hans Küng. *Dichtung und Religion: Pascal, Gryphius, Lessing, Hölderlin, Novalis, Kierkegaard, Dostojewski, Kafka*. Munich: Piper, 1988.

Kantzenbach, Friedrich Wilhelm. "Der Abbau der Offenbarungsvorstellung und die Konzeption G. E. Lessings." In *Protestantisches Christentum im Zeitalter der Aufklärung*, 148–69. Gütersloh: Gerd Mohn, 1965.

Kofink, Heinrich. *Lessings Anschauung über die Unsterblichkeit und Seelenwanderung*. Berlin: Druck von Georg Reimer, 1911.

Lamport, F. J. *Lessing and the Drama*. Oxford: Clarendon Press, 1981.

Leisegang, Hans. *Lessings Weltanschauung*. Leipzig: Felix Meiner, 1931.

Liepert, Anita. "Der Spinozismus Lessings (1729–1781)." *Deutsche Zeitschrift für Philosophie* 27 (1979): 59–70.

Liepmann, Hans W. *Lessing und die mittelalterliche Philosophie*. Stuttgart: W. Kohlhammer, 1931.

Loewenich, Walther von. *Luther und Lessing*. Tübingen: J. C. B. Mohr, 1960.

Loofs, Friedrich. *Lessings Stellung zum Christentum*. Halle: Waisenhauser, 1910.

Lüpke, Johannes von. *Wege der Weisheit: Studien zu Lessings Theologiekritik*. Göttingen: Vandenhoeck & Ruprecht, 1989.

Mann, Otto. *Lessing: Sein und Leistung*. Berlin: Walter de Gruyter, 1965.

———. "Neue Lessing-Forschung." *Zeitschrift für deutsche Philologie* 59 (1935): 374–80.

Mehring, Franz. *Die Lessing-Legende: Zur Geschichte und Kritik des preussischen Despotismus und der klassischen Literatur*. Berlin: Dietz Verlag, 1953.

Michalson, Gordon E., Jr. *Lessing's "Ugly Ditch": A Study of Theology and History*. University Park and London: Pennsylvania State University Press, 1985.

Niewöhner, Friedrich. *Veritas sive Varietas: Lessings Toleranzparabel und das Buch von den drei Betrügern*. Heidelberg: Verlag Lambert Schneider, 1988.

Nigg, Walter. *Das Buch der Ketzer*. 6th ed. Zurich: Artemis Verlag, 1981.

Nisbet, H. B. "Lessing and the Search for Truth." *Publications of the English Goethe Society* 43 (1972–73): 72–95.

Nölle, Volker. *Subjektivität und Wirklichkeit in Lessings dramatischem und theologischem Werk*. Berlin: Erich Schmidt Verlag, 1977.

Nolte, Fred O. "Voltaire's 'Mahomet' as a Source of Lessing's 'Nathan der Weise' and 'Emilia Galotti'." *Modern Language Notes* 48 (1933): 152–56.

Oehlke, Waldemar. *Lessing und seine Zeit*. 2 vols. Munich: C. H. Beck'sche Verlagsbuchhandlung, 1919.

Oelmüller, Willi. *Die unbefriedigte Aufklärung: Beiträge zu einer Theorie der Moderne von Lessing, Kant und Hegel*. Frankfurt am Main: Suhrkamp, 1979.

Pätzold, Detlev. "Lessing und Spinoza. Zum Beginn des Pantheismus-Streit in der deutschen Literatur des 18. Jahrhunderts." In *Aufklärung-Gesellschaft-Kritik*. Edited by M. Buhr and W. Forster, 298–355. Berlin/DDR, 1985.

Pelters, Wilm. *Lessings Standort: Sinndeutung der Geschichte als Kern seines Denkens.* Heidelberg: Lothar Stiehm Verlag, 1972.

Pons, Georges. *Gotthold Ephraim Lessing et le Christianisme.* Paris: Marcel Didier, 1964.

————. "Lessings Auseinandersetzung mit der Apologetik." *Zeitschrift für Theologie und Kirche* 77 (1980): 381–411.

Quapp, Erwin. *Lessings Theologie statt Jacobis Spinozismus.* Bern: Peter Lang, 1992.

Regner, Friedemann. "Lessings Spinozismus." *Zeitschrift für Theologie und Kirche* 68 (1971): 351–75.

Reventlow, Hennig Graf. "Die Auffassung vom Alten Testament bei Hermann Samuel Reimarus und Gotthold Ephraim Lessing." *Evangelische Theologie* 25 (1965): 429–48.

Rilla, Paul. *Lessing und sein Zeitalter.* In Gotthold Ephraim Lessing's *Gesammelte Werke,* vol. 10. Berlin and Weimar: Aufbau-Verlag, 1968.

Rohrmoser, Günter. "Aufklärung und Offenbarungsglaube (Lessing-Kant)." In *Emanzipation und Freiheit,* 30–61. Munich: Wilhelm Goldmann Verlag, 1970.

Rolleston, T. W. *Life of Gotthold Ephraim Lessing.* London: Walter Scott, 1889.

Schellong, Dieter. "Lessings Frage an die Theologie." *Evangelische Theologie* 30 (1970): 418–32.

Schilson, Arno. "Gotthold Ephraim Lessing und die Theologie. Zum Stand der Forschung." *Theologie und Philosophie* 47 (1972): 409–28.

————. *Geschichte im Horizont der Vorsehung: G. E. Lessings Beitrag zu einer Theologie der Geschichte.* Mainz: Matthias-Grünewald-Verlag, 1974.

————. "Lessing und die Aufklärung: Notizen zur Forschung." *Theologie und Philosophie* 54 (1979): 379–405.

————. *Lessings Christentum.* Göttingen: Vandenhoeck & Ruprecht, 1980.

————. "Lessings 'Kritik der Vernunft.' Versuch einer 'Aufklärung' über die Aufklärung." *Theologische Quartalschrift* 162 (1982): 24–30.

Schlegel, Friedrich. "Über Lessing." In *Gotthold Ephraim Lessing.* Wege der Forschung, vol. 211. Edited by Gerhard and Sibylle Bauer, 8–35. Darmstadt: Wissenschaftliche Buchgesellschaft, 1968.

Schmidt, Erich. *Lessing: Geschichte seines Lebens und seiner Schriften.* 4th ed. 2 vols. Berlin: Weidmannsche Buchhandlung, 1923; reprint, Hildesheim: Georg Olms Verlag, 1983.

————, ed. *Goezes Streitschriften gegen Lessing.* Stuttgart: G. J. Göschen'sche Verlagshandlung, 1893.

Schneider, Heinrich. *Lessing: Zwölf biographische Studien.* Munich: Leo Lehnen Verlag, 1951.

Schneider, Johannes. *Lessings Stellung zur Theologie: Vor der Herausgabe der Wolfenbüttler Fragmente.* The Hague: Uitgeverij Excelsior, 1953.

Scholz, Heinrich, ed. "Einleitung." In *Die Hauptschriften zum Pantheismusstreit zwischen Jacobi und Mendelssohn.* Berlin: Verlag von Reuther & Reichard, 1916.

Schöne, Albrecht. "In Sachen des Ungenannten: Lessing contra Goeze." *Text + Kritik* 26/27 (1975): 1–25.

Schrempf, Christoph. *Lessing als Philosoph.* 2d ed. Stuttgart: Fr. Frommanns Verlag, 1921.

————. "Lessing." In *Gesammelte Werke.* Vol. 5, *Auseinandersetzungen I: Kant-Lessing,* 297–468. Stuttgart: Fr. Frommanns Verlag, 1931.

Schultze, Harald. *Lessings Toleranzbegriff: Eine theologische Studie.* Göttingen: Vandenhoeck & Ruprecht, 1969.

————. "Lessings Auseinandersetzung mit Theologen und Deisten um die 'innere Wahrheit'." In *Lessing in heutiger Sicht*, 179–83. Beiträge zur Internationalen Lessing-Konferenz Cincinnati, Ohio 1976. Edited by Edward P. Harris and Richard E. Schade. Bremen and Wolfenbüttel: Jacobi Verlag, 1977.

Schwarz, Carl. *Gotthold Ephraim Lessing als Theologe*. Halle: C. E. M. Pfeffer, 1854.

Schwarz, Reinhard. "Lessings 'Spinozismus'." *Zeitschrift für Theologie und Kirche* 65 (1968): 271–90.

Sell, Karl. *Die Religion unserer Klassiker: Lessing-Herder-Schiller-Goethe*. Tübingen: J. C. B. Mohr, 1904; 2d ed., Tübingen: J. C. B. Mohr, 1910.

Smend, Rudolf. "Gotthold Ephraim Lessing." In *Gestalten der Kirchengeschichte*. Vol. 8, *Die Aufklärung*, edited by Martin Greschat, 281–97. Stuttgart: Verlag W. Kohlhammer, 1983.

Specht, Rolf. *Die Rhetorik in Lessings "Anti-Goeze": Ein Beitrag zur Phänomenologie der Polemik*. Bern: Peter Lang, 1986.

Spicker, Gideon. *Lessing's Weltanschauung*. Leipzig: Verlag von Georg Wigand, 1883.

Stamm, Israel S. "Lessing and Religion." *Germanic Review* 43 (1968): 239–57.

Stange, Carl. "Lessings Erziehung des Menschengeschlechts." *Zeitschrift für systematische Theologie* 1 (1923): 153–67.

Steiger, Lothar. "Die 'gymnastische' Wahrheitsfrage: Lessing und Goeze." *Evangelische Theologie* 43 (1983): 430–45.

Steinmetz, Horst. "Gotthold Ephraim Lessing." In *Deutsche Dichter des 18. Jahrhunderts: Ihr Leben und Werk*, edited by Benno von Wiese, 210–48. Berlin: Erich Schmidt Verlag, 1977.

Stockum, Th. C. van. *Lessing Absconditus*. Amsterdam: H. J. Paris, 1929.

————. *Spinoza-Jacobi-Lessing*. Groningen: P. Noordhoff, 1916.

Strohschneider-Kohrs, Ingrid. *Vernunft als Weisheit: Studien zum späten Lessing*. Tübingen: Max Niemeyer Verlag, 1991.

Thielicke, Helmut. *Offenbarung, Vernunft und Existenz: Studien zur Religionsphilosophie Lessings*. 4th ed. Gütersloh: Gerd Mohn, 1957.

————. *Vernunft und Existenz bei Lessing: Das Unbedingte in der Geschichte*. Göttingen: Vandenhoeck & Ruprecht, 1981.

————. *Glauben und Denken in der Neuzeit*. Tübingen: J. C. B. Mohr, 1983.

Tillich, Paul. "Lessing und die Idee einer Erziehung des Menschengeschlechts." In *Gesammelte Werke*. Vol. 12, *Begegnungen*, 97–111. Stuttgart: Evangelisches Verlagswerk, 1971.

Timm, Eitel. *Ketzer und Dichter: Lessing, Goethe, Thomas Mann und die Postmoderne in der Tradition des Häresiegedankens*. Heidelberg: Carl Winter Universitätsverlag, 1989.

Timm, Hermann. *Gott und die Freiheit: Studien zur Religionsphilosophie der Goethezeit*. Vol. 1, *Die Spinozarenaissance*. Frankfurt am Main: Vittorio Klostermann, 1974.

————. "Eine theologische Tragikomödie: Lessings Neuinszenierung der Geistesgeschichte." *Zeitschrift für Religions- und Geistesgeschichte* 34 (1982): 1–17.

————. "Der dreieinige Ring. Lessings parabolischer Gottesbeweis mit der Ringparabel des Nathan." *Euphorion* 77 (1983): 113–26.

Trillhaas, Wolfgang. "Zur Wirkungsgeschichte Lessings in der evangelischen Theologie." In *WSA*. Vol. 9, *Das Bild Lessings in der Geschichte*. Edited by Herbert G. Göpfert. Heidelberg: Verlag Lambert Schneider, 1981.

Traub, Friedrich. "Geschichtswahrheiten und Vernunftwahrheiten." *Zeitschrift für Theologie und Kirche* 1 (1920): 193–207.

Ullmann, Wolfgang. "Wahrheit des Herzens oder Wahrheit der Geschichte? Zur Interpretation von Lessings Schrift 'Über den Beweis des Geistes und der Kraft' (1777)." *Theologische Versuche* 3 (1971): 121–33.

Vallée, Gérard. "Introduction." In *The Spinoza Conversations between Lessing and Jacobi: Text with Excerpts from the Ensuing Controversy.* Translated by G. Vallée, J. B. Lawson, and C. G. Chapple. Lanham, New York and London: University Press of America, 1988.

Wagner, Albert Malte. *Lessing: Das Erwachen des deutschen Geistes.* Leipzig and Berlin: Horen-Verlag, 1931.

———. "A Century of Research on Lessing. Past and Future of Modern Languages." *Modern Languages* 25 (1943–44): 5–19.

Waller, Martha. *Lessings Erziehung des Menschengeschlechts: Interpretation und Darstellung ihres rationalen und irrationalen Gehaltes.* Berlin: Verlag Dr. Emil Ebering, 1935.

Wernle, Paul. *Lessing und das Christentum.* Tübingen: J. C. B. Mohr, 1912.

Wessell, Leonard P. G. E. *Lessing's Theology: A Reinterpretation.* The Hague: Mouton & Co., 1977.

Wiese, Benno von. *Lessing: Dichtung, Aesthetik, Philosophie.* Leipzig: Verlag Quelle & Meyer, 1931.

———. "Dichtung und Geistesgeschichte des 18. Jahrhunderts." *Deutsche Vierteljahrschrift für Literaturwissenschaft und Geistesgeschichte* 12 (1934): 470–78.

Zeeden, Ernst Walter. *The Legacy of Luther.* Translated by Ruth Mary Bethell. London: Hollis & Carter, 1954.

Zimmermann, Robert. "Leibnitz und Lessing." In *Sitzungsberichte der Wiener Akademie der Wissenschaften.* Philosophisch-historische Classe. Vol. 16, 326–91. Vienna: K. K. Hof- und Staatsdruckerei, 1855.

Zscharnack, Leopold. *Lessing und Semler: Ein Beitrag zur Entstehungsgeschichte des Rationalismus und der kritischen Theologie.* Giesen: Verlag von Alfred Töpelmann, 1905.

———. "Lessing." In *RGG*, 1st ed. Tübingen: J. C. B. Mohr, 1912. Vol. 3, cols. 2073–78.

———, ed. "Einleitung des Herausgebers." In Gotthold Ephraim Lessing, *Werke.* Edited by Julius Petersen and Waldemar von Olshausen. Vol. 17, edited by Leopold Zscharnack. Hildesheim and New York: Georg Olms, 1970.

V. *Other Works*

Aiton, Eric John. *Leibniz: A Biography.* Bristol and Boston: Adam Hilger Ltd., 1985.

Althaus, Paul. "Seelenwanderung. 2. Dogmatisch." In *RGG*, 3d ed. Vol. 5, cols. 1639–40. Tübingen: J. C. B. Mohr, 1961.

Arendt, Hannah. *Men in Dark Times.* New York: Harcourt, Brace & World, 1968.

Baumer, Franklin L. *Main Currents of Western Thought.* New Haven and London: Yale University Press, 1978.

Baumgartner, Hans Michael. "Wandlungen des Vernunftbegriffs in der Geschichte des europäischen Denkens." In *Grenzfragen.* Vol. 16, *Rationalität: Ihre Entwicklung und ihre Grenzen*, 167–203. Freiburg & Munich, 1989.

Benz, Ernst. *Evolution and Christian Hope: Man's Concept of the Future, from the Early Fathers to Teilhard de Chardin.* Garden City, New York: Doubleday & Co., 1968.

Beyschlag, Karlmann. *Evangelium als Schicksal: Fünf Studien zur Geschichte der Alten Kirche.* Munich: Claudius Verlag, 1979.

————. *Grundriß der Dogmengeschichte.* Vol. 1, *Gott und Welt.* Darmstadt: Wissenschaftliche Buchgesellschaft, 1988.

Blumenberg, Hans. *Arbeit am Mythos,* 5th ed. Frankfurt am Main: Suhrkamp, 1990.

Bornkamm, Heinrich. *Luther im Spiegel der deutschen Geistesgeschichte.* Göttingen: Vandenhoeck & Ruprecht, 1970.

Brown, Colin. *Jesus in European Protestant Thought 1778–1860.* Grand Rapids, Michigan: Baker Book House, 1985.

Bruford, W. H. *Germany in the Eighteenth Century: The Social Background of the Literary Revival.* Cambridge: Cambridge University Press, 1935; reprint, 1952.

Creed, John Martin and John Sandwith Boyssmith, eds. *Religious Thought in the Eighteenth Century.* Cambridge: Cambridge University Press, 1934.

Daniélou, Jean. *Origen.* Translated by Walter Mitchell. New York: Sheed and Ward, 1955.

Diem, Hermann. *Theologie als kirchliche Wissenschaft.* Vol. 2, *Dogmatik: Ihr Weg zwischen Historismus und Existentialismus.* Munich: Chr. Kaiser Verlag, 1955.

Dierse, U. and W. Schröder. "Panentheismus." In *Historisches Wörterbuch der Philosophie.* Vol. 7, col. 48. Darmstadt: Wissenschaftliche Buchgesellschaft, 1989.

Dilthey, Wilhelm. *Gesammelte Schriften.* 5th ed. Vol. 2, *Weltanschauung und Analyse des Menschen seit Renaissance und Reformation.* Stuttgart: B. G. Teubner Verlagsgesellschaft, 1957.

Dupuy, Maurice. *La philosophie allemande.* Collection Que Sais-Je? no. 1466. Paris: Presses Universitaires de France, 1972.

————. *Doitsu Tetsugakushi* (History of German philosophy). Translated by Yoshihiko Harada. Tokyo: Hakusuisha, 1995.

Ferguson, Adam. *Essay on the History of Civil Society.* Edinburgh: A. Millar & T. Caddel, 1767.

————. *Institutes of Moral Philosophy.* Edinburgh: A. Kincaid & J. Bell, 1769.

Franz, Erich. *Deutsche Klassik und Reformation.* Halle: Max Niemeyer Verlag, 1937.

Gerrish, Brian A. *Continuing the Reformation: Essays on Modern Religious Thought.* Chicago: University of Chicago Press, 1993.

Goppelt, Leonhard. *Theologie des Neuen Testaments.* 3d ed. Göttingen: Vandenhoeck & Ruprecht, 1978.

Graf, Friedrich Wilhelm. *Theonomie: Fallstudien zum Integrationsanspruch neuzeitlicher Theologie.* Gütersloh: Gerd Mohn, 1987.

Hammacher, Klaus. *Die Philosophie Friedrich Heinrich Jacobis.* Munich: Wilhelm Fink Verlag, 1969.

————, ed. *Friedrich Heinrich Jacobi: Philosoph und Literat der Goethezeit.* Beiträge einer Tagung in Düsseldorf (16.–19.10.1969) aus Anlaß seines 150. Todestages und Berichte. Frankfurt am Main: Vittorio Klostermann, 1971.

Hartshorne, Charles and William L. Reese, eds. *Philosophers Speak of God.* Chicago and London: University of Chicago Press, 1953.

Harvey, Van A. *The Historian and the Believer: The Morality of Historical Knowledge and Christian Belief.* Philadelphia: Westminster Press, 1966.

Heimsoeth, Heinz. *Die sechs großen Themen der abendländischen Metaphysik und der Ausgang des Mittelalters.* 8th ed. Darmstadt: Wissenschaftliche Buchgesellschaft, 1987.

Hirsch, Emanuel. *Geschichte der neuern evangelischen Theologie.* 5 vols. Gütersloh: C. Bertelsmann Verlag, 1949–54.

Hodgson, Peter C. *Winds of the Spirit: A Constructive Christian Theology.* Louisville, Kentucky: Westminster John Knox Press, 1994.

Hoffmeister, Johannes, ed. *Wörterbuch der philosophischen Begriffe.* 2d ed. Hamburg: Felix Meiner, 1955.

Hornig, G. "Akkommodation." In *Historisches Wörterbuch der Philosophie.* Edited by Joachim Ritter. Darmstadt: Wissenschaftliche Buchgesellschaft, 1971. Vol. 1, cols. 125–26.

Kaufmann, Walter. *Hegel: Reinterpretation, Texts, and Commentary.* New York: Doubleday & Co., 1965.

Knoll, Renate. *Johann Georg Hamann und Friedrich Heinrich Jacobi.* Heidelberg: Carl Winter Universitätsverlag, 1963.

Kogishi, Akira. *Risan suru Yudayajin* (Jews in dispersal). Tokyo: Iwanami, 1997.

Kopitzsch, Franklin. "Politische Orthodoxie: Johann Melchior Goeze 1717–1786." In *Profile des neuzeitlichen Protestantismus.* Edited by Friedrich Wilhelm Graf. Vol. 1, *Aufklärung-Idealismus-Vormärz,* 71–85. Gütersloh: Gerd Mohn, 1990.

Korff, H. A. *Geist der Goethezeit: Versuch einer ideellen Entwicklung der klassisch-romantischen Literaturgeschichte.* 2d ed. Leipzig: Koehler & Amelang, 1955.

Kupferberg, Herbert. *The Mendelssohns: Three Generations of Genius.* New York: Charles Scribner's Sons, 1972.

Lohse, Bernhard. "Johann Melchior Goeze als Theologe des 18. Jahrhunderts." In *Johann Melchior Goeze, 1717–1786: Abhandlungen und Vorträge.* Edited by Heimo Reinitzer. Hamburg: Friedrich Wittig Verlag, 1986.

Lütgert, Wilhelm. *Die Religion des deutschen Idealismus und ihre Ende.* Vol. 1, *Die religiöse Krise des deutschen Idealismus.* Gütersloh: Gerd Mohn, 1923; reprint, Hildesheim: Georg Olms, 1967.

McGrath, Alister E. *The Making of Modern German Christology, 1750–1990.* Grand Rapids, Michigan: Zondervan Publishing House, 1994.

Mandelbaum, Maurice. *History, Man, and Reason: A Study in Nineteenth-Century Thought.* Baltimore and London: Johns Hopkins University Press, 1971.

Manuel, Frank E. *Shapes of Philosophical History.* Stanford: Stanford University Press, 1965.

Mayer, Hans. *Outsiders: A Study in Life and Letters.* Translated by Denis M. Sweet. Cambridge, Massachusetts and London: MIT Press, 1982.

Mizugaki, Wataru. *Shūkyōteki Tankyū no Mondai* (The problem of religious quest). Tokyo: Sōbunsha, 1984.

———. "Kami no Jiko Nijūka ni tsuite" (On God's self-replication). In *Naze Kirisutokyō ka* (Why Christianity?). Edited by Yasuo Furuya, 127–52. Tokyo: Sōbunsha, 1993.

Moore, George Foot. *Metempsychosis.* Cambridge: Harvard University Press, 1914.

Niebuhr, H. Richard. *The Meaning of Revelation.* New York: Macmillan Publishing Co., 1941; paperback ed., 1960.

Nigg, Walter. *Das Ewige Reich: Geschichte einer Hoffnung.* 2d ed. Zurich: Artemis Verlag, 1954.

Origen. *Contra Celsum.* Translated by Henry Chadwick. Cambridge: Cambridge University Press, 1980.

Origène. *Contre Celse,* Tome 1, 1, 2. Sources Chrétiennes 132. Paris: Les Editions du Cerf, 1967.

Pannenberg, Wolfhart. *Ethik und Ekklesiologie.* Göttingen: Vandenhoeck & Ruprecht, 1977.

Piepmeier, R. "Erziehung des Menschengeschlechts." In *Historisches Wörterbuch der*

Philosophie. Vol. 2, cols. 735–39. Edited by Joachim Ritter. Darmstadt: Wissenschaftliche Buchgesellschaft, 1972.

Plessner, Helmuth. *Die verspätete Nation: Über die politische Verführbarkeit bürgerlichen Geistes*. Frankfurt am Main: Suhrkamp, 1994.

Reeves, Marjorie and Warwick Gould. *Joachim of Fiore and the Myth of the Eternal Evangel in the Nineteenth Century*. Oxford: Clarendon Press, 1987.

Reinitzer, Heimo, ed. *Johann Melchior Goeze, 1717–1786: Abhandlungen und Vorträge*. Vestigia Bibliae, no. 8. Hamburg: Friedrich Wittig Verlag, 1986.

———— and Walter Sparn, eds. *Verspätete Orthodoxie: Über D. Johann Melchior Goeze*. Wolfenbütteler Forschungen, vol. 45. Wiesbaden: Otto Harrassowitz, 1989.

Reill, Peter Hanns. *The German Enlightenment and the Rise of Historicism*. Berkeley, Los Angeles and London: University of California Press, 1975.

Reist, Benjamin A. *Processive Revelation*. Louisville: Westminster/John Knox Press, 1992.

Satō, Tsugitaka. *Isuramu no "Eiyū" Saradin: Jūjigun to Tatakatta Otoko* (Saladin the hero of Islam: A man who fought against the crusades). Tokyo: Kōdansha, 1996.

Schlegel, Friedrich. *Romanha Bungakuron* (Essays on the literature of Romanticism). Translated by Sadasuke Yamamoto. Tokyo: Fūzanbō, 1978.

Scholem, Gershom. *Major Trends in Jewish Mysticism*. 6th ed. New York: Schocken Publishing, 1972.

Schweitzer, Albert. *Geschichte der Leben-Jesu-Forschung*. Vol. 1. Hamburg: Siebenstern Taschenbuch Verlag, 1972.

Strauss, Leo. *The Rebirth of Classical Political Rationalism*. Selected and introduced by Thomas L. Pangle. Chicago and London: University of Chicago Press, 1989.

Toland, John. *Christentum ohne Geheimnis*. Translated by W. Lunde. Edited by Leopold Zscharnack. Giessen: Töpelmann, 1908.

————. *Christianity Not Mysterious: or, A treatise shewing, that there is nothing in the gospel contrary to reason, nor above it: and that no Christian doctrine can be properly call'd a mystery*. London, 1696; reprint, *Christianity Not Mysterious*. New York: Garland, 1978.

Troeltsch, Ernst. *Die Bedeutung des Protestantismus für die Entstehung der modernen Welt*. Munich and Berlin: R. Oldenbourg, 1911; reprint, Aalen: Otto Zeller, 1963.

————. "Der deutsche Idealismus." In *Gesammelte Schriften*. Vol. 4, *Aufsätze zur Geistesgeschichte und Religionssoziologie*, edited by Hans Baron, 532–87. Tübingen: J. C. B. Mohr, 1925; reprint, Aalen: Scientia Verlag, 1966.

————. "Glaube: 4. Glaube und Geschichte." In *RGG*. Vol. 2, cols. 1447–56. Tübingen: J. C. B. Mohr, 1910.

————. *Glaubenslehre*. Nach Heidelberger Vorlesungen aus den Jahren 1911 und 1912. Edited by Gertrud von le Fort. Munich and Leipzig: Verlag von Duncker & Humblot, 1925.

————. "Praktische christliche Ethik: Diktate zur Vorlesung im Wintersemester 1911/12. Aus dem Nachlaß Gertrud le Forts herausgegeben von Elenore von la Chevallerie und Friedrich Wilhelm Graf." In *Mitteilungen der Ernst-Troeltsch-Gesellschaft*. Vol. 6, 129–74. Augsburg, 1991.

————. *Protestantisches Christentum und Kirche in der Neuzeit*. In *Die Kultur der Gegenwart*. Edited by Paul Hinneberg. Part 1/4, vol. 1, *Geschichte der christlichen Religion*. Einleitung: Die israelitisch-jüdischen Religion, 431–755. 2d ed. Berlin and Leipzig: B. G. Teubner, 1909.

————. *Protestantism and Progress: The Significance of Protestantism for the Rise of the Modern World*. Philadelphia: Fortress Press, 1986.

————. "Religionswissenschaft und Theologie des 18. Jahrhunderts." *Preussische Jahrbücher* 114 (1903): 30–56.

Vielhauer, Philipp. *Geschichte der urchristlichen Literatur.* 4th ed. Berlin: Walter de Gruyter & Co., 1975.

Welch, Claude. *Protestant Thought in the Nineteenth Century.* Vol. 1, *1799–1870.* New Haven and London: Yale University Press, 1972.

Williams, George H. "Introduction." In *Spiritual and Anabaptist Writers.* Edited by G. H. Williams and A. M. Mergal. Philadelphia: Westminster Press, 1957.

Windelband, Wilhelm. *Die Geschichte der neueren Philosophie.* 2 vols. Leipzig: Breitkopf & Härtel, 1878; reprint, Karben: Verlag Petra Wald, 1996.

Wollgast, Siegfried. *Der deutsche Pantheismus im 16. Jahrhundert: Sebastian Franck und seine Wirkungen auf die Entwicklung der pantheistischen Philosophie in Deutschland.* Berlin: VEB Deutscher Verlag der Wissenschaften, 1972.

Yamashita, Hajime. *Doitsu-Yudaya Seishinshi Kenkyū* (A study of German-Jewish intellectual history). Tokyo: Yūshindō, 1980.

Yasukata, Toshimasa. *Ernst Troeltsch: Systematic Theologian of Radical Historicality.* American Academy of Religion Academy Series, no. 55. Atlanta: Scholars Press, 1986.

————. *Lessing to Doitsu Keimō: Lessing Shūkyō Tetsugaku no Kenkyū* (Lessing and the German Enlightenment: A study of Lessing's philosophy of religion). Tokyo: Sōbunsha, 1998.

Index